Weirdsville USA

The Obsessive Universe of David Lynch

Paul A. Woods

Plexus, London

British Library Cataloguing in Publication Data
Woods, Paul A.
  Weirdsville USA : the obsessive universe of David
Lynch
  1. Lynch, David, 1946 - Criticism and interpretation
  2. Motion picture producers and directors - United
States - Biography
  I. Title
  791. 4'3'0233'092

  ISBN 0859652556

Cover designed by Phil Smee
Book designed by Mitchell Associates
Cover photograph by Andrew Mcpherson
Printed by Hillman Printers

Acknowledgements
For research support and facilities I would like to
acknowledge BFI information and Library Services;
and the following film production companies:
    The American Film Institute; Asymmetrical
Pictures; Brooksfilms; CiBy 2000; Dino de Laurentiis;
EMI Films; Kino Link; Mainline Productions;
Polygram Filmed Entertainment; Propaganda Films;
Superior Pictures; Universal Pictures; Worldvision
Enterprises Inc.
    Film stills are courtesy of the British Film Institute
Stills, Posters and Designs; All Action; the Institute of
Contemporary Arts; Paul Woods; American Film
Institute; Brooksfilms; Universal Pictures; De
Laurentiis Entertainment; Erato Films; Propaganda
Films in association with Worldvision Enterprises;
Polygram Filmed Entertainment; CiBy 2000;
Worldvision Enterprises; Asymmetrical Productions
and Propaganda Films; HBO Productions; Kino Link
Productions.
    The following books and documentaries proved
invaluable in doing research: *For One Week Only –
With Jonathan Ross*. 'David Lynch Special' (Channel X
Television 1990); Howell, Michael and Ford, Peter. *The
True His tory of the Elephant Man*. Allison & Busby
1980; Kuhn, Joy. *The Elephant Man – The Book of the
Film*. Book Club Associates 1981; Gifford, Barry. *Wild
At Heart: The Story of Sailor and Lula*. Atlantic Monthly
1986; Lynch, Jennifer. *The Secret Diary of Laura Palmer*.
Pocket Books 1990; Lynch, David and Gifford, Barry.
Lost Highway – the original screenplay. Faber & Faber
1997; Lynch, David and Frost, Mark. *One Saliva
Bubble*. First draft: 20/5/87.
    I would like to give special thanks to David Elliott,
for his assistance and encouragement.

Contents

Introduction

Ease your foot off the brake slowly. Let the pick-up roll back through that narrow gap in the sycamores. Once you're through there, you can move onto the dirt road and make for the main highway.

But there's a heck of a distance to travel before you're home free. In the city of your dreams.

Take one last look at the woods before you leave 'em behind. In the balmy glow of daytime, the criss-crossing grain of the trees holds strange faces inside its ancient bark. The orange bowl of the sun reflects on the nearby lake; its colours move through liquefied contortions, then disappear into the darkness within the trees.

The low sunset makes a roof over the forest, but soon it will be dark. All the wildness and craziness will come together in the darkness. It's thrilling, but it's kinda scary. You can't put a name or a face to it, but you can feel it out there in the air. Just like you were a little kid again.

Driving back through the old town, you feel like maybe parking by someone's front lawn and just lying there below the sky. Let the golden memories dance on the backs of your eyelids, like lukewarm sunshine massaging your face. But that was when things were pure; days were long; nights held the sweetest dreams.

Now it's dark. Now, you would feel all the evil and decay radiating upwards from the neatly mowed grass. Feel the dark mystery behind every set of four walls in that quiet street. One dream is as beautiful as the next – whether it's of blue skies and aeroplanes, or entering a strange, dark world of murder.

But you have other memories to visit before you can move on. So you down the gas pedal and take the truck out on the highway.

The main highway takes you away from dreams of childhood. As you reach the outskirts of the city, you're no longer driving a truck – you're at the wheel of an old VW. The car is a reliable old friend, but her exhaust is starting to rattle; her suspension shudders under the weight of so much memory and dream, all piled up heavy on the extended roof rack.

The windows smear with black emissions, floating on the breeze from industrial chimney stacks. You recognise the black soot as the essence of your own fears; scared to wind down the windows, you can only pump the gas a little harder and hope to pass quickly by the perimeter of the city.

But something makes the dream last a little longer. You feel curiously reassured by the electric pylons, railway viaducts and derelict warehouses. Those fears were of a different time – the dreams of a less worldly, insecure dreamer.

Casting the corner of one eye over the slowly-passing scenery, you can see how much of yourself has been given to the place: dark subway tunnels echo with howls from another world, a passage to some dark adventure; the rumbling, belching factories hold your life history in their raw materials.

Corroding metal waste-pipes intersect the nearby industrial site, like umbilical cords linking your memory back to the mysteries and fascination of childbirth. Their liquefying vapour forms fluid patches as the night air cools – like the sweat of a delivering mother or a sick infant.

By the time you reach the hills that surround the city of lights, you find yourself in the middle of a different dream.

Now, it's hard to reconcile the memories that shape your landscape with the life you're living. The spluttering old jalopy you were driving is now a brand new Chevy. But, now you've parked the car up on the peak of a nearby cliff, you can catch glimpses of your own memories and obsessions in the flashing neon and headlamps just over the hill. You sense love very nearby, in the air, but also strangeness, sex, murder. On the last short stretch of your night-time drive, you have the feeling that the wild pain in the hills is calling you to where you've been headed since way, way back.

But if you take one wrong turn, you could be lost out on that highway forever, with no way to even be sure of your own identity . . .

CHAPTER ONE

All-American Martian Boy

States don't come much more united than Montana. At the geographical heart of the American union, its skies provide a deep blue ceiling over part of God's little acre. Out there in the Pacific North-Western tall-timber country, the oaks, cedars and sycamores watch over the children in the neat little houses surrounding the woodland perimeter – like petrified giants, or ancient Native American gods.

As our subject would say, it's 'about as American as you can get'.

It was here, during the cautious optimism of the immediate post-war years, that three children – David, John, Margaret – were raised in what the firstborn recalls as an 'extremely happy' family. The eldest boy of that contented progeny, David, was born to the Lynch family in Missoula, Montana on 20 January, 1946, within a few short months of the Allies winning World War Two and his mother country winning the economic peace.

These were rich times for a middle-American child to grow up in. Too young to feel the unease among many returning servicemen at the end of the war, David Lynch was raised in a pastoral version of the American dream. 'I had sort of a golden childhood,' he'd later admit, half-embarrassed. His earliest memories are of long sunny days; bright flowers and neatly-tended lawns; early morning birdsong and family visits; gifts from grandparents and good-natured sibling games; family camping vacations and winning Eagle Scout badges.

In this bright, clean world, surface was all – and the surface was darned near-perfect. When little David lay among the long grass, listening to the chirruping crickets in the undergrowth and watching the humming aeroplane overhead, his young heart instinctively knew he lived in the best of all possible worlds – built by the harmonious marriage of human industry and nature.

Home, sweet home, was a textbook example in how to live clean and live well, back in those apple pie an' A-Bomb days of the 1950s.

Mom and Dad neither drank nor smoked. They never argued, they never fought. For many young kids – especially those who lived in the dark undergrowth of this golden era – this would have been a childhood dream of heavenly security.

Little David Lynch, however, was developing an inner life at odds with his own peaches-and-cream affability and innocence. To his way of looking at it, Mom and Dad were behaving so nice and perfect it was making him a little twitchily self-conscious.

'There were lots of advertisements in magazines when you see a well-dressed woman bringing a pie out of the oven,' he recalls of the decade which nurtured him, 'and a certain smile on her face – or a couple smiling, walking together up to their house with a picket fence. Those smiles were pretty much all I saw.

'It's a strange smile. It's the smile of the way the world should be or could be. They really made me dream like crazy.' Within such an upstanding, middle-American family, little David might be mistaken for a miniature bundle of neuroses. He recalls a bout of agoraphobia, occurring long before the age most sufferers of the dysfunction have popped their first Valium: 'Luckily, school came about. But I had a touch of that disease where you are afraid to go out.' As a pre-school-age neurotic, the boy might have been considered a suitable case for ongoing treatment. With hindsight, however, all signposts point to a warping of that idyllic small-town existence, within a highly subjective inner life.

Dad was a common-sense, hard-working type, but he was no ordinary workaday Joe. No, sir – Mom may have been a regular housewife and mother, but young Dave's old man was a research scientist with the Forest Service, and he introduced his young fellow to the private worlds that existed beyond the town limits.

'He would drive me through the woods in his green Forest Service truck,' his grown-up son recalls, 'over dirt roads, through the most beautiful forests where the trees are very tall and shafts of sunlight come down, and in the mountain streams the rainbow trout leap out and their little trout sides catch glimpses of light. Then my father would drop me off in the woods and go off. It was a weird, comforting feeling being in the woods. There were odd, mysterious things. That's the kind of world I grew up in.'

But the topography of his private universe was opening up. As a small-town boy, he had fed his imagination on the beauty and mystery of the forest; as he grew, however, he would increasingly branch out into Big City, USA, which began to assert an altogether more primal, much more horrifying fascination.

'I kept coming to Brooklyn to visit my grandparents, and that was part of the horror,' admits Lynch. 'In a large city I realised there was a large amount of fear. Coming from the North-West, it kind of hits you like a train. Like a subway.

'In fact, going into the subway, I felt I was really going down into Hell. As I went down the steps – going deeper into it – I realised it was almost as difficult to go back up and get out of than to go through with this ride. It was the total fear of the unknown: the wind from those trains, the sounds, the smells and the different lights and mood, that was really special in a traumatic way.'

The fascination with contrasting places and environments grew steadily from the time of those exhilaratingly chilly visits to New York City. For the first time, the boy felt himself growing obsessed by the indefinable, by what, in adult life, he would describe as 'a force, a sort of wild pain and decay accompanying everything'. The young Lynch felt – but was not able to articulate – an inherent tendency to corrosion, obsolescence and self-destruction polluting the atmosphere of all modern industrial environments: 'Whenever you finish something, it starts decaying. Instantly. Just like New York City. The roads, the buildings, the bridges are falling apart. New ones are going up, and they're not built the same way.'

Which was no reason for dismay or despair. Quite the opposite. In the young man's mind, organic and man-made environments were starting to mesh in a mutated, aesthetic hybrid.

In his early teens, Dad's work started a short cycle of upheaval and displacement. None of which seemed to have any adverse effect on the well-adjusted, young obsessive – though the sense of rootlessness can only have added to his unspoken sense of unease, to the 'wild pain'.

First, the Lynch family moved to Spokane, a suburb of Washington, DC, then to Durham, South Carolina, then to Sandpoint and Boise, Idaho, to be followed by one more move further south to Alexandria, Virginia.

High school in Virginia was not a happy time – if not actually plagued by any great trauma. The new kid in town encountered classic minor alienation, never quite able to fit in. Having been brought up to be an all-round kind of guy and general good apple, he tried to take place in school activities but, not being the athletic kind, was never likely to win much applause. Running for the post of class treasurer with a nifty little slogan, 'Save With Dave', he still didn't make the grade.

(As an all-American Eagle Scout, however, the anxious young boy spent his fifteenth birthday helping to seat VIPs for President John F. Kennedy's inauguration ceremony at the White House. Even young people from as conservative a background as Dave Lynch could sense the momentousness of electing a new, youthful, charismatic leader – and a war hero to boot – for a new era, even if he was a Democrat. But, as young Dave might have told them, had anyone had the remarkable foresight to ask, there's always a force, a wild pain abroad in the air – it's unpredictable, and it's out of control.)

'I was like a regular person,' he recalls of his early teens. 'There wasn't much happening upstairs. I didn't really think at all – not that I can remember – until I was about nineteen.'

But something surely was going on upstairs – albeit on an intuitive, non-intellectual level. In the interim period, before Lynch was able to recognise that his internal world and way of thinking were just the teeniest bit different from Joe Shmoe's, daydreams would slowly transmute into positive activity. Alongside his new best school-friend, Jack Luton, he would indulge plans for a productive and fascinating adulthood: the 'Art Life'.

The catalyst that moved the dream a degree closer to reality was a real, live, honest-to-goodness artist. Bushnell Keeler, who young Dave met by chance while still at high school, had just about the niftiest lifestyle of any fellow he'd met, as far as his young admirer was concerned. Uninterested in attitude, posturing or the trappings of bohemianism, the dreamy high school kid was impressed by the single main factor: this guy could spend a big part of his life just *creating*.

He also had a studio, from which, with a little wide-eyed persuasion, he was willing to hire out floor-space at a nominal fee. The young artist-*manqué* jumped at the opportunity. His small world electrified by creativity, he began to share the studio-within-a-studio with best buddy Jack. At weekends he would live the dream further, heading downstate to study painting at the Corcoran School of Art in Washington, DC.

After high school, by now fully committed to the Art Life, young David enrolled at the Boston Museum School of Art. Somehow, however, the nascent artist felt far less electrified and stimulated than he believed he had a right to. After all, living for art full-time was supposed to be the pursuit of a dream.

Finding his tenure less than productive in terms of developing a personal vision, he played the role of art student for no more than a year. Still, he wasn't about to give up – in fact, the perverse optimism that would carry his darker side like a life-raft was only just coming into its own.

Next on the artistic agenda was what had been an antique 'broadening experience' for the sons of the English and, later, the American moneyed classes: the European tour. The young American – along with Jack, still his best friend and constant companion – had taken pains to arrange a visit to the home of Austrian Expressionist painter Oskar Kokoscha, then in his late fifties. Supported by their families, their stay abroad was scheduled for three years. It lasted fifteen days.

'Europe', in the typically insular American vernacular, took in anywhere from West Germany to London – the two areas Kokoscha was dividing his life and work between. In any case, despite his fondness for the artist's vividly colourful, expressionistic recreation of everyday events and street scenes, young Lynch found little in the Old World to connect with his personal obsessions.

'I didn't take to Europe,' he recalls, understatedly, of this further episode of disappointment. 'I was all the time thinking, "This is where I'm going to be painting." And there was no inspiration there at all for the kind of work I wanted to do.'

Young Dave's abrupt retreat from the Old World had been no 'return of the prodigal . . .' Disturbed by his son's lack of a game plan for life, devoutly commonsensical Dad cut off his allowance. So began the trawl through a menial working life. A job in an art store here, selling picture-frames there.

'And I kept getting fired from these jobs,' he wistfully admitted, 'because I couldn't get up in the morning.' The final strained artistic link snapped when he got himself fired from the picture-frame store for scratching one of its specialised products. The manager – who went under the modest *nom de plume* of Michelangelo – was at least sympathetic enough to re-hire the dreamy wastrel. But this time around, young Dave was to gain a true taste of how wider society regards the dreamer, and how it generously seeks to include him into its social scheme. Thanks to Michelangelo, he now enjoyed the post of building janitor – with a bell installed in his apartment so his employer could wake him each morning.

Like one of those diligent, Depression-era bums with a placard saying 'Will Work For Food' tied around his neck, that was the only living cost he was paid in his new sinecure.

'Then he would make me show him my food,' Lynch remembers of his employer's paternal regime, 'because he didn't want me spending it on paint, and not eating. Well, I wasn't going to do that. I mean, I was hungry.'

Hungry, and content to live on the artery-clogging soul-food of the hard-up: peanut butter sandwiches and milk.

By now, it was 1965.

Young men in the full bloom of youth, like 19-year-old David Lynch, were being formally invited to participate in a little unfinished business of Uncle Sam's over in south-east Asia. Despite pockets of student resistance, it was assumed that every able-bodied young man would heed his country's call. So it was that one morning at 4.30 a.m., best buddy Jack Luton turned up to ensure Dave Lynch would be on time to attend his physical exam for the draft.

As both young men had got the call to defend democracy and Coca Cola, they rode the bus together out of town to the draft induction centre. It was then that Jack told Dave about how he was maintaining his own personal Art Life: attending the Pennsylvania Academy of Fine Arts, in Philadelphia.

Whether it was the prospect of avoiding the draft as a full-time student, or whether his interest was simply fired by the last chance to pursue the Art Life on a career level, is not known. What's certain is that it threw Dave into a sudden spate of activity. He assembled his portfolio, borrowed a little money from his father, reassuring him that this time – really, this time – he was going to pursue art as a career, and took a bus to the city of Philadelphia.

By the end of the year, he had enrolled at the Academy.

'It was a great time to be at the Academy,' recalled Lynch of a period which finally lived up to his youthful expectations. 'Schools have waves, and it just happened that I hit on a really rising, giant wave. There were so many good people at the school. And that really started everything rolling. I kind of got a feeling for things in terms of painting, and my own style kind of clicked in.'

His own style began to develop from the supposedly radical *mélange* of modernism: post-Pollock action painting; primitivist drawing. To these dominant anti-conventions, Lynch would bring what were then his stylistic trademarks – geometrical shape and mechanical structure – to create what he termed 'industrial symphony' drawings: a concept that would echo like a factory whistle through his life and career.

Via a diverted route, Lynch had arrived at the threshold of the Art Life; having already rejected the study of fine art twice over, in its most narrow careerist terms, he now had the luxury of an academic career he considered meaningful, relevant to his own internal vision.

'They call it rebellion,' Lynch reflects on his youthful attitude, pre-Academy and beyond. 'I just didn't want anything to do with anything except painting and living the Art Life. Nothing else was fun.'

He estimates his own period of – for want of a better word – 'rebellion' as lasting until the end of his state-subsidised work. In other words, up until the age of 30. Lynch has reflected long on his sustained burst of youthful idealism: 'My theory is that most people rebel that long these days, because, not counting accidents or strange diseases, we're built to live longer. And so all the stages consequently last longer. And so you're going to find people living at home, going through these strange rebellions. And maybe they'll be 60 before they realise they're an adult and get serious about things.'

As for the trappings of the Art Life, Lynch and his fellow students were living a marginal form of bohemianism on the outskirts of the city. 'We lived in strange ways and in strange parts of town,' he recalls of a period before adult responsibilities – when his student girlfriend, Peggy, was still part of the art school crowd, not the central figure she would soon become in his life.

'One time I was walking around at night with a stick with nails driven through it, and a squad car pulls up alongside of me, and a cop says, "What've you got there?" And I showed him this stick with nails driven through it. He said, "Good for you, bud," and took off.'

Too early for the nationwide youth rebellion that accompanied psychedelia, Lynch was closer to the tradition of eccentric individuality than hippiedom – still occasionally tolerated in a nation where the pioneer spirit often loses out to the tradition of puritan conformity.

By the time of his second year at the Academy, young David Lynch felt confident enough to make a particularly idiosyncratic entry in the annual experimental painting and sculpture competition. The raw material was his own facial features – three plaster casts of his head made, life-mask style, by Jack Luton. (Now known as Fisk, after a family name-change.) Added to this, however, was intercut cinefilm of his own changing expression, plus three other visages photographed from purely human sources – with attendant torsos to match all six heads. In layman's terms, the young painter had mixed his media to an extent where the end product was most easily defined as 'film'.

At this point of his life, Lynch asserts, it was fine art rather than cinema that shone his guiding light. Only a handful of movies exerted a long-term influence: *Sunset Boulevard* (1950), Billy Wilder's grotesque, neo-gothic classic about a faded movie queen; *La Strada*

(1954), Fellini's tragicomic romance between a female clown and a brutish strongman who mistreats her up until the point of death; *Lolita* (1962), Kubrick's sharp but sanitised adaptation of Nabokov's elegant black comic novel of sexual obsession with a minor; and the films of Jacques Tati, the Parisian actor/director, displaying a gentle, absurdist humour, reliant on sound effects for aural accompaniment rather than scripted speech.

The determinedly bizarre competition entry was certainly not intended as a film in itself, even in the experimental sense, but was most accurately described as a 'moving painting'. The six heads – part sculpted, part animated, part natural – ran through a rapid series of reactions on a film sequence lasting less than a minute, accompanied by the wail of a siren. With the film on a self-winding loop, however, the moving figures would live out the 'wild pain' – distorting, catching fire, expanding and bloating, vomiting – *ad infinitum*.

As even its maker concedes, it may have raised the odd eyebrow but it didn't play like any precursor of things to come. 'That was going to be the end of my film-making experience,' testified Lynch. 'The entire "film" cost me $200, and that was just too expensive. It was much nicer to paint than to make these movies. But this was one of those things – a crossroads.'

In fact, Lynch was at a crossroads where every aspect of his life seemed to be diverging in separate directions. 'He was in art school, wanting to take on the world with his painting and film,' recalled Jack Fisk, 'and suddenly his girlfriend was pregnant. And he found himself with a baby, and I think it was like, "Oh no, my life is ended, I'm gonna be an adult."'

Towards the end of his tenure at the Academy of Fine Arts, Lynch's sense of responsibility led him to marry Peggy, moving to an apartment in a decaying, crime-ridden area of Philadelphia. After leaving the Academy, he would take a job as a printer, reproducing art engravings. In 1968, after Lynch had turned 22, Peggy gave birth to a daughter, Jennifer. Despite his holding down a regular job, the knack of raising a family on one small income would prove a precarious one.

'It takes two to tango, and this is what happened to me,' Lynch recalls of the period when his artist's ideals got frozen in the headlights of oncoming reality. Mercifully, he keeps the changes to his young adult life in perspective, refusing to play the victim of circumstance: 'It was tough. But again, absolutely good and meant to be. Sometimes a jolt of electricity at a certain point of your life is helpful. It forces you a little bit more awake.'

Meanwhile, Lynch's 'moving painting' had been witnessed by one H. Barton Wasserman – millionaire painter and Academy competition panel member.

Deciding he'd like to own a similar artefact, he approached the young artist with an offer of funding a similar project to the tune of just under a thousand dollars. Grateful of the interest, Lynch set to work on 'moving painting' number two, utilising exactly the same methodology: animated scenes on an endless tape loop, to be projected onto a shaped and sculpted screen.

Using his own natural flair for creative handiwork, the artist built and animated the figures over a period of two months. But this time, however, his fumbling lack of experience with a camera was too great a flaw. When the film was developed and returned from the lab, it was nothing more than a blur. Embarrassed, Lynch called up his patron to explain and apologise, but found his generosity not yet exhausted. When told, 'Take the rest of the money and do whatever you want,' he decided to tackle cinematic technique on a more ambitious, albeit just as experimental level. Raising the rest of the budget from his father, in return for a completed print of the film, Lynch set to work not on a loop, but on a self-contained, animated, four-minute short – *The Alphabet*, credited as 'An H. Barton Wasserman Production'.

As its maker recalls: '*The Alphabet* is a little nightmare about the fear connected with learning. It's very abstract – a pretty dense little film.'

The Alphabet [1968]

A long-haired girl (Peggy Lynch) lies prostrate in bed, illuminated by expressionistic, almost monochromatic lighting. Children's voices chant 'A – B – C!' on the soundtrack. The image of the girl is briefly intercut with that of a mannequin-like, female face wearing dark shades.

The alphabet itself is an animated version of Lynch's early 'industrial symphonies': a strangely organic electrical circuit, consisting of the 26 letters. The dominant letter 'A' gives birth to squealing baby 'A's. The animated figure of a be-suited part-man (resembling the works of Magritte and the Austrian artist Korab) transforms into a piece of feminine sculpture, which is then brought to life by the mask-like features of the girl. Knowledge is fed directly into her cranium by an animated heart, until her head erupts in a fountain of gaudy, paintbox blood. Assimilating information is a painful, frightening process.

'Please remember you are dealing with the human form,' announces a female voice, against the terrified image of the bed-ridden girl. An exaggerated, life-mask-type plaster frieze of her features makes her appear both pitiful and grotesque. She simultaneously flails against and reaches for the painted letters of the alphabet which hang in the air, tangling herself in the twine which suspends them.

As off-kilter as *The Alphabet* may have seemed, its reception quickly resulted in Lynch's elevation from the mainstream art school fraternity.

Bushnell Keeler, whose encouragement and sharing of facilities had pointed young Dave towards the Art Life in the first place, was generous of spirit enough to give further pointers. He told him about the American Film Institute, a public body for nurturing home-grown cinematic talent which his brother-in-law had helped to establish. 'You ought to apply for a grant,' Keeler told him. 'All you have to do is write a script for a film you want to do and send them previous work.'

Lynch was intrigued, but not so enamoured of the medium that he was prepared to opt for a conventional narrative approach. In his own words, the outline which he sent to the AFI in Washington, along with a print of *The Alphabet*, was not strictly a script, but it was 'very weird . . . it was just little images and stuff, sort of like shorthand and poetry'.

For a short while, the upstart art student suspected himself of arrogance, becoming increasingly and painfully aware that many of the other applicants had already built reputations as film-makers. ('I was so embarrassed that I even applied,' he admitted.)

This particular bout of insecurity was cancelled out, however, by a phone call received one day at the printing plant from AFI directors George Stevens, Jr. (son of the *Shane* director) and Tony Vellani.

Stevens recalled that the various films received by AFI grant applicants that year were divided into categories, all sitting in separate piles, apart from one which stood on its own: *The Alphabet*. 'We gotta give this guy a grant,' is how he remembers the consensus of the time.

The only slight obstacle was the budget – Lynch had submitted a detailed budget of $7,118, whereas the AFI wanted to know if he could deliver the film for $5,000. 'You got it,' was Lynch's reply. As ever, all that was needed were a few words of encouragement to boost fragile optimism and belief in his own 'can-do'.

In any case, though the budget proved inadequate further down the line, the AFI would be encouraged enough by his progress to grant him another $2,200 to complete. Almost immediately, he was able to start work on the project which, in a logical progression from the techniques of *The Alphabet*, mixed live action with animation – although the preference for sound effects and music, instead of dialogue, brought the 34-minute end product closer to a disturbing mixed-media experience than anything conventionally recognised as a film.

In creating the sound effects, Lynch decided to solicit more help this time round from Calvin Productions, a local industrial films production company. The sound engineer who had previously mixed his home-made effects for *The Alphabet* was not available, however, and pointed the young film-maker towards his assistant, Alan Splet.

'I thought, "Oh brother, I'm being shunted off to his assistant,"' Lynch remembered. 'And Alan – he's a strange-looking guy. He's very, very thin, and he had a synthetic black suit and real short hair and a strange look to him. I shook his hand, and I felt all the bones shaking in his arm. I thought, "This guy is an oddball. This isn't going to work."' So began a creative partnership which would have a huge influence throughout Lynch's first seminal – in more ways than one – major project, and beyond.

The Grandmother [1970]

The Grandmother *opens against a crude animated background. Three human beings – father (Robert Chadwick), mother (Virginia Maitland), boy (Richard White) – are born by a kind of mutant photosynthesis, pushed out of the ground by a spermatozic plant undergrowth. All have pale, clown-like faces and express themselves non-verbally, via discordant sound effects.*

The brutish father is hostile to the boy. The fertilisation stem in the undergrowth which gave birth to them all is blocked up, indicating his wish to sire no more children. The slovenly parents sit at a table which is covered by the refuse of their lives: breakfast items, clothes-lines, glasses of clear liquid (booze). Every seedy detail of their existence is expressionistically exaggerated.

The crudely drawn, animated sun comes up on a major organ chord. The boy has wet his bed, displayed by a huge yellow circle

His slatternly young mother tries to show affection to the unhappy boy, her groping and pouting obscenely suggestive of sexual abuse.

Drawn by a high-pitched whistling noise, the boy finds a sack of seeds in an attic room of their dark apartment house. He grows the head of an old woman from a mound of earth on the bedside table.

Major-key organ chords herald the birth of the grandmother (Dorothy McGinnis). She ascends from the animated undergrowth to the vulvic earth passage in the upstairs room. The boy is relieved when she smiles at him and shows grandmaternal affection.

At the dinner table, the boy is expected to enjoy the garbage-can remains of various greasy foods. The table overflows with soil and wild flora, realising Lynch's association of physical decay with invading plant life

In the middle of the night, the boy is awakened by the grandmother calling to him with an owl-like hoot. Making his way up the stairs, he is spotted by his two shrieking, grunting parents. His open mouth reveals a sprouting, tentacular, animated tongue.

On a stage created by his own imagination, he becomes a cone-hatted executioner, decapitating the animated figure of his father; he drops a boulder onto the stomach of his mother's figure. The piss stain on the boy's bed grows until it becomes a deep ocean pool between two rocks. The figures of the mother and father are bloated and elongated by pipes which feed into their bodies, until they crack into pieces and fall away.

The boy takes refuge in the grandmother's room. They communicate with body language, touching and prodding, accompanied by a simple-but-haunting female voice and organ theme by the band Tractor.

Transported back into the surreal, animated world of the undergrowth, the grandmother works hard to produce more plant life. Her neck grows long, she raises a giant, cactus-like plant, from whose flowering head comes a great bird. Flying insects rise from the plant life; spermatozic white streaks fertilise the plants and throw life out into the 'real' world.

Lying in bed, the grandmother undergoes flickering convulsions. The boy hears her strange whistle and runs up the darkened stairway to help her. She goes into frantic, fast-cutting convulsions, spinning around the room.

In a black and white sequence at a cemetery, the mournful boy comes to gaze on the grave of the grandmother. He seems not to notice that she sits in front of her own gravestone in a rocking chair. Her head falls back and she goes into a final convulsion; the boy's eyes screw up as he suddenly feels her pain.

At home, the despondent little boy lies on his bed. A large, crustacean-like creature – resembling the grandma-pod as it grew from the soil – hangs over his head, roots or branches filling the air around him.

The Grandmother went on to win competition prizes at the 1970 San Francisco, Belleview and Atlanta film festivals. It also made Critics' Choice in that year's best sponsored film-makers competition at the AFI.

At the same time, the family viewing – the film being a minor family affair, with sister Margaret assisting on script supervision and sound effects – was just a little tense. 'When my parents saw *The Grandmother*, they were very upset,' admits Lynch, 'because they didn't know where it came from.'

Recalling his almost bizarrely idyllic childhood, he admits, 'I longed for some sort of . . . not a catastrophe but something out of the ordinary to happen. Something so that everyone will feel sorry for you. And you'll be like a victim. You know, if there was a tremendous accident and you were left alone. It's kind of like a nice dream. But things kept on going normally, forward.'

While this disarming confession of a childhood longing to be orphaned also speaks of an early wish to buy into the 'victim culture', it's clear that, instead of some misplaced sense of self-pity, the morbid daydreams opened an important, dark door in the young Lynch's imagination. One through which he could glimpse the inner world of other anxious little guys – people somehow like himself, but standing at 180 degrees to him in terms of their potential for happiness. All these characters would ever have to compensate them was their own imagination.

The Grandmother emphasised subconscious themes – the pains of childhood, the horrors of bad parenthood and loneliness, the organic strangeness of birth, taking refuge from a waking nightmare inside more personal dreams – that would be obsessively replayed. The measure of obsession lay in the unwillingness of the new 'film sculptor' to edit or interpret his subconscious mind. Whereas what lies repressed may come roaring back a thousandfold, the preoccupations of life's dreamers are no more likely to go away simply because they get a regular airing.

And the medium of communication for this particular obsessive dreamer was hereby destined to be film.

When the initial AFI budget for *The Grandmother* had become exhausted, director Tony Vellani paid a visit to Philadelphia to observe its painstaking production. Encouraged by what he saw, he approved the further payment of $2,200, and recommended the promising experimental director contact the Centre for Advanced Film Studies, recently set up by the AFI in Los Angeles.

Now following, instead of fighting, the flow which had taken him from the mainstream visual art world, Lynch was to apply twice to the Centre. Rejected in its first year simply on account of lack of space, he was invited to use their facilities for project development in 1972. It was another crossroads, but this time he would never be able to retrace his route.

Biting hard, he handed in notice to quit his job, prepared his supportive young wife and their little girl for relocation, and left Philadelphia for LA – a new life in a new town.

But Philadelphia was to remain for a long time the city of his dreams, as we shall see.

ERASERHEAD

A FILM BY DAVID LYNCH

CHAPTER TWO

Eraserhead:

A Dream of Dark and Troubling Things

People do not dream: they are dreamt.
We undergo our dreams.
Carl Jung

I — A Long Gestation Period

The Centre for Advanced Film Studies is based in the centre of Hollywood. Run by the public-funded American Film Institute, it exists to impart an academic approach to the most instinct-driven sector of the modern communications industry. Aspect by aspect, step by step, the Centre's cinematically-literate tutors break the creative process of film-making down to a series of functional components.

In the early 1970s, when the Centre ran from the Greystone mansion in Beverly Hills, its methods were less regulated. Aspiring young film-makers were offered a grab-bag of tutorials, seminars and hands-on film-making assignments more likely to fire their imaginations – if not actually turn them into the new wave of American 'auteurs' most dreamt of becoming.

Among the wide-eyed, long-haired hopefuls of the time was the foppish, young, mid-Western art school drop-out, David K. Lynch. 'I'm thankful that I went when it was loose,' he recalls of his formative years behind the camera. 'If you wanted to learn something, somebody would be around to tell you about somebody else – or you could drop in on a class if you wanted to. But you could do a lot of your own work.'

In his application to the Centre, the young celluloid painter had to submit previous work and a working script. *The Grandmother*, as his most substantial 'moving painting' so far, was naturally the completed work; the script was a formative piece called *Gardenback*, which, with the Centre's encouragement, the new entrant was to spend most of his first year expanding and revising.

During this early period, the agreeably genteel young face of the *avant-garde* received almost unprecedented encouragement from a major studio. Via the Centre, Lynch was introduced to a 20th Century Fox producer who became interested in expanding *Gardenback* into a feature.

'But I couldn't think in a regular enough way, with regular enough dialogue, to make it work for them,' Lynch admitted. With the admirable perversity of youth, he was to shrug it off. 'A lot of people tried to help me, but the bits that I liked started floating further apart, and in between was the stuff I didn't like.'

The original idea for *Gardenback* was the story of Henry and Mary, a sympathetic though geeky oddball couple, and the strain which adultery places on their relationship. 'When you look at a girl, something crosses from her to you,' explains Lynch, expanding the sketchy original storyline into a concept. 'And in this story, that something was an insect which grew in this man's attic, which was like his mind. The house was like his head. And the thing grew and metamorphosed into this monster which overtook him. He didn't become it, but he had to deal with it, and it drove him to completely ruining his home.'

Urged by friends to add realistic dialogue and conventional plot structure to make the Kafka-esque fantasy viable, he found his enthusiasm fading fast: 'I had worked on it so long that it had sort of killed the spark for me.' Ultimately, these feelings were spelled out to his mentors at the American Film Institute: 'They said I could do anything I wanted to, and that's how *Eraserhead* started.'

The title came from a random visual idea frozen in the nascent film-maker's mind: 'My original image was of a man's head bouncing on the ground, being picked up by a boy and taken to a pencil factory. I don't know where that came from.' As we will see, it came from the same subterranean territory which bred the rest of the film's stark surrealism.

One final obstacle remained for this quirkiest of student projects. The AFI's directors had assumed, on the basis of Lynch's 21-page script, that *Eraserhead* was intended as a short, as per *The Grandmother* and most other student films. Cautious after recently losing money on a first feature, they worked on an arbitrary typescript–screentime ratio and instructed their protégé to budget for a film 21 minutes long. 'I think it's going to be a bit longer than that,' he demurred, to be answered by the random compromise, 'Well, okay, 42 minutes.'

No allowance had been made for what would become abundantly obvious during filming – that the script had been so slender because Lynch purposely neglected dialogue in favour of imagery. In fact, Lynch had also wilfully neglected narrative, realism and rationalism in favour of a painstakingly constructed descent into the unconscious. It was, as the self-explanatory subtitle read on his original 21-page typescript, 'A Dream of Dark and Troubling Things'.

The young aspiring artist made one significant gesture to his financially cautious backers. Significant, in that the calculated nice-guy compromise he offered was, for him, no sacrifice at all. In return for letting him shoot on high-quality 35mm stock, he offered to forgo colour for cheaper black and white. It had been, of course, his intention to create a waking dream in sharply defined monochrome all along.

'I think black and white makes things seem not so normal,' Lynch explained. 'Because we're used to seeing in colour, it removes you one step from a normal feeling. It makes it easier to go into another world.' Monochrome was also an aesthetic decision, dictated by a graphic artist's eye: 'It seems to make you see more clearly. To me, a frame in black and white is purer than a colour frame. It's less distracting, you'd probably be more apt to see the character and hear the character in black and white.'

With a minimal $10,000 budget granted by the AFI, 25-year-old David Lynch's first feature was almost ready to roll. First of all, however, came the matter of acquiring cast and crew, and undertaking pre-production chores, all on a budget of next to nothing. As well as a temporarily indomitable optimism, and an obsessively personalised imagination that revealed itself by slow degree, Lynch would also demonstrate the most vital quality needed to get his film off the ground: the 'can-do' spirit of the practical mid-Western handyman.

In early 1972, Lynch was permitted regular access to several buildings set amongst grounds owned by the Centre for Advanced Film Studies, including stables and garages. Due to the grounds' use by the Beverly Hills parks department, director and crew made a joint decision to shoot nocturnally in order to avoid the constant noise of vehicles and dayworkers. As per the supposed condescension of shooting in black and white, this in itself was a welcome expedient, conducive to the conception of a truly dark aesthetic.

Assisted by his brother, John, and Alan Splet, sound engineer on *The Grandmother* and now *Eraserhead*, Lynch set about building sets for the claustrophobic interior shots which constitute about 90 per cent of the film. As the type of near-demented DIY man who sees the meaning of life in a handful of tacks, he was proud of his sleight of hand, building supposedly solid brick walls entirely from flimsy papier-mâché. This ability to deceive the human eye using minimal resources would display itself more vividly in the slowly-evolving special effects.

'That's what I loved about the whole *Eraserhead* thing,' he'd recall fondly. 'Faking it. But still taking the time to get it right and get the mood.' Where a $35-set was considered expensive, however, time was always going to be a more abundant commodity than money.

The small but loyal crew began to come together, none of them aware just how unfeasibly large a bite this film would take out of their lives. As Lynch perceived the scope of this ambitious, low-budget project was going to take camera duties out of his hands, he took up Splet's suggestion to approach Herb Cardwell – an industrial film-maker Lynch had met back in Philadelphia. Cardwell duly acceded, and put industrial information films behind him in favour of post-industrial surrealism.

The importance of Cardwell – and his successor, Fred Elmes, who took over camerawork when Cardwell left – in bringing Henry's dark and troubling inner world to the screen cannot be understated. Lynch had already surmised that the translation from imagination to viewing theatre could only be achieved with the stark contrasts of monochrome. For their contribution to this most obsessive of personal visions, Cardwell and Elmes would be lauded for creating the most effective black and white photography since the 1940s heyday of film *noir*.

'The dailies would come back from CFI [the development lab],' remembered production manager Doreen Small, 'and they'd say, "Are you shooting this with one candle in a tunnel?" And David would send them back saying, "Not dark enough. I want this darker."'

Similarly, the painstaking work of sound engineer Alan Splet can be accorded the tribute of placing *Eraserhead* apart from anything else in contemporary cinema. Lynch's new-found conviction was that sound should not be subordinated to the primacy of the visual image. In acknowledgement, Splet created an relentlessly droning aural collage of industrial noise, exaggerated incidental sounds and anachronistic jazz organ accompaniment. Lynch's own conception of soundtrack noise was that music is 'brittle', whereas sound effects are 'liquid'.

Rather than trying to communicate what he was aiming for, Lynch preferred to work through the film piecemeal, trusting that his small crew's professionalism and experience would communicate a non-verbal concept. 'You can do a whole load of stuff scene by scene,' he says. 'If it has resonance on different levels, you can talk mainly on one level, and if it's true, the validity will carry onto the other levels. But you don't ever have to really talk about this.'

Fred Elmes suggests Lynch kept him on the periphery of the film's meaning, but still communicated enough to make his work possible: 'He gave me little clues as to what it meant. He gave me enough to keep me involved – to keep me hooked with it.'

Before the individual elements could come into their own, however, the cast and crew needed to be completed.

Doreen Small had worked on a blaxploitation movie called *Cool Breeze* (1972) with Lynch's best buddy, Jack Fisk (formerly Luton). Fisk, who would assume the physically agonising role of the Man in the Planet as a favour, recommended to her that David would appreciate the type of manager who went scouting around for cheap props. She duly found several items to decorate Henry's grim, shadow-swathed apartment and private universe, including a picture of an atomic mushroom cloud, which hangs upon his wall like other 9-to-5ers have a Pacific Island or Paris street scene, and a 'kind of sticky, oily, hair stuff' found at a 'kind of oil well over on Robertson Avenue'. She was quickly inducted.

The recruitment of the cast was pure, peachy-keen serendipity. All roles were filled by the first actors Lynch auditioned. Given the film's tortuous production history, it has to be assumed that the right people presented themselves (a perverse compliment, in itself), rather than that the director was unduly hasty.

In fact, one of the most remarkable aspects of *Eraserhead* is how keenly a group of badly-paid, experienced but unknown actors took to playing a group of grotesques in a psychotic world, their alienated, non-communicative mode of speech suggesting they recognised – as Samuel Beckett surely did – that most everyday conversation is simply the sound of one hand clapping. While the film's dark comedy was severely underrated on first release, there's little doubt that a sense of fun permeated the set when things were running smoothly.

Also remarkable was the fact that cast and crew were granted bare subsistence money (with the exception of cinematographer Herb Cardwell, who received a proper union salary) from a budget whose meagre size seemed to preclude it.

'I had worked on other AFI films,' recalls production assistant Catherine Coulson (who would much later become the Log Lady in *Twin Peaks*), 'where it was just assumed that the actors and technicians worked for free, but David took his initial money from AFI and paid everybody. I was making $25 a week, but when we ran real low on money, we cut everybody's salary in half. I put it all back into the food; we would all kind of pool our money to some extent. It really did seem like our film, even though it was David's film. There was a sense of collaboration.'

The lead role, that of Henry Spencer (now granted a surname), the subconsciously-stranded geek with the vertical bouffant, went to Jack (then billed as John) Nance. Never has an actor become such an iconic screen figure while remaining so barely known – but then, on *Eraserhead*, few of cinema's rules had any application.

Nance, a reliable Texas-raised trouper, had made a negative progression from the stage to a number of cheapo action pictures. But he almost didn't get the part.

'We didn't have that great an interview,' Lynch would admit. Catherine Coulson – Nance's wife at that time – explained, understatedly, that 'Jack is not the kind of person who gets very enthusiastic unless something really catches his imagination.'

Nance himself was more than a little wary of Lynch. The rest of the cast and crew all found their young director immediately agreeable – he was boyishly charming, polite, with quaint manners formed in the pre-rock 'n' roll 1950s of his early childhood, making casual use of unhip terms like 'neat' and 'nifty'.

To Nance, however, the student director had a faint whiff of self-conscious wackiness about him. At a time when the gaudy, unrestrained self-expression of the late '60s had

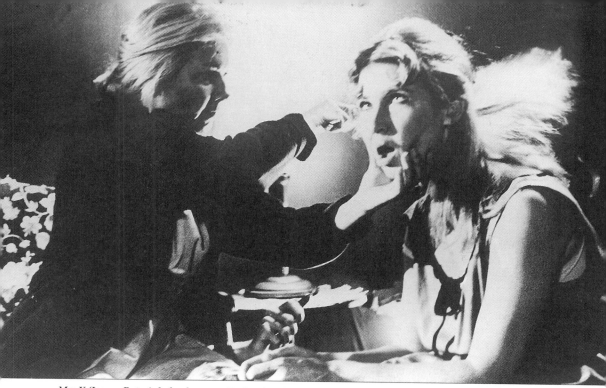

Mrs X (Jeanne Bates) shakes her neurotic daughter Mary (Charlotte Stewart) out of a catatonic trance in Lynch's classic debut feature **Eraserhead** *(1976). Jeanne Bates was formerly cast as 'nice young mothers' in 22 pictures under contract for Columbia; to shed her former image, she donned false moles and matted hair.*

become a dreary uniform of lank, long hair and yards of blue denim, the young David Lynch came across as affectedly foppish, rather than as an identikit hippy. By the time shooting on *Eraserhead* was well underway, the débutant director regularly donned an old straw hat and no less than three wide, '70s-style ties around his neck.

'We kept our distance at first,' recalls Nance of his first impression. 'Lynch wasn't sure, and I wasn't sure.' It was only as they were taking leave of each other in the car park that Nance made the chance comment which cemented a working relationship and an enduring friendship. He spotted an old Volkswagen which had been fitted with a big, home-made wooden roof-rack: 'It was kind of an ingenious design. You could probably load as much on the VW as you could on a truck. I thought, "What a neat thing." So I said, "Boy, whoever built that thing must be on the ball." And David said, "Thank you, Jack. I did that, and you're hired."'

For his own part, Nance was becoming fascinated by Lynch's provincial vision of urban hell for reasons of his own. 'I was reading all of these strange images in the script,' he recalled. 'And then I got to the final scene where there's the giant baby head. I was struck by that because it was describing, in some detail, a sort of hallucination I had at one time when I was very sick and running a fever . . . I was in a hotel room in Great Bend, Kansas, in a blizzard, dying, and I had a terrible nightmarish kind of hallucination. When I was reading that scene I thought, "My God, this is exactly like that time in Great Bend." And then later, when he introduced me to the Baby, I said, "That's it."'

Just for an hour or two, at least, Jack Nance had known what it was like to actually *be* Henry Spencer.

As for Catherine Coulson, she was to become every bit as essential a component of the *Eraserhead* ensemble as her husband, though she would not occupy a moment's screen-time of the final cut.

Initially cast in the part of the disgusted nurse who hands over Henry and Mary's premature, mutated baby, she auditioned for the part wearing 'a prim little dress and my hair tied back very severely', and was hired instantly. Ms Coulson soon found herself occupying a similar production assistant/jack-of-all-trades position to Doreen Small.

'Well, since you're going to be here,' Lynch would suggest to her, 'would you like to hold the boom or push the dolly?' As a consequence of new-found dedication, she later found herself in the perverse position of adjudging her own scene as inessential and insisting it be cut, when production time and money were running out.

'We became like a family,' she remembered fondly. 'Basically Jack's and my home life became *Eraserhead*, and oftentimes, after we were through shooting, David would come over, and we would eat pancakes at our house. Peggy and Jenny used to come down to the stables, and Jenny would ask David if she could go play with the Baby [the working model]. I remember spending New Year's Eve at the stables. We were all drinking champagne and Jack gave Jenny, who was about four, a couple of sips of champagne so she would go to sleep. We all listened to music and had a real nice time in our little home away from home.'

Within a year of that idyllic holiday scene, the same little nuclear family would split. The fact that even New Year's Eve was spent at the *Eraserhead* studios was symptomatic of the obsession which drove the project. In 1973, that positive obsessiveness would be tempered with desperation, as it became a grinding, seemingly futile ordeal just to keep going.

The marriage of David and Peggy Lynch did not survive this intense period. More positively, although he neither did nor could take direct responsibility for the raising of his daughter, Jennifer Lynch remained 'Daddy's girl', always close to her father – his influence on her life becoming ever more marked as she grew to adulthood.

Once casting was complete, the fresh-faced helmsman began theatrical rehearsals on the first shot: the tragicomic scene where Henry arrives home at his apartment to find Mary having great difficulty feeding their malformed offspring. With no experience to measure his provisional schedule against, Lynch asked Catherine Coulson to time the scene with a stopwatch. But the running time of one scene is no indication of a film's length of production.

'It was supposed to take a few weeks to shoot,' she remembered in amused disbelief. 'I think the original shooting schedule was six weeks.'

The first shot of the production went entirely without a hitch, performed in a single take on 29 May, 1972. A small delegation of AFI directors showed up to witness the shoot, and, as Lynch recalled: 'They thought everything was under control. It looked like we were really rolling – and we were.'

Despite the provisional six-week schedule, shooting would continue semi-regularly into the early part of the next year. By the time the film had finished shooting, been through post-production and received its preview screening, it would be more than four years since David Lynch pieced together his crew and began pre-production work.

'I always say I met David as a young woman,' stated Catherine Coulson cheerfully, 'and by the time I had finished *Eraserhead*, I had aged.'

Requests for further funding, as the project stretched on into the next calendar year, were met with little more than goodwill. 'I ran out of the Institute's money, and had to raise more myself,' remembered Lynch with lingering frustration. 'Because we needed more and they'd already given quite a bit, they said that they didn't want to stop it. They just said, "We can only help you now in terms of equipment. You're going to have to get the money somewhere else."'

'It finally took about five years from the time I started shooting to the time it was released. The shooting took about two years, and the rest of the time was spent raising money.'

Another potential crisis – the resignation of cinematographer Herb Cardwell in

February 1973, when Lynch could no longer afford to pay him – was deflected by the hiring of Fred Elmes. Working on a similar peppercorn stipend to the rest of the crew, Elmes' enthusiasm was initially sparked by the sheer otherworldliness of the project.

'They selected a couple of reels of film to give me a feel of what was happening – to see if I wanted to be involved. They started with the real tame stuff: Henry in his room, walking outside and so on. And then they got to the Baby, which they saved for the end, and God, I didn't know what to make of it. It was bizarre, but captivating at the same time. I just didn't know what I was getting involved in. But I really was hooked right from the beginning.'

At his first day on set, Elmes soon discovered that, despite the cast and crew's dedication, *Eraserhead* was still very much the child of one man. 'Everybody knew what to do and what not to do,' he'd later recall. 'So I went into it the way I normally would, which is in a very quiet way, taking charge of what needs to be done and to do it myself.

'We were doing a close-up of the Baby, and David had looked through the camera and lined it up, and it was all ready to go. And I went over to the table, and I moved this little prop over so that it was not hidden so much by something else. And Catherine turned to me and said, "Fred, we don't move things on that table." And I said, "Well, it's just that it was blocked, and I wanted to see it more clearly." And she said, "Well, David has never moved anything on the table." So I put it back. Heaven forbid David should see!' Elmes laughed, in recollection of the dedicated obsessiveness he became part of.

By this second calendar year of production, cast and crew were ensconced in Lynch's surreal vision of urban, industrial existence.

Early in the film, one of the most basic and significant effects was used to illustrate what eventually became a personal Lynch motif: floating – adrift; alone; on the edges of consciousness and chance. When the haunting figure of Henry Spencer opens the film, bobbing unsupported through his personal stratosphere, it signifies that we are to follow him on the currents of unconsciousness, and that he is a passive player in his own existence.

For the opening, Elmes and his crew placed the camera sideways, upside down, every which way against the motionless Jack Nance. 'But we couldn't get him to float right,' he recalled. 'We knew where he was going to go in the shot; we knew what the move was, and how long. We just didn't know how to get it. We shot it a couple of different ways, and ended up with him sitting upright and the camera sideways. We locked the camera off, and he sat on the dolly, and we just dollied him back and forth – bobbing up and down against a black background.'

Similar, but more elaborate techniques would be used at the end of the film. Once more, the figure of Henry was to be filmed against a black background, this time a black curtain spattered with small lights representing distant star belts. This is for the climactic scene where 'reality' – or at least that part of Henry's private universe we recognise most easily – starts to destabilise, ending in the implosion of his apartment. The curtain was 20 feet high by 60 feet wide, with lights at the rear to shine through a series of holes for the stars. Given the expanse of the background, the scene had to play as an outdoor shot.

'And it could only be done at a weekend,' remembers Elmes, 'because the only area available was the gardeners' area down at the stables. There was no way we could interrupt their schedule, so Friday at 4 p.m., when they left, we moved in and hung the curtain, and we put up the dolly track and started lighting it. It took the whole weekend to do it, so we actually shot it that Monday at 3 a.m. We had to work very quickly, grab the shot, then clean up real fast so we'd disappear by the time the gardeners came in at 7 a.m.

'I don't know when I slept sometimes. We were on a night schedule, partly because a lot of it had to be shot at night, and partly because David enjoyed working at night more. I would be at the

AFI all day, working on other films, and then at 5.30 p.m. we'd watch dailies from the night before, and then start shooting – until 3 or 4 a.m. And everyone did this. It just became a way of life.'

Such conviction beyond the call of duty was no guarantee of anything running smoothly. After the frenzied weekend rush to film Henry in front of the star curtain, the daily rushes revealed a malfunction on one of the high-speed cameras. Sure enough, the whole process had to start again the following weekend, regardless of time and money already spent.

'At the time all those problems were earth-shattering,' testified Elmes, 'because we didn't always have the money to reshoot something, and we hadn't had the years of experience to know exactly what it was that went wrong.'

After more than half a century of technical progress in the cinema, the director and crew of *Eraserhead* were utilising the same paste, paint and push techniques as the pioneer of film illusion, former stage magician Georges Melies, back in the late 1890s / early 1900s.

Despite all the degrees of obsession, loyalty and sacrifice, in the spring of 1973 filming shuddered to a halt. Describing this dark period in his life, Lynch recalls, 'The project was like an animal dying in the desert. At first, the birds stay very far away, and then, little by little, they come in and start taking bites. And you're just too weak to get them off you.'

For these ravenous carrion, read the AFI.

'I really thought it was the end,' he recalled, clearly not quite over the experience after years of contemplation. 'They'd come down and take some piece of equipment, and it would be a horror. Then they'd come down and take something else, and I'd say, "You're going to bring it back?" And they'd say, "Sure, we're going to bring it back." They would never come back.'

As the by-now dedicated cast and crew drifted back to their civilian lives, David Lynch found himself adrift in the world of his imagination again – but without the means to externalise it, or to dredge anything up from its depths.

'I worked in a restaurant, and David would come down in the afternoon and do some jobs in exchange for a grilled cheese sandwich and fries,' recalls Catherine Coulson. 'He was always doing odd jobs; we found him lots of things to do to support himself.'

Lynch himself described how he survived during this period: 'My landlord had several buildings and he found out that I very much enjoyed installing hot water heaters. And then I was building sheds, that didn't make any money, and I was delivering the *Wall Street Journal*, for the big bucks. I was making $48.02 a week.'

Fred Elmes was kept busy on his next project, cinematography for John Cassavettes' *The Killing of a Chinese Bookie*. However, he kept the faith and kept in touch. 'David and I used to live a block from each other. Even in the time we were not shooting, we were planning. We would have so many napkins and place mats that had block diagrams and little storyboards written on them as to how we were going to do effects, and what we would have to build in order to do the effect.'

'I was quite desperate at times,' admitted Lynch. Desperation fostered a yearning for the simpler, art school days of *The Alphabet* and *The Grandmother*, and the animation techniques used to create them. 'I even wanted to build an eight-inch tall Henry and animate – or stop-motion – him through sets to connect the scenes that hadn't been finished.'

But slowly, over the remaining months of 1973, those patiently, persistently oiled wheels were to start moving again.

Once again, all of the endlessly-loyal ensemble dug in. Personal loans were obtained from family and friends; deferments were negotiated on production costs; the equipment which the AFI had reclaimed was begged back; agreement was reached via an AFI board member with CFI, the processing lab, whereby they would develop the film's negative. Shooting would eventually resume on 29 May, 1974, two years to the day after it had begun.

Meanwhile, David Lynch's personal life had fragmented.

He separated from his wife Peggy in 1973, leaving her and their young daughter at the marital apartment. Much as it's presumptuous to attribute the break-up to the tortuous gestation of *Eraserhead*, it can be assumed that the constant financial pressure, and the aspiring artist's near-insane dedication to his creation, cannot have helped in any way.

Since production stalled in 1973, Lynch had remained ensconced in the dark world of *Eraserhead* as much out of necessity as obsession. With nowhere else to live, he had taken up residence in the set of Henry's apartment room at the AFI stables. 'I love going into another world,' testified Lynch, snatching something positive from the ashes of a very intense period. 'And film provides that opportunity. *Eraserhead* way more than any other film, because I really did live in that world. I lived on the set, and in my mind I lived in that world. And the sets, the lighting, the mood of it helped. And since it took so much time, I really sank into it.'

One final production crisis was still to come. It originated with the American Film Institute, backtracking on their earlier acceptance of *Eraserhead* as a feature film. Acceptance had been implicitly given by their funding of the project, prior to the drying-up of funds which stopped shooting in the first year.

'But then around that time,' Lynch remembered, 'the unions told them, "If you're going to have us come in and help you, give seminars, and help bring these people along, we don't want you making films that are going to compete with ours. You can't make feature films."

'We kind of got kicked out of AFI. After two or three years of being down there, they suddenly gave us this unrealistic, ridiculous deadline.'

With an estimated 30 hours of shooting still to take place, the *Eraserhead* ensemble were given 30 straight hours to get the whole thing finished. With one break for the director's *Wall Street Journal* deliveries, the film came in, incredibly, on time.

'We were totally exhausted, but we got everything done,' Lynch recalled with mixed feeling. 'But we weren't used to shooting like that, being under the gun. There are a lot of things that you might think of along the way if you have time, but we had to just race through it.'

Gradually, production was drawing to a close on one of the most unusual projects in cinematic history, where the uncompromising images on screen were almost matched by extremes of obsessive forbearance and sacrifice, not least on the part of the film's originator.

'I feel that I shouldn't have spent so much time on *Eraserhead*,' Lynch would later reflect. 'I should like to have made more films in that time, but it wasn't happening.'

As tribute to his all-American 'can-do', however, Lynch had brought to the screen a startling series of images no commercial production company would possibly have backed.

II — ERASERHEAD (1976) — 'A Dream of Dark and Troubling Things'

A 30-year-old man floats horizontally against a black background. The shock-headed man, Henry, regards a planetoid which hangs suspended in space.

The Man in the Planet sits in a desolate basement by a grimy, cracked window – he may be the janitor of Hell, or a malevolent God. Much of the Man's face and naked torso is badly burned, his skin hanging from him in flaps. He pulls levers which release a huge, sperm-like creature from Henry's mouth.

The Man in the Planet sequences, which begin and end the film, were shot in one day. Art director Jack Fisk, Lynch's good friend and husband of then-obscure actress Sissy Spacek (both of whom put money into the project), took the part as a favour to his

The Man in the Planet: the deformed janitor who wields God-like influence over Henry's universe. Played by Lynch's lifelong friend, Jack Fisk, in uncomfortable body make-up.

struggling mid-Western friend. 'I'd just started growing a beard,' remembered Fisk with good humour, 'and I'd had it for about two weeks. David got this stuff to cover my beard, but make my skin look kind of deformed. When I went home after doing this, I tried to get it out. Sissy didn't want me to shave my beard off, so I was in a tub of hot water, pulling it out a little piece at a time. I've never really forgiven David for that.'

The creature falls to earth, splashing down in a puddle. It is daylight. Henry is walking through the grey, industrial landscape. He steps directly in the muddy puddle where the creature has fallen. His hair stands five or six inches above his head; his black suit is neat but at least one size too small. His perambulatory odyssey – past deserted factories and derelict houses – is accompanied by the murmur of machinery.

Henry Spencer's mutated 1950s fashion sense is, for many, one of the endearing, lighter touches of the film. In the early days of production, during the sloppy early '70s, Henry's appearance was guaranteed to mark him as uncool. However, given Lynch's own pop-aesthetic sensibilities, veering defiantly between the '50s and the present day, it's clear he always regarded Henry as more than a caricature nerd.

By the time of the movie's late '70s release, in the punk era, Henry came over as so anti-hippy he was hip. Second-hand thrift-store fashion was a style statement for youth who disdained mass-produced '60s hangover threads or Travolta-esque discowear. As Lynch recalled, poor, tormented working stiff Henry was almost a proto-punk in this respect: 'Henry's whole wardrobe was gotten at Goodwill. [Goodwill Industries, the US charity store.] It was like we were going shopping, and we got his shoes and his socks and his pants, his penholder and all his pens, and got him all geared up with his little tie tack and his tie.'

Rather than any kind of rock 'n' roller, however, Henry's persona is closer to a tragic clown figure. With his half-mast trousers and comical walk, he calls up distant echoes of Jacques Tati, one of his creator's few self-confessed cinematic heroes. In this light, Henry is a visual comedian, cut adrift in the darkest recesses of his own subconscious. (Jack Nance's assertion that he found himself copying Lynch idiosyncrasies, like speaking all his dialogue as if he was merely muttering to himself, identifies the character as the darker side of the director's own subconscious.)

The classic Henry hairstyle is an original Lynch design, with modifications. His directions to Nance were to keep it short at the sides, with about two inches of hair brushed thickly back on top. As Nance had last had his hair cut about two weeks prior to shooting, he enlisted his wife's aid on the first night, who admitted to 'a kind of maniacal pleasure from backcombing his hair'.

Nance, unafraid to look geekish for his art, was stuck with the wild neo-pompadour for several years. As Catherine Coulson remembered: 'One of the hardest things was keeping Jack's haircut all those years. When he wasn't shooting for a while, he would let it go, but then poor Jack would have to have another haircut before starting to shoot again. My family didn't know him any other way really, except with that goofy hair.'

Inside Henry's room, all is darkness except for the glow of a single light-bulb. The window faces directly onto a brick wall. Fungus and wild flora grow in patches; a miniature tree grows from a mound of earth without a plant pot. He searches his chest of drawers for a single photo of Mary, which is torn in two pieces. The chest is covered in seaweed. The radiator hisses threateningly and gives off steam.

To emphasise the time that elapsed during shooting, Lynch pointed out the otherwise invisible join between two early scenes: 'There's a scene where Henry, the main character, is walking down a hall and he opens the door to his apartment. And then there's a cut to the interior of the room to show him walking in. Well, he walked in a year and a half after the shot in the hall was done.'

Henry's path to the house of Mary X and her family runs along the railway track. Industrial noise alarms him. He recoils from the growls of unseen wild dogs.

The home of the X family is separated from the railway tracks by a high wire fence. Inside, shuddering vibrations from the nearby railway cuttings are continually heard and felt. Metal pipes litter the decaying rooms. A litter of puppies suckle at their mother's teats on the kitchen floor. Grandma X sits catatonically in the kitchen, a lit cigarette placed between her unmoving lips burning away to ash. All the while, malfunctioning lights flicker.

Mary begins to slip into an epileptic fit, and is brought out of it by Mrs X. Henry is introduced to Mary's father, Bill X, a plumber and affable imbecile. Bill has seen the area pass from a meadows to 'the hell-hole it is today'. He put in most of the metal piping himself, whining. 'People think pipes grow on trees. They don't!' (Though in Henry's universe, pipes could be the only things which grow on trees.) Conversational repertoire exhausted, he makes mindless smalltalk. 'Well, Henry, what do you know?' he asks, inanely grinning. 'Oh, I don't know much of anything,' Henry replies anxiously.

As the AFI grant money ran out, Lynch and the crew tried to raise funding by showing the first completely edited, soundtracked scene to an unidentified producer. The scene was the first part of Henry's visit to the X household, as described above. Jack Nance remembers: 'The producer blew his stack. He was enraged; he was offended. He went storming out of the screening room, and he was yelling, "People don't talk like that! People don't act like that! You people are crazy! What do you think you're doing?"'

Much later, when the film had achieved cult status, many viewers squirmed in their seats at the recognition that people do, in fact, talk like that. Henry's visit to the X house is every stiff, awkward meeting with the family of a close friend or partner, amplified *ad absurdum*.

The family are fed individual, fist-sized, man-made chickens. 'Strange damn things,' says Bill, 'but they're new!' Henry is invited to carve. The minute chicklet he tries to dismember goes into a synthetic death agony, emitting a thick, dark gunk which could as easily be 3-in-1 Oil as blood. Mrs X follows her daughter into convulsions, hysterical at the sight of the discharging chicken.

Mrs X enquires, 'Did you and Mary have sexual intercourse?' Henry is too terrified to answer. She licks his face, and has to be pulled off him. The stress gives Henry a nosebleed. She announces he's left Mary with child, their baby about to be sent home from the city hospital. 'Mother,' Mary cries, 'they're not even sure if it is a baby!' 'It's premature, but it is a baby,' retorts Mother.

Henry returns home. Checking his mailbox, he finds a wriggling animated worm inside. He enters, giving a faint smile to mother and child. The Baby is a malformed amphibian of unspecified gender, limbless, with bandages binding its bell-shaped torso, its neck pencil thin, unable to support its slimy, oval head. It constantly gives out a haunting, discordant cry for attention.

Equal extremes of pathos and revulsion are born from the fact that the Baby appears so intolerably real – at least, it's a credible representation of how a foetus might appear if not allowed to develop beyond the pre-human stage. For this, the credit, as with much else, belongs to Lynch. Having designed and built the Baby, he then maximised its original impact by ensuring that no stills of it were released during the publicity stage.

'In a way, nobody designs anything,' reflected Lynch, when credited with one of the most haunting non-human beings in cinema. 'All these shapes are found in nature. They are archetypes that everyone can relate to even if they can't intellectualise why.'

Mary returns to her parents' house 'to get a night's sleep before I go crazy'. Henry's concerned when the Baby spontaneously develops a suppurating rash and respiratory problems, nursing it back to health. But whenever he tries to leave the apartment it screams for him to come back.

That night, Henry finds Mary back in bed with him. He reaches for her, but touches the little spermazoid monsters emanating from her body. As he stares at their crushed remains, the small cabinet beside them opens to reveal the worm from the mailbox. Its mouth opens to swallow the camera's point of view.

For the 'spermazoids', the semi-foetal invaders of Henry's unconscious, Lynch procured his raw material from the maternity ward itself. Specifically, he got the resourceful Catherine Coulson to bring back a supply of freshly-cut umbilical cords from a local hospital. 'There's nothing like the real thing,' he disarmingly explained his fascination with organs and viscera.

'I was under the bed to keep tension on the umbilicals,' remembered Doreen Small of this most visceral effect. 'The "billy cords", as Jack would call them. And Jack pulled, and we sort of missed, and one of them landed in his shoe. He got so grossed out that we had to stop shooting for a couple of days.'

When Henry wakes again in the morning, he finds Mary is not with him. As he sits immobile in

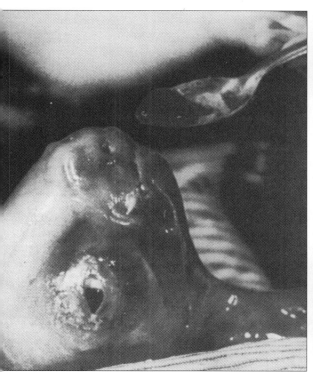

*The Baby: pitiful amphibian personification of Lynch's fears of parenthood and responsibility. Repulsively lifelike, the director's foetal design found echoes in movie creatures from the gestating **Alien** (1979) to **ET** (1982).*

his storm-beaten apartment, the Baby no longer shrieks at him but laughs – whether contentedly or mockingly is not clear. He gazes longingly at the light-well behind the radiator, and a small stage opens up to him. The Lady in the Radiator enters the stage, a beaming, peroxide-blonde cutesy-pie, who smiles coyly at Henry while clasping her hands and dancing an awkward, shuffling step to cheesy old vaudeville muzak. Close up, she has grossly swollen and scarred cheeks. Her stage is fired with spermazoids by the Man in the Planet. She never stops smiling, nor misses a step, just stomps the sperm-shaped creatures into white pools on the floor.

As Lynch admits, the original tone of the film was relentlessly dark and nihilistic; as Doreen Small recalled, 'It was much less of a dream and much more of a nightmare when we began.' Its bleak, no-hope feel suited the trapped, pessimistic way Lynch himself felt beneath his light, boyish exterior – 'an insecurity thing', as he almost dismissively terms it. Living on caffeine and nicotine (his drugs of choice to this day, albeit in more moderate doses), every setback, major or minor, wore heavily on his nerves. His temper was becoming brittle, his mood misanthropic. 'I had everything going for me,' he recalls, 'I was supposedly doing what I wanted to do more than anything else: making films. I practically had my own little studio, and we were working: but I just wasn't happy.'

Lynch discovered meditation, a non-chemical way of maintaining mental equilibrium which he continued to practise for many years. He remembers the moment when he decided there was no reason why the physical ugliness of Henry's universe should not conceal a little tarnished beauty: 'One day I was sitting in the food room, and I just drew this little lady, and little foetuses were falling out of her. And I thought she would live in the radiator, where it's nice and warm, and this would be a real comfort for Henry. So, I went running into this set, which was just across the hall, and I looked at the radiator, and lo and behold, there was this little square in it. It was perfect. And not only that – we had shot scenes with Henry looking at the radiator two different times; there was nothing extra we had to shoot. It fit in perfectly.'

The Lady herself was a genuine showgirl – Laurel Near, part of a three-sister singing trio, was introduced to Lynch by Catherine Coulson. 'I thought I was just going to dance across the stage,' she asserted, but she soon found herself subjected to the Lynch facial plastics kit. Lovingly, he built on her fair cheekbones until symmetrical lumps of plaster and putty suggested swelling tumours and scar tissue. 'My face hurt a lot after the sessions,' she recalled without bitterness.

Henry is visited by the Beautiful Woman Across the Hall. They embrace on his bed, as it becomes a deep pool of vaporous liquid. The Baby screams as they embrace; the Beautiful Woman tries to look over her shoulder but Henry prevents her as they sink into the liquid.

Alone again, Henry watches another stage performance by the Lady in the Radiator. She sings to reassure him, her repetitive rhyme becoming almost mantra-like:

'In Heaven, everything is fine.

You got your good things, and I got mine.'

She disappears in a blinding flash, to be replaced by the Man in the Planet. A leafless tree wheels itself onto the stage. Henry's head falls off slipping through a thick pool of blood as if passing through an oil fountain, hitting the sidewalk outside. A young boy claims the severed head; he hurries along to a nearby factory workshop, where the manager considers it as raw material. The men lift open the split scalp and remove a piece of Henry's brain. It is loaded into a machine. The machine's conveyor system fills pencil ends with erasers.

In this most entertainingly macabre of scenes – like a kid's version of *Un Chien Andalou* produced by Disney – which grants the film's prosaically surreal title, Lynch displays the morbid, phobic night terrors of an insecure man, transformed into something approaching slapstick comedy.

However much psychological conjecture has been spent on the 'meaning' of *Eraserhead*, it's little remarked upon that the eraserhead sequence itself is only a few hallucinatory degrees removed from an uninterpreted presentation of insecurity nightmares, such as the random crumbling of teeth or suddenly finding oneself stark naked in a crowded public place.

Eraser shavings fly into the air, where they transform into star constellations.

Henry is back at the grim apartment block. Outside his apartment door, the Beautiful Woman Across the Hall goes to her room with a sleazy, moustached man. She sees Henry with the Baby's screaming, amphibian head instead of his own. Downstairs, someone is having the hell beaten out of him by a group of attackers. The Baby's cry is subdued by its respiratory illness. Henry approaches gingerly, cutting the bandages from around the child's torso. To his horror, its cardio-vascular system is revealed to him. Maddened, he takes the scissors and plunges them into the Baby's exposed, beating heart.

Gushing toxic discharge emits from the dying Baby's body. Henry is menaced by a gigantic double of the little Baby's head. The Man in the Planet maniacally throws levers, but the planet explodes.

Lights rapidly short-circuit and spark; the faithful Lady in the Radiator steps forward to meet the terrified awake-dreamer in an embrace, his suffering over.

Henry's waking nightmare: his displaced head lies on the floor, while the mutant Baby's head takes over his body. The scene takes place on the stage vacated by his dream woman, the Lady in the Radiator.

III – EXAMINING THE AFTERBIRTH

Just as *Eraserhead* can be defined as a journey into a damaged psyche, so its action takes place in a universe where the organic meshes viscerally with the mechanical, the environment is equal parts psycho-sexual and post-industrial. In its setting, we glimpse a rare, semi-autobiographical element in a work which otherwise eschews realism.

As already recounted, Lynch lived his poorest, most desperate pre-film school years in the city of Philadelphia. Ill at ease among the urban sprawl, the nervous young man still managed to remain for five years – to meet and marry his first wife, Peggy, and to become a father for the first time, to his daughter Jennifer, in 1968.

Under these circumstances, Philadelphia was not so much a city as a state of mind. The Lynch family lived in an industrial area that was already foreshadowing the economic recession of the '70s, like some municipal ghost-of-things-to-come. Its deserted factories, condemned tenement blocks, ghostly streets, trundling railway tracks and sooty windows loomed large in the young man's daydreaming mind.

As if to complement the environment, the nearer side of human grotesquerie never seemed far away: the Lynchs' apartment block ran parallel with the local morgue, and that less fortunate morbid obsessive, Edgar Allan Poe, agonised and drank himself crazy just a few blocks away, while working on a local newspaper.

Lynch would tell of an incident reflected in the later scenes of *Eraserhead*, when we briefly glimpse a man being attacked at the bottom of Henry's apartment block: 'I happened

31

The boy (Thomas Coulson) cradles Henry's head like a glittering prize. A vividly old-fashioned prop, with jelly spread on the neck stump, its very artificiality adds to the film's dream quality.

to be upstairs, painting the third floor black. And my wife at the time, Peggy, was taking my daughter, Jennifer, who was one, out in this perambulator. It was like the Cadillac of perambulators that we got at Goodwill for about a buck. It had springs – it had a ride like a giant Cadillac. Anyway, Peggy was taking this down the steps. And a large family across the street was going to a christening. And a gang came swooping down and attacked the family. And in the family there was a teenage son who tried to defend the whole bunch, and they beat him down, and they shot him in the back of the head. Those kind of things will spoil the atmosphere – *permanently* – and bring it way down.

'*Eraserhead* is the real *Philadelphia Story*. Philadelphia was a place I never wanted to go to – ever,' confessed a sensitive Lynch. 'It was really a frightening city. It has an atmosphere of fear, just all-pervading fear.' To evoke W. C. Fields, for many years, 'On the whole, I'd rather be in Philadelphia' was a comparison David Lynch would only apply favourably to death.

In more recent years, he has gathered enough of a perspective to make him soften towards the old place. At least, he now regards it as the single greatest influence on his life and work. 'There were places there that had been allowed to decay,' he recalled with fascination, 'where there was so much fear and crime that just for a moment there was an opening to another world. It was fear, but it was so strong, and so magical, like a magnet, that your imagination was always sparking in Philadelphia.'

Eraserhead is not about living in Philadelphia, however, not even on a metaphorical level – just as it is not specifically about anything. Anyone searching for a subject, theme, or even just a little direct interpretation has traditionally received little help from its creator. 'I don't know where it really came from,' he habitually claims. 'It was just ideas that popped into my head and were strung together.'

There's no reason to doubt that the film's brilliantly-realised images occurred randomly to the young director; that the imagery went totally unanalysed in its transference to the screen. It's this very neglect of his rational and critical faculties – no striving to make things clearer, no wilful misinterpretation of what his subconscious is saying – which ensures that what we see on screen is, quite genuinely, one man's unadulterated psychic slime.

Years later, Lynch would admit: 'People have – at least I have – habit patterns, and I wanted to look into one particular one. It was disturbing to me and others,' he offers semi-candidly, without giving too much away. 'So I decided I would go see this psychiatrist who was recommended by a friend . . . Then I asked him if it could negatively affect my creativity – and he said, "Maybe." That was it. I could see how, if you disturb the nest too much, you're liable to . . . you don't know what could happen. What it does is, it destroys the mystery, this kind of magical quality. I can be reduced down to certain neuroses or certain things, and since it's now named and defined, it's lost its mystery and the potential for a vast, infinite experience.'

Eraserhead is the rarest cinematic entity, a film that is not about dreams, but which, in its faithfulness to dream logic and undiluted subconscious imagery, actually *is* a dream. The censorship of rationality or intellect never intercedes between the image and its appearance on screen – even though, in some cases, it took many painstaking months to visually realise those images.

While the very many strands of *Eraserhead*, both personal and artistic, cannot be broken down to a simple equation of surrealism plus horror or film *noir*, one assumed influence can perhaps be completely written off. When the film eventually made its cult breakthrough in the late '70s, some critics, unable to forget memories of their own 1960s youth, opted for the lazy argument that *Eraserhead* must have something to do with hallucinogenic drugs.

Lynch, however, who was too busy scavenging for raw materials and delivering newspapers between shoots to go tripping round his own head, owns up to a rather more all-American abuse of mind-altering substances: 'Things got bleak at times, but they were bleak in a fun way. I think it was sugar that helped me a lot. I went to Bob's Big Boy, which is a restaurant out here. Every afternoon at 2.30 was Bob's time. I'd have a chocolate shake and several cups of coffee. I got such a rush from the sugar that a lot of times I felt much happier than I really was.' So much for the rock 'n' roll type who insisted the maker of *Eraserhead* must have been locked in a dark cupboard and fed peyote buttons.

The governing aesthetic of *Eraserhead* is ultimately one of fascination, not disgust. In its visualisation of both the post-industrial environment and the viscous, organic world of the sexual subconscious, it echoes the belief of Lynch's fellow obsessive, modernist SF author J. G. Ballard, that the only alien world worth exploring is the one we live in.

'If you set a new piece of steel out in a vacant lot,' Lynch would later explain, well versed in the mechanics, as well as the aesthetics, of decay, 'at first it doesn't have a lot going for it. It might be nice, but it's sort of a slow area. Then nature starts to work on it, and pretty soon it's a fantastic thing. It all started for me back in Philadelphia because it's old enough, and it's got enough things in the air, so that it can really go to work on itself. It's decaying, but it's fantastically beautiful. It gives you ideas. All the interactions of these chemicals and nature on things produce something that you could never get unless man and nature sort of worked together.'

In many ways, though *Eraserhead* is an otherworldly hybrid of industry and flesh, it's the biological details which linger in the mind of sensitive audience members – particularly the viscerally exposed Baby, as Henry pops its helpless little heart. Lynch, ever the obsessive, explained how he researched the subhuman Baby's interior, as the result of an aborted scene featuring a dead cat in a puddle.

'It was an experience,' he reflected. 'I examined all parts of it, like membranes and hair and skin, and there are so many textures that on one side are pretty gross, but isolated in an abstract way, they are totally beautiful. It's the kind of thing where, if you don't name it, it's beautiful. But as soon as you do, all kinds of associations become attached to it, and people will be turned off. To me, a lot of these things are really beautiful. And somehow, I think other people find the beauty in something that could be ugly in *Eraserhead*.

'Just like you talk about a piece of decaying meat. If you happen upon it in a certain setting, you could almost hear people *ooh*ing and *aah*ing about its beauty. Until they realised what it was. Then they would not find it beautiful anymore. As soon as it had a name to it.'

As for interpretations of the fleshy, organic side of *Eraserhead*, for a long time the consensus was a Freudian one: repressed sexuality, grown twisted and diseased; relived adolescent trauma; fear of both female and male genitalia.

Henry certainly seems frozen in a permanent adolescence. His relationship with the world is that of a passive, bemused onlooker – he cannot be said to have any true place in it. His desires are many, but frustrated. To compensate for the privations he's forced to accept, he spends most of his time alone in his room, daydreaming.

The moist, viscous detritus which litters his apartment – the uprooted plants, seaweed, containers of water – seem like some maladjusted displacement of fascination for the pudenda, and the need for physical contact. The sexual climate seems determined by the perception of a boy undergoing a particularly difficult puberty, who finds sex simultaneously alluring and nauseating, projecting his feelings onto fantasised images of disgust.

At the beginning of the film, the casting of the anthropomorphised sperm, out of the planet and, via an intense white light, into a puddle (or very literal gene pool), is as obvious a science fiction metaphor for conception as one could imagine. When eventually shown, the Baby itself is not much genetically advanced on the spermazoid, underlining what the film's Freudian enthusiasts have pinpointed as the horror or trauma of birth.

Similarly, Henry's climactic, harrowing murder of his helpless mutant child has been interpreted as the negating of his own sexuality – literally, mutilating his own penis. However, this seems much too narrowly Freudian an interpretation.

Though, for many years, Lynch avoided commenting on any biographical element the Baby may have represented, he was happy enough to number birth among his biological fixations. 'For a long time, and I suppose still, the idea of birth was a mysterious and fascinating thing, involving, again like sex, just pure meat and blood and hair. And then at the same time, this feeling of life and the spiritual thing. There's too many things going on there not to be fascinated. It's the weirdest thing.'

Jennifer Lynch had just about reached her fourth birthday when *Eraserhead* began production. Living with her mom and dad in a cramped one-bedroom apartment, she saw them separate when she was little more than a year older. Among the attendant pressures that can contribute to any marital breakdown, the strain felt by a couple of young parents when the male partner is only halfway out of training school, working on a pet artistic project and earning little money must be more than a little intense.

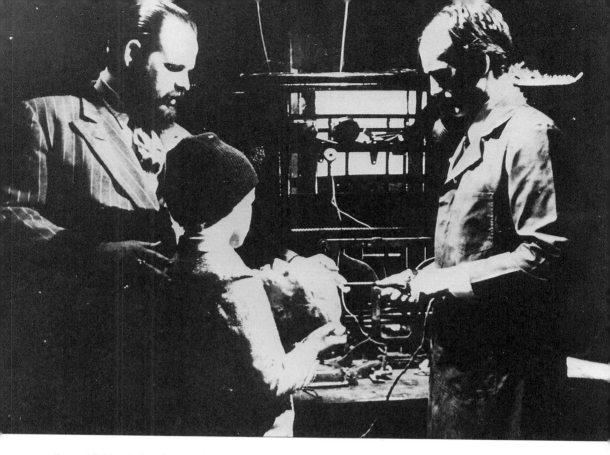

'I am stifled by the fear that I might wake up in the morning after a restless night's sleep to find there's nothing more than a stump left where my head was before.' – Traume *(Dreams), Friedrich Huch, 1904. The defining moment of the film: Henry's head is considered as raw material by the eraser factory boss and his machine operator (Neil Moran / Hal Landon, Jr.).*

'I think one of the main misconceptions,' the grown-up Jennifer Lynch would explain, 'especially as of late, is that the prime idea for *Eraserhead* came out of my birth. Although without a doubt it was inspired by my conception and birth, because David in no uncertain terms did not want a family. It was not his idea to get married, nor was it his idea to have children. But . . . it happened.

'I was born with clubbed feet, and people have made insinuations to the fact that because the baby in *Eraserhead* is deformed and all of this, certainly it had a lot to do subconsciously, as any event that takes place in life has a lot to do with things, but I don't think David credits that directly to where *Eraserhead* comes from. I think that if I had to interpret it solely, I'd say yes, that was influential, but a lot of it was as it is in the film: a very simple man who's thrown into a relationship and thrown into fatherhood, parenthood, is confused, and everything around him seems so immediately dark and strange, and he longs for this sort of clean, pure childhood image he had before all this happened to him.'

Perhaps the final overlooked aspect of *Eraserhead* is the humour. Granted, the film is not exactly a laugh-a-minute; but then, neither is it the unbearably bleak experience many imagined it to be on first viewing.

Henry's universe may be an extended nightmare, but he blunders through it with the childish bewilderment of Jacques Tati, Buster Keaton (that poker face, the world falling around him while he remains impassive), or even Stan Laurel (those vertical tufts of hair, the childlike inability to deal with an adult world).

Similarly, the X family may be grotesques, but they're also comical domestic characters. While the dream-logic exaggeration means that they behave nauseatingly at dinner (the comatose grandma with her cigarette, mother becoming orgasmic over the absurd man-made chicken), there's no doubt Lynch was having fun with them.

Their grotesquerie, like the corrosive anti-beauty of the industrial landscape, is actually one of the more enjoyable parts of Henry's grim universe. When mad Bill, the plumber, corners Henry in smalltalk, Henry defensively pleading 'I don't know much of anything at all,' the trademark whimper of Laurel, defending himself against a wild-eyed Ben Turpin, can almost be heard.

At the time, though, it all just seemed so overpoweringly dark.

IV — OUT OF THE WOMB

David Lynch had written the original working script for *Eraserhead* when he was a 26-year-old film student. By the time it premiered in Los Angeles, the city in which he was resident, he had recently turned 30.

Alan Splet recalled the spring 1976 rush to have the film ready for the Cannes Film Festival: 'I remember at some very late date, David and I finally agreed to do it, and it meant really working almost around the clock. I was sleeping in the same room that I was editing in. So for about a month and a half, I would work until 3 a.m., then I'd crash right away, get up the next morning, eat breakfast, go right back in and cut again.'

Their 'baby' was within a hair's breadth of its entry deadline. 'The film was a rough cut, but they said they would take one,' recalled Lynch. 'I got some money to go to New York — it was part of the *Eraserhead* money. And I got a shopping cart from the Farmer's Market; the owner let me have the cart to take the film to New York and back. I had 24 reels: twelve of sound and twelve of picture. I took it to New York, and I screened it for those people, but I never saw their faces. There were supposed to be three heavy-duty Cannes guys in this little screening room in some weird place in New York. All day I waited for my turn to show *Eraserhead*. Later, I found out that the Cannes guys went back the day before. I had flown all the way to New York and there wasn't anybody in the room.'

Chastened but unbowed, he then sent the rough cut by mail to the panel of the New York Film Festival. It was turned down, as it would be again the subsequent year. 'We figured that maybe it would get into some festivals. And that's all . . . I thought, there's no way I'm even going to get into festivals with this,' Lynch recalled soberly.

By this time, the aspirant (not to say desperate) director had remarried, this time around to Mary Fisk, sister of best friend Jack. With family and friends in the film industry, she decided to think positively on her husband's behalf, and urged him to enter it for LA's Filmex festival.

'It was the last day one could apply, and my wife said, "We're going to get in the car and drive over there and you're going to turn it in. You've got to give it a try." And I said, "Well, yeah, I'll just go over and get rejected again." So I went in and set the film down, and I said, "Look, this has been rejected from Cannes, it's been rejected from New York; you guys take a look at it." But he said, "We don't care where it's been rejected from. We're our own people. We're going to look at it, and we'll let you know."'

Eraserhead premiered at the 1976 LA Filmex festival, in a 110-minute cut. Beforehand, however, it received a private screening at the American Film Institute for cast, crew and AFI members (plus family, including Lynch's parents and daughter).

'The theatre was so quiet after screening,' remembered Fred Elmes. 'It was a little bit spooky. No one knew quite what to say. No one had seen it except for a couple of people, and nobody saw the whole movie together. And it was sort of different than anyone had imagined it to be. It was really a shock. It does take your breath away, and it's hard to know how to respond to it, which I think depressed David, because he was expecting some response.'

After the screening, the film's creator felt pressurised into drastic action. If the cast and crew could be shocked by something they themselves had laboured long and hard over, the prospect of an appreciative audience seemed further away than ever.

'The pacing is slow in *Eraserhead*, and that's great,' Lynch opined, reflecting on the final creative hurdle. 'I love the feel of it, but I think some scenes were dragging it down to where the pacing was painful. It was pushing you out of the film. I stayed out of the room at Filmex, but I could feel that it was too long. Fred was in there, and he said that people weren't reacting.

'So that night, I made a decision. In my heart, I knew some of these scenes had to go. I'd never been able to quite do it, but when you feel an audience not reacting, then you can do it. So out they came.'

In the first, Catherine Coulson appeared in a brief but sinister S&M scenario – originally recruited to play a nurse, this was the only scene with her that was actually shot.

'My friend and I were lying on a bed, bound by these kind of battery cables,' describes Ms Coulson. 'And the guy with the black box walks toward us with these prongs. It wasn't sexy; it was David's sexy, which is always kind of pristine in a way. And what happened was Henry hears these strange noises, and walks down the hall. He opens the door a crack, and this is his vision of what he sees. The women look at him, and he quickly shuts the door.'

Lynch described the second and most lengthy scene to be excised. 'Henry hears this sort of calling and he looks out his window. It's daytime, the wind is blowing dust, and there's the little kid out in the alley. He suddenly sees this shiny thing in the dirt, and he gets down and starts digging, and he finds these rows of dimes. So, he really starts digging, and Henry sees this. Henry runs out of the room, but the Baby starts crying; but he's got a good run going and he makes it to the elevator. He's pushing the button, but the elevator won't come. So he runs down the stairs. He runs into the lobby, and we see the elevator door is propped open with a mop. There's a mop bucket in there, and the landlady has been cleaning. That's why he couldn't get the elevator.

'But because the door's open, the Baby's crying is real loud and echoing all through the elevator shaft. So Henry gets frustrated and kicks the couch in the lobby, and the landlady comes and says, "Don't kick my wood." She starts into this landlady-tenant thing. So Henry leaves her and goes back upstairs. He looks out the window, and more people have come, and they're digging, and the dust is blowing. By night there's fighting going on out there.' All that's left of this 'gold-rush' scene is the brief glimpse of someone being beaten up.

One other scene cut from the final print deals with a strange kind of psychic disturbance: food horror. Henry is seen rushing to a drawer to look for a vaporiser to aid his wheezing Baby; the drawer is full of an unspecified, mulchy food, the stuff of many dyspeptic dreams.

'So the problem was how to make a drawerful of vanilla pudding,' recalled Catherine Coulson. 'Doreen and I went out to the grocery store, and we tried to figure out what kind of vanilla pudding would mix up the fastest. So we hand-beat instant vanilla pudding, filled this drawer with it, and then put these green peas on top of it.'

Lynch never specified the reasons for excision of specific scenes, bar the film's length and pacing. But somehow, the brief image described above sounds as if it might have had an altogether more discomfiting effect on the viewer than much of what surrounded it.

Now, twenty years down the line, with a plethora of 'special edition' releases of science fiction films on video, padded out with footage from the cutting room floor, the time seems overdue for a genuine director's cut of *Eraserhead*.

After Filmex, despite the director's fears, the film found itself an appropriate distributor. Ben Barenholtz, of Libra Films in New York City, had already made cult successes of Waters' *Pink Flamingos* (1972) and Jodorowsky's *El Topo* (1969) by playing the 1970s Midnight Movie circuit.

'The major studios will put a film out for a week and if it doesn't make so many dollars, they'll pull it forever,' Lynch explained. 'Well, Ben puts a film out, and just kind of weathers it. First, the real weirdos will see it; they'll see anything if it's running at midnight. And if it clicks with them, it'll enter the next phase, which is a slightly bigger group of people. And all these transitional areas are critical. But you can't tell how long it will take for the word to spread and for people to respond. The first night in New York, there were 25 people in the theatre. I think it went down to 24 the next night. But the next weekend, it got more and more people. And it went from there.'

'Dismal American Film Institute exercise in gore,' ran the sadly typical *Variety* review of 10 February 1977. 'Commercial prospects nil.' Blasting Lynch for what Filmex accurately claimed to be 'one of the most repugnant scenes in film history' (the murder of the Baby), the shell-shocked reviewer went on to puzzle at how he could spend five years of his life completing such a reprehensible film.

Ironically, it was the 'Pope of Sleaze', whose films were regular Midnight Movie crowd pleasers, who helped the film to find an audience which stood a chance of appreciating it.

'When *Eraserhead* opened, John Waters' film, *Desperate Living*, was opening at the same time,' Lynch recalled. 'At a personal appearance, he told the audience that his favourite film was *Eraserhead* and recommended that everyone see it. He really helped the film out.'

Slowly, almost imperceptibly, things happened. Word got back that the film had won both a jury award and a special award at the Avoriaz Film Festival in France. Stanley Kubrick was said to be deeply impressed by the film, viewed from a festival print in Britain. Most important of all, it was at last taken seriously in the press.

Jack Kroll's groundbreaking review in *Newsweek* told of poor Henry's journey through 'deliquescence', how the film depicted 'the ultimate corruption of matter itself throughout the universe', and ended in an 'internal apocalypse'. Unexpected as the acclaim may have been, Lynch would find from hereon that it was impossible for any reviewer not to treat his film seriously. *Eraserhead* was, at very least, acclaimed for being 'completely *sui generis*', as *Cinefantastique*'s K. George Godwin would write – one in a genre of one.

Most conducive to Lynch's askew vision were, oddly enough, the rock music press. In the years since Lynch had begun the film, there had been a sea change in youthful philosophy and fashion. Termed the 'Cold Wave' by the British rock paper *Sounds*, a disparate grouping of neo-musicians, would-be artists and acolytes found common ground in a determination to apply conceptual theory while avoiding the utopian dogma of the '60s; to move into darker, sometimes taboo areas; to experiment with 'sound', as opposed to music (few were actual musicians anyway); and a marked preference for industrial (or anything displeasing to conventional) aesthetics.

Eraserhead could have been made for them. *Sounds* raved about the film on a page normally reserved for news about the most fashionable bands, recommending it to those who enjoyed the stark, angular rhythms of Wire and Siouxsie and the Banshees.

The hippest bands were quick to echo the lip service, and *Eraserhead* began to seep its oily way into the cultural landscape. The US art-rock band Pere Ubu – who took their name from the proto-surrealist play, *Ubu Roi* – had a chubby singer in ill-fitting suits who, though much more rotund than Jack Nance, was frequently compared in appearance with Henry Spencer.

T-shirts showing the film title and Henry's startled face, against the legend A Dream of Dark and Troubling Things, abounded among young 'aesthetic nihilists'; art school poseurs cultivated the tight-suit-and-vertical-bird's-nest-coiffure look. An *Eraserhead* tribute single was one of the first independent 45s to be recorded by a lone performer on cheap electronic keyboards and drum machine, using early sound samples – in this case, of the screaming mutant baby.

In short, *Eraserhead* was the type of phenomenon which makes jaded pundits look back and say 'how very late '70s' it all was – failing to appreciate how the film's industrial and organic decay were personal obsessions which David Lynch pursued throughout the entire decade, and have still not left him.

By the early 1980s, Lynch repaid the film's devoted following among the sub-commercial underground by issuing an *Eraserhead* soundtrack album. Amidst spartan bursts of music, including Fats Waller's organ playing and Peter Ivers' eerily minimalist 'Lady in the Radiator Song', came long periods of stereophonically-balanced industrial noise. Though it might have seemed like a post-modern joke, it was a very timely nod to bands all over the West who were placing the sounds of industry on an equal or superior footing to rhythm and melody: Throbbing Gristle, Non, Einstanze Neubaten, SPK, Test Department – even UK electro-pop combo Depeche Mode would incorporate metal bashing into their better '80s recordings.

Though attitudes to Lynch's foray into the alternative music world were mixed, it would gain him enough respect for later direct musical collaborations. Meanwhile, the *Eraserhead* fetish among the 'nihilist generation' took a long while to abate, with noise-guitar band the Pixies making a stage staple of the 'Lady in the Radiator Song' in the late '80s.

In the late December 1979 issue of *Melody Maker*, various big names and gonna-bes were asked what their personal hopes were for the looming 1980s. Hard to imagine now, but the coming decade had a semi-futuristic feel – the 21st century was finally in sight, and all David Bowie desired to see the new era in with was then the rarest of artefacts: a personal videotape of *Eraserhead*.

Looking back over the ensuing decades, the cast and crew can be forgiven any self-satisfaction they feel at being a part of that period.

'It seemed like we were never going to finish the film,' remembered Jack Nance, at the time of playing the character Pete Martell on the *Twin Peaks* TV series. 'We had to scrap an awful lot, and we failed an awful lot. But we were kids then. Now we're old,' he mused philosophically.

'I think it never got any better than *Eraserhead* got,' said Doreen Small. 'Maybe it'll feel as good, but I don't think it can feel better that that. So committed to something, so proud of something . . . We were all hand-maidens to genius.'

In retrospect, Lynch even considers the American Film Institute's baling out of the project, and the subsequent financial hardship, to be a blessing in disguise. 'And every film that's made there now, AFI owns lock, stock and barrel, has all the rights, everything. I am a very lucky person. I was able to retain the rights to my film.'

Lynch still has to pay a profit percentage to the AFI, in return for their original expenditure plus loan of premises and equipment. Still, he regards it as a small price. Most remarkable of all, for the motion picture industry, Gentleman Dave from the tall timber country has honoured his long-term promise to treat every one of the loyal cast and crew fairly.

'Because he couldn't pay us, David offered us a percentage of the profit of the film – if and when it should ever make money,' remembered Fred Elmes. 'I certainly wasn't in it for the money, and we were all certain that it was not possible for the film to make any substantial amount of money. So, it's a welcome surprise that there's some money coming back.'

'There was a sense of collaboration,' recalled Catherine Coulson, 'which is why David gave us all such a nice percentage of the film – something we did not even write down until after the film started making money. The reward, artistically and emotionally, was great, but to be able to get some money back from it – a healthy cheque each quarter – is a real rarity in this particular business.'

So where was David Lynch, back in the late 1970s, when his monumental film was making its first waves?

Once business picked up, he was riding on a modest tide of optimism. After veering maniacally between obsessive productivity on the film and despair of its commercial chances, he'd decided the life of a full-time painter was no longer for him.

'Sound and picture – there are two senses involved,' he enthused. 'It can really do something. It covers so many different things. You can't get the same feeling for any other form. I really want to explore it in a "feeling" way, really learn about this business of pacing and what goes next to what, and think in terms of sound and picture real close together.'

To continue with his new-found career, however, he would have to find his first commercial backer. There was no stampede. Those few producers who had bothered to visit the arthouses were too vexed by the obvious question: where does a film-maker go after something like *this*? And they were not going to be the ones who financed the risk of producing something just as extreme.

David Lynch had spent half a decade totally devoting his life to a film which very nearly did not get made; after the initial stunned reactions, there was a gradual wave of recognition that this was the most remarkable independent film of the 1970s; it was becoming a huge cult among the more cerebral sections of non-conformist youth.

And he was going absolutely nowhere. For now, it was time to take refuge in the Metaphysics of Manual Labour once more.

CHAPTER THREE

The Elephant Man:

A Study in Human Dignity

While *Eraserhead* turned heads in the city of its birth, its creator was dividing his time between manual labour and writing a new screenplay. Though *Eraserhead* was a magnet for mainstream industry hostility, it also encouraged devotion among its more awe-struck converts. One comment, by an attendee of the film's LA premiere at the Nuart Theatre, is typical of the latter faction: 'I thought it was the best film I'd ever seen and certainly the most unique.'

The admirer was Stuart Cornfeld, an aspiring film producer. So impressed was he by the realisation of Henry's universe that he obtained David Lynch's phone number from the American Film Institute, to compliment him personally.

'I said, "Listen, I just wanted to tell you I thought your film was incredible,"' he recalls. 'Lynch thanked me, and I asked him what he was doing, and he said he was fixing roofs – that the initial reception that the film had was somewhat disappointing, and that he hadn't received any offers to do anything.'

Amazed by the industry's indifference to such a unique vision, Cornfeld got together with Lynch to commiserate. The two men got on just fine and dandy, and pretty soon met on a regular basis to kick around ideas for mutual projects.

Lynch already had another very personal baby in gestation: *Ronnie Rocket*, his latest script (see Chapter Four). For a while, Cornfeld proposed producing the project, until deterred by the executives he regarded as potential backers.

'I thought it would be commercial,' remembered Lynch, 'but other people who have track records predicting this didn't think so.' So for now, the pet project was shelved – albeit only temporarily, so far as Lynch was concerned. As we will see, however, it would be far from the last time he met resistance to the idea.

Once Lynch made his willing to compromise known to Cornfeld, wheels started moving. Within a few weeks, Cornfeld had met with another aspirant producer, Jonathan Sanger,

David Lynch on the set of **The Elephant Man** *(1980), returned to Europe, age 33, for the first time since his teenage years, with John Hurt, head shaven for his long ordeal in the make-up chair.*

who owned the rights to an original screenplay by writers Christopher De Vore and Eric Bergren. Cornfeld was loaned the script, impressed by its sensitive treatment of a grotesque subject, and immediately suggested his new friend Lynch as a suitably sympathetic director.

By this time, Lynch had also read the screenplay, while Sanger had taken the trouble to delve a little further into his creative background. 'We just started talking about the script, and everything I felt about it he felt about it too,' remembers Sanger. He recalled his first impression of the strange creativity he believed Lynch would bring to the project. 'When I saw *Eraserhead*, it was the kind of movie where just his use of film technique to me was astonishing for somebody who'd never had very much film experience before. And when I saw *The Grandmother*, I said, "Jesus, he's not a flash in the pan. This is somebody who has a real consistency of vision."'

Lynch was equally impressed with De Vore and Bergren's screenplay. Entitled *The Elephant Man*, it was a slightly fictionalised bioscript of Joseph Carey (renamed John, in the script) Merrick: a doomed Victorian from the era of the Industrial Revolution, who earned his title by being the most radically deformed person in recorded history.

Lynch admitted to not having heard of Merrick's pitiful story at the time, although as soon as he heard Cornfeld juxtapose the words 'elephant' and 'man', they 'made a little noise in my head'.

Born 1863, Leicester, in the English Midlands, Joseph Merrick is believed to have been a life-long sufferer from the incurable disease neurofibromatosis ('von Recklinghausen's disease' – not elephantiasis, which is a form of gigantism – but an alarmingly common condition which, while it has never distorted any other human being the way it did Merrick, is estimated to affect one in 3,000), causing huge, cauliflower-like growths on his bones and sacks of decaying 'elephant skin' on his torso. A literate and sensitive young man, he first worked as a cartographer but was forced to give up the job when his already severe but progressive deformity prevented him holding a pen. Like many other disabled people pre-Welfare State, he sold matches before entering the workhouse after the death of his mother.

Reliant on his own limited means, Merrick was persuaded by a travelling showman, calling himself 'the Silver King', to belie his essentially civilised and gentle nature by exhibiting himself across the country in freak shows. The two formed a partnership – far more congenial a relationship than that depicted in the screenplay, but which still ended in grief. In 1886, the Silver King absconded with all their funds while they toured Belgium. Merrick was released from the 'carny' treadmill by Dr Frederick Treves, a prominent surgeon who had examined him two years before. Treves' more benevolent method of exploitation made him a freakish celebrity to the British aristocracy, and Merrick died in a private room allocated to him at the Royal London Hospital, aged 27.

'I saw this strange-looking flesh,' Lynch would later reflect on the concept, ' with this beautiful soul inside, happening in the middle of industry, and I just was caught.'

Soon after, in the summer of 1979, Bernard Pomerance's play, also entitled *The Elephant Man*, would open on Broadway. But even the success of the play seemed to breed greater caution among movie executives paid specifically not to make independent decisions, but to wait to climb aboard the bandwagon of someone else's next big thing. (Some may have been convinced they were being asked to finance that surest of box office poisons, a theatrical adaptation. As we will see, that was not the only complication caused by the interchangeability of stage and screen titles.)

But the cavalry eventually rode in, in the unlikeliest of forms.

At this time, Stuart Cornfeld was working as associate producer on *The History of the World Part I* (1981), the latest excess-fest from Mel Brooks, ex-TV gag writer, stand-up comic, and writer-director.

'For years, people have been coming up to me and asking for my participation and/or help with their projects,' testified Brooks at the time. 'Well, I went through hell to get my first film, *The Producers*, made.'

Never forgetting his frustrating start in the industry, the comedian always harboured the kind of conviction most of its success stories soon forsake, that one day they will 'put something back'. 'I've always felt that I owed that to others. And so I formed a company with an idea that I would at least provide some seed money, at least take a chance and pay some Writers' Guild minimums to young people who wanted to write and direct films; people who I thought were worthy of this kind of attention.

'Jonathan Sanger, who was my first assistant director on *High Anxiety*, knew I was doing this kind of thing, financing scripts, etc. So he brought a rough draft of something called *The Elephant Man* to me. I called him at page 38 and said, "I don't have to read another word, I want to do this film, I want to finance it, this story must be told."'

Brooks recalled checking the track record of the new director his colleagues had told him so much about. 'I was flabbergasted,' is how he remembered his first viewing of *Eraserhead*, appraising it as a work of absurdist high art. 'You have to be a fool to love it, but I fell head over heels in love with this film. The symbolism, like Samuel Beckett's, was very clear to me, the story was incredibly moving, I thought the photography was brilliant, and I said, "This man is a major director."'

Like Sanger, Brooks somehow expected the creator of this unique vision to wear his obsessions on his sleeve. No sirree, Bob. Lynch turned up in his smart-casualwear, looking like a Joe Everyman symbol of the imminent 1980s: slightly shorter but still floppy light brown hair; Chino-style pleated slacks; tennis shoes; cotton shirt buttoned all the way up to the neck.

'I expected to meet a grotesque,' laughed Brooks, 'a fat little German with fat stains running down his chin. Instead, there's this clean American WASP kid, like Jimmy Stewart 35 years ago . . . Jimmy Stewart from Mars.'

Any doubts that Brooks would be totally behind this melancholic lament of a story were dispelled. While he went about raising the finance, the producers were given the green light for Lynch to develop the script further with the two original writers, introducing his own visual ideas wherever possible.

Once a $5 million production deal was in place, via distribution by Paramount (US) and EMI (UK), vital questions of casting arose.

For Lynch, thus far used to the devoted co-operation of B-movie stalwarts, fringe theatre players and non-actors, the luxury of considering internationally-acclaimed actors and then directing them in a foreign land was a daunting prospect.

'I was like, from Missoula, Montana,' stresses Lynch, 'making this Victorian drama in England with actors that were known the world over. That's another kind of pressure that you wouldn't want to wish on anyone.'

Brooks kept the casting process democratic, with input from all the main helmsmen. He remembers casting for the all-important, physically uncomfortable role of Merrick himself.

'Well, we all had our hands up waving at the teacher at once. We all said John Hurt, because we had all seen his exquisite performance as Quentin Crisp in *The Naked Civil Servant*, we were the first people in America to see a tape of his performance as Caligula in *I, Claudius*. We all felt he is the most incredibly complex actor in the world.

'So we talked to John, I told him the story and he was nearly in tears at the end. And then I showed him the death masks of the Elephant Man (obtained from Merrick's former home, the Royal London Hospital), which I had blown up to show him the detail. And he was overwhelmed. He said he must do it.'

Other notable Brit theatricals, recently migrated to the more lucrative silver screen, included Anthony Hopkins in the crucial balancing role of Dr Frederick Treves – the very spirit of decency and Victorian charity, as if he himself were a distorted mirror image of the gentle Merrick which filtered away the corrupted flesh, showing only the soul.

(Hopkins was gratified to find at roll call one morning, booked in for make-up a half-hour before him, one Frederick Treves – great-nephew of the doctor, expressing his approval by playing the bit part of an alderman.)

Other old Brit reliables fit perfectly into secondary roles: Freddie Jones slimes it up splendidly as the sleazily Dickensian Bytes, a semi-fictionalised version of Merrick's real-life manager, the Silver King (just as unscrupulous though less brutal than Bytes, who is portrayed as the Elephant Man's 'keeper'); Dame Wendy Hiller is Mothershead, tight-lipped matron of the Royal London, whose initial distaste at the hospital being used to house a freak gives way to a kind of maternal 'tough love'; Michael Elphick is a convincing, bullying chief porter, whose moronic surliness reminds Merrick that he can never be truly free of the type of person who treats him like a baited bear

Among such a stalwart British cast, the only American 'name' was Anne Bancroft, bringing a mature sensuality to the part of Mrs Madge Kendal, the actress who perversely championed Merrick as a 'society figure', much to his uncomplaining joy. As Mrs Mel

Brooks, she found a copy of the script lying around the house and took the polite step of approaching the day-to-day producer, instead of demanding the role from her husband.

The Elephant Man finally began shooting at Lee International Studios, Greater London, on 8 October 1979.

It was the first time Lynch had been to Europe since his ill-fated trip to study under former north London resident Oskar Kokoscha, in 1964. Production would last just under three months, including location shooting in and around London.

Shortly before production, however, playwright Bernard Pomerance, author of the film's lauded theatrical namesake, had slapped a writ on Brooksfilms to stop them using the title.

In truth, it's been accurately noted that De Vore and Bergren had completed their original (pre-Lynch) screenplay before the theatrical *Elephant Man* saw its opening night; that the play presents a far more incisive, less sentimental treatment of the main characters, Merrick and Treves, than the film, which communicated much of its emotional effect by expressionistic imagery not easily obtained in the theatre; that the impact of Merrick's almost sacredly distorted appearance was achieved by diametrically-opposed means: in the film, John Hurt emotes to the heavens behind a suit of tumescent, crepuscular make-up, ensuring only the most soulful use of his voice, eyes and physical gestures will allow him to communicate; in the play, a perfectly fit and healthy actor gradually contorts his naked body piece by piece, in the scene where Treves introduces Merrick's wretched predicament to the Pathological Society, until his twisted shape becomes a more humanoid simulacrum of the (genuine) Elephant Man's body as projected onto a screen behind him.

Still, despite their essential stylistic differences, many episodes in the narrative of both play and screenplay were interchangeable. Brooksfilms were in combative mood, however, counter-suing for repeated interference with the financing, production and distribution of the film. Immediately prior to the cameras rolling in October, Mel Brooks was able to defiantly announce, 'We are definitely making the movie and the title *will* be *The Elephant Man*.'

Ultimately, the dispute would be settled without lengthy litigation by a disclaimer added to the end of the film credits. Stressing that it was not adapted from the Broadway play of the same name, it identified the film's historical sources as two books: *The Elephant Man and Other Reminiscences,* by Sir Frederick Treves, written in the 1890s when he was a knight of the realm and personal physician to Queen Victoria (also the source for the repeated anomaly of Merrick's name, with Treves rather eccentrically insisting on referring to his charge, Joseph, as 'John'); and *The Elephant Man – A Study in Human Dignity* by Ashley Montagu, published in 1973.

Given that Pomerance's play used exactly the same sources, it's easy to detect the overlap in the narrative action, if not in the tone, of both play and film. Equally similar, though both film and play were presumed (or, in the film's case, had claimed) to tell the factual story, both give highly interpretative accounts, most notably in the case of the cinematic version.

By the time production was underway, its director had long since won the same aesthetic concession as with his subsidised first feature.

'Early on we decided with David Lynch that the film should be in black and white,' stated Brooks, 'to hold back some of the more horrible aspects of the deformity. Also, I think black and white gives you a more authentic look for a period film.'

Monochrome was considered appropriate for grimy, smoggy Victorian London, and also to minimise any nauseated distraction the viewer might feel at the sight of Merrick's decaying features – particularly true of the Belgian carnival scene, where the fungoid extremity of his rotting torso is exposed.

Ultimately, however, this was another triumph for the director's visual sensibilities, still addicted to pure light and dark.

'It's very hard to find the best black-and-white cameraman in the world,' opined Brooks, 'because they're all very good. But I said the best black-and-white film I've ever seen (in terms of cinematography) is *Sons and Lovers* (1960). Jack Cardiff was the director and Freddie Francis the cameraman.

'So we called Freddie Francis just on a whim,' recalled Brooks, 'sent him the script and he said he wanted to do it. This guy even remembers what the bath water should be for black and white.'

Despite his penchant for richly-detailed monochrome, however, Francis had spent most of the last two decades as the director of garishly gaudy British horror films from the studios of Hammer and Amicus.

Francis's restrained, chiaroscuro lighting would bring John Merrick's world to life as a piece of visual Expressionism. To all visual extents and purposes, his contribution ensured the film played like a horror movie – but the classic, German-inspired Hollywood horror of the 1930s, rather than the plasma-paint melodramas of his own 'bread and butter' work at Hammer.

Clearly, Lynch was moving into a different league of film-making. At the same time, however, he hardly seemed to realise it, thinking nothing of continuing the home-made effects approach of his earlier films.

'I love doing stuff like that,' he confirmed. 'It's fun to try to think of solutions to problems and to do these things yourself. But then you find out that in Hollywood (*The Elephant Man* being essentially a Hollywood film, despite its British location, cast and crew) some of the fun is taken out of it because you're not the one doing it. There are people that specialise in this, and people that specialise in that, and it does save time.'

Nonetheless, Lynch hoped to continue the Chaney-esque tradition of applying experimental make-up, as he had done with the Man in the Planet and the Lady in the Radiator in *Eraserhead*, and to create the Elephant Man's physiology himself. 'I had an idea for a suit which would look really organic, and wouldn't require five hours of make-up every day. In theory, it was incredibly perfect. But what I did was a total flop,' he admitted. 'I was making this sort of skin, and in theory, it was a nifty idea; this skin would float over something, move and look like real skin.'

Lynch's body-suit, the exterior of which was to be layered with artificial skin, was so rigid it made Hurt look as if he 'was working inside of a helmet, a diving mask', as if made up for one of the schlockier, 1950s sci-fi monster movies.

'There was like a ten-thousandth of a second when I put it on John Hurt the first time that it looked right. And then in the next ten-thousandth of a second, it hit me so hard that there was no way. And the next week and a half was one of the darkest times of my life.'

Lynch was eventually rescued by the action any jaded veteran would have taken immediately: bringing in the experts. Make-up artist Christopher Tucker was a mainstream worker much respected in the film and television industry. In the twisted, overblown, distorted figure of John Merrick, Tucker would have his greatest professional challenge – and easily his finest hour.

Contrary to the director's early hopes, the make-up would take six hours a day – rather than five – to apply and remove, with Hurt only called to endure the ordeal on alternate days for reasons of safety. His Oscar-nominated make-up (kept under wraps to avoid any diminution of its initial screen impact) was closely based on the figure of Merrick himself, as per the full-sized photographs in front of which the normal-bodied actor distorts himself in Pomerance's play.

Most helpful of all, Tucker was able to make a close study of the Elephant Man's tumescent skull and twisted bodily stance, via a cast of his head and shoulders made from the skeleton still held behind glass at the London Hospital, which Lynch and Sanger had got from its officials after a great deal of persuasion.

'Frankly, I was hostile,' admitted Percy G. Nunn, assistant curator at the hospital's medical college. 'This is an emotive profession. Sir Frederick Treves was a humanitarian and he felt that he should take the Elephant Man away from the public gaze and give him sanctuary here. For the short period that he lived here he was given peace of mind. I felt very strongly that this should be followed up, where Merrick's skeleton and cast were concerned.

'So when David and Jonathan first came to me, saying that they needed pictures of the skeleton and cast, I wasn't at all sympathetic. I felt that it was an invasion of the privacy of the museum – and of poor Merrick's memory.

'And then, slowly, I began to change my mind. I began to realise, after talking to the two of them, that this was to be a serious study of Merrick's story.'

Christopher Tucker took eight weeks to design a 'genetic make-up' based on Merrick's earthly remains, at one point working obsessively for a period of 49 hours. With John Hurt's head shaved, a cast of his own features had Merrick's deformities added painstakingly to it, until he was ready to be subjected to the full transformation.

Ultimately, the full bodily make-up was the perfect device for presenting the romantic tragedy of a young man, a poetic soul, trapped in a world and a body that seemed compounded of all the physical corruption in eternity.

The Elephant Man (1980)

A beautiful, dark-haired young woman convulses in terror at the trumpeting of rampaging elephants. Their hoofs raise and their trunks flail, signifying an attack on her helpless body beneath them. The scene ends with a dense cloud of smoke and the sound of a baby crying.

An illusionist's fire introduces a Victorian London sideshow. As a top-coated gentleman follows the path of policemen in the process of closing down 'the greatest freak in the world', an outraged official tells Bytes, the exhibitor, that 'Freaks are one thing, but this is monstrous!'

The genteel patron, Dr Frederick Treves, tracks Bytes down to an East End backstreet in order to view the man whose deformities he has heard about. Given a melodramatic introduction by his 'keeper' – 'the terrible . . . Elephant . . . MAN!' – the camera only part-glimpses what Treves can see in the shadows. A tear trickles from Treves' eye.

Treves pays Bytes to deliver the Elephant Man to the London Hospital. Nightmarishly conspicuous in a long, dishevelled cape, burlap hood with one eyehole cut and tilted workman's cap, wheezing ferociously, he gives off a malodorous smell.

At a meeting of the Pathological Society, Treves describes the condition of this 'perverted and degraded version of the human male' – 21-year-old John Merrick, concealed behind a screen but clearly silhouetted. Tumescent growths on the skull have rendered his head almost insupportable by his body, making it essential for him to sleep upright for fear of asphyxiation; his spine is twisted; fungoid growths on the skin are literally making him rot away; his right arm is withered. As an afterthought, Treves notes that his genitals are perfectly formed and functional – a black joke of God or nature.

When he goes back to Bytes, Merrick becomes the subject of a drunken attack by his 'keeper'. The boy assistant calls on Treves to help Merrick, who is scarcely able to breathe. He takes him back to the hospital, threatening to have Bytes arrested if he dares interfere.

47

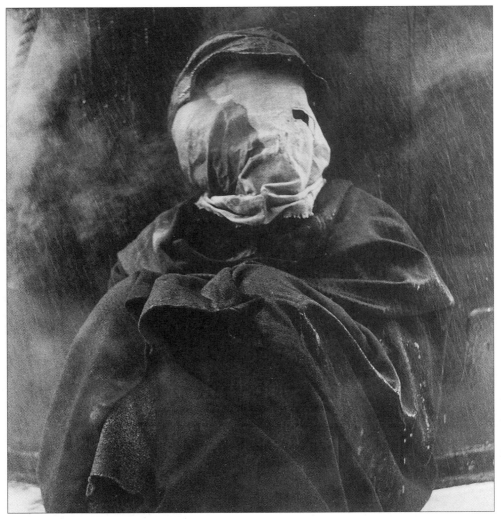

*The mysterious archetype of **The Elephant Man**: the much-parodied apparel of cape and burlap hood conceals the humanity of a tortured soul, as well as one of the cinema's most grotesque cosmetic creations.*

The camera focuses on Merrick's features for the first time when a nervous young nurse is sent upstairs to take him his food. His head is hideously outgrown, his mouth distorted, but he is every bit as unnerved by her screams.

Treves requests of Carr Gomm, chief surgeon and director of the Royal London, that the deformed man be granted a long-term stay. Without dismissing the idea, the director opines the hospital is no place for an imbecile. Their informal interview goes badly, but Gomm is called back by Treves when he hears their subject making a word-perfect recitation of the 23rd Psalm. Both surgeons realise they are dealing with an intelligent man in a corrupted body. Gomm ponders on what life has been like for John Merrick: 'I don't think anyone can possibly imagine.'

Treves takes John home to visit his wife. Elegantly dressed in a frock-coat and wing-collar, he is courteous and charming to the nervous Mrs Treves. He shows her a locket containing a cameo portrait of his mother – the dark-haired young woman terrorised by elephants. His hostess exclaims how beautiful she is, drawing tears from John.

Perusing The Times, *esteemed actress and socialite Mrs Madge Kendal reads of both the afflictions and the sensitivity of the Elephant Man and decides she would like to visit him. Treves accompanies her to John's private room, where he is fashioning an intricately-detailed matchstick model of the nearby church. She presents him with a copy of* Romeo and Juliet, *and they read verse from Shakespeare's romantic tragedy together. She astounds him by planting a kiss on his deformed cheek, telling him that he is not an Elephant Man, but Romeo.*

John becomes the recipient of many visits from upper-crust London 'society'. Matron Mothershead makes the observation that he is being gawped at every bit as much as if he were in a freak show.

The hospital's patron, HRH Princess Alexandra, carries a letter from Queen Victoria, expressing her trust that the hospital will continue to care for 'one of England's most unfortunate sons'. John is overjoyed to be told by Treves that he now has a permanent home. He later confesses there has been one other question on his mind – whether his friend can cure him. Treves admits that they cannot. 'No. I didn't think so,' John replies without a hint of bitterness.

'A perverted and degraded version of the human male': John Merrick's silhouetted introduction by Treves (Anthony Hopkins) to the Pathological Society heightens the tension before his sudden visual exposure.

Still, there are those who will exploit him, even in his new-found sanctuary. One night, a drunken rabble from a local pub enter the room with the night porter. The porter forces whiskey down John's throat, then holds a mirror to his face so that his own visage is the first thing he sees when reopening his eyes. As they leave, a lingerer remains: Bytes, who has come to reclaim his livelihood.

John is transported by Bytes to a freak show in Belgium. Physically ailing, he presents a sorry spectacle to the customers who turn away in dismay. Drunkenly, Bytes punishes him by locking him in a baboon cage. As he retires, the carnival's other freaks release him and take him to a ferry bound for London.

At Liverpool Street station, a group of everyday Joes pursue the 'freak' into the men's toilet. Before they beat him up, one of them pulls the hood from his head: they're shocked to see his rapidly decaying features. The attack stalled by his anguished cry that he is not an animal, but a man, the police arrive to break it up.

Treves is deeply moved by the return of his friend and patient, apologising for letting him come to harm, but John stresses he is happy every moment of the day. Quietly aside, Treves confirms to the young nurse who was once terrified by his appearance that John is dying.

At the theatre, they see an elaborate Victorian pantomime which seems to John to be quite magical. Mrs Kendal draws attention to the presence of her friend, seated in the Royal Box. The audience give him a standing ovation.

Come bedtime, John completes the last minor details of his model church and resolves that tonight he will sleep like other people, like the little boy in the portrait on his wall. Aware he's risking asphyxiation, he focuses upon the face of his mother, whose voice promises him that 'nothing ever really dies', and upon the starry cosmos which opens up to envelop him.

For *Eraserhead* cultists who feared that Hollywood – albeit transported overseas – might flatten their new hero's style, the macabre, expressionistic elements of *The Elephant Man* averted severe disappointment.

'It's way more conventional, for sure,' the director had reported back from the set of his first big-budget feature. 'But there are things about it which make it similar in some ways to *Eraserhead* . . . which was, you know, only me.

'There's a real good chance to build a mood that's totally different from now,' he enthused, finding the far-away setting of Victorian London stimulating in its alienation. 'It's back in time, and he lived in strange places. It's just a whole other world. And John Merrick, the Elephant Man, is such a strange, wonderful, innocent guy.'

In retrospect, it's hard to fault the immediate decision of Cornfeld, Sanger and Brooks to put Lynch in charge of the script rewrite, and ultimately the film itself. The basic narrative, however moving and compassionate, is almost stultifyingly linear; in the scenes where horror is absent, and the expressionistic photography concentrates on speaking actors rather than imagery, the film comes perilously close to those British-made costume dramas that US networks regard as 'quality TV'.

But the elements Lynch brought to bear were separate from the main narrative – richer in personal symbolism and visual motif, bringing imaginative depth to his approximation of Merrick's 19th-century world. Stylistically, the film does, as its director claims, bear many of the marks of *Eraserhead* – in particular, dream sequences presented as subjective reality.

The opening scene – where a small herd of stampeding elephants threatens to crush Merrick's young mother underfoot, suggestive of both inter-species rape, and, with the dream's epilogue of a baby crying, difficult childbirth – is presented verbatim, without the quotation marks of stressing this is a sideshow yarn used to explain the Elephant Man's disfigurement, which Merrick himself apparently came to believe in. By omitting so much

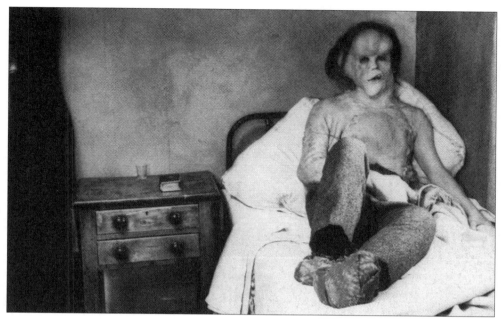

Freak, or frightened child? The sensitive John Merrick (John Hurt) is fully exposed for the first time.

as one single reference to his disfiguring disease, *The Elephant Man* lends more credence to its title character's strange belief, becoming a kind of semi-real dream biography.

In the genuine words of Joseph Carey Merrick: '. . . My mother was going along the street when a procession of animals were passing by, there was a terrible crush of people to see them, and unfortunately she was pushed under the elephant's feet which frightened her very much; this occurring during a time of pregnancy was the cause of my deformity.' Merrick's belief in the yarn is likely to have been a heartfelt attempt to understand his own misfortune. The opening of Lynch's film, however, emphasises the mythological nature of so personal a belief, the semi-rape by an entire small herd of pachyderms being way beyond even the wildest happenings of a circus parade in Leicester.

In the second dream sequence, the camera closes in on Merrick's hood and passes through the eyehole, re-emerging on the other side as per the worm's-eye point of view in *Eraserhead*; Merrick melancholically acknowledges his reflection in a window (mirrors are barred from his room as a small, practical mercy); waking dream images of the industrial symbiosis of man and machine culminate in a group of men pushing a dark plate towards the screen, which becomes a mirror wherein he views the face of himself as a child – smaller but, distressingly, just as hideously malformed.

The final scene, in which Merrick, aware of his own deteriorating condition, lies down to sleep like a little child, though he knows it will mean his own death, is the most audaciously fantastic of the film; rather than portraying his asphyxiated death throes, as does Pomerance in his more literal but less grotesque treatment, Lynch shows Merrick's consciousness ascending into a starry sky, the nearest lights of our own solar system filling the screen as he's reconciled with the dream image of his lost mother, promising him 'the heart beats . . . nothing dies'. Its obvious predecessor is Henry in *Eraserhead* standing startled against a constellation of stars, as the material squalor around him capitulates to the chaos of his dream world.

Other striking similarities between Lynch's respective mainstream and underground first features include: physical ugliness depicted with such fascination that it has a transcendent beauty; clouds of steam filling the screen in the film's most dream-like moments, emanating from some sweatshop hell-hole, or wrapping the beswathed dream figure of Merrick in a mysterious fog; men and industry shown working in tandem, the workers exerting their muscles as primitive machines grind noisily away – as if Lynch wishes to insinuate that John Merrick is a son of the earliest part of our own, ambivalent industrial age, and that the environmental poisoning caused by our necessary progress is just as likely the origin of his deforming disease as some apocryphal event involving his unfortunate mother and a herd of elephants.

In many ways, the post-Industrial Revolution world inhabited by the Elephant Man is the blueprint for the post-industrial nightmare endured by Henry Spencer. The all-defining difference lies in their existential tone: the internal reality of *Eraserhead* is a world – indeed, a universe – of no escape, where even Henry's last refuge, his dreams, can turn against him at any moment. The world of the Elephant Man is more realistically brutal, its privations and spiritual sickness already known from historical texts, e.g. from the literary *oeuvre* of Dickens – the visual comparison of workers and machines with elephants is suggested in *Hard Times*, where elephants are the simile used to describe the endlessly grinding northern mills.

But it is also a world of hope. The facts of Merrick's salvation – of his being found a home at the Royal London Hospital, his compliance with the 'genteel freak' status bestowed upon him by upper-crust London society, his enjoyment of an upper-middle-class lifestyle denied to his former proletarian tormentors – are there in the official records of the story. As realised by Lynch, they made for a winning new taste on the cinematic palate. Below the nightmare surface of *Eraserhead* – far more visible in the lesser-seen *Grandmother* – was an integral aspect of Lynch's personality, now openly on display for the first time: the sentimentalist of the grotesque.

The Elephant Man was released to much delighted surprise from the mainstream cinema industry, which had formerly considered Lynch too murky a maverick to handle a subject delicately.

'Lynch commendably avoids summoning feelings of disgust, as he did in his loathsome first feature,' quoth the unforgiving *Variety*, '. . . an unusually serious and gripping treatment of a subject that could have easily been cheapened,' while one British cinema magazine acclaimed the film as 'one of the most moving and dignified love stories the English-speaking cinema has produced in a long time' – all the more remarkable an assessment considering that love is a platonic one between two men, a doctor and a disfigured patient.

Moreover, the film with the 'screwball', otherwise-unemployable director, was nominated for eight Oscars – including John Hurt, for best leading actor – in the 1980 Academy Awards. Almost unbelievably, it did not win one single award – not even in incontrovertible areas of technical excellence such as Freddie Francis's pristine black-and-white cinematography, Christopher Tucker's extraordinary make-up, the production design by Stuart Craig which belied the film's relatively low budget, or John Morris's lush, romantic original score, all of which were nominated.

At the awards ceremony that year, flop-fringed, baby-faced newcomer David Lynch made a boyish contrast to more seasoned veterans of the industry, shifting in his seat with

An exaggeratedly brutal version of the real Merrick's business partner, Bytes (Freddie Jones) attacks his corrupted, decaying body.

This poetically grotesque procession, as the Belgian carnival freaks rescue Merrick, seems to be a sentimental inversion of the climax of Tod Browning's classic Freaks (1932).

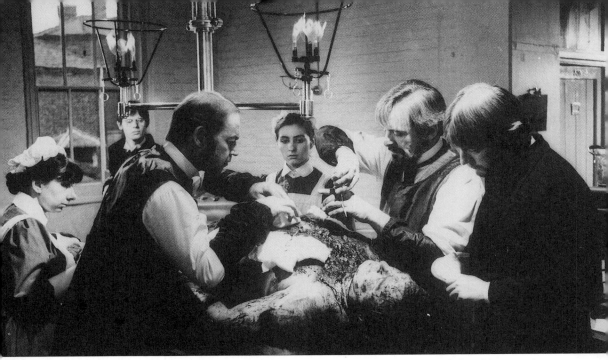

'We're going to see a lot more of these': Treves (Antony Hopkins) treats a critically-wounded machine operative. Under a historical pretext, Lynch indulges his fascination with the relationship of man and industry.

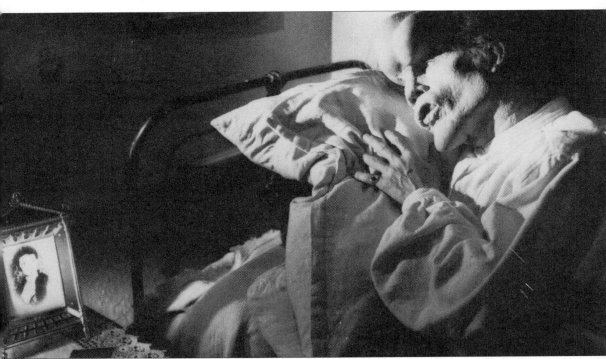

Merrick (John Hurt) regards the photo-portrait of his mother before laying down to rest for the last time. As the starry sky envelops him, Lynch's personal sentimentalism becomes far more visible than it had been in Eraserhead.

excitement. The most exceptional nominations for both best film and best director, by a very long distance, were two black-and-white movies: *The Elephant Man* and Martin Scorsese's *Raging Bull*. (Which, by way of coincidence, has a scene where the factual main character – middle-weight boxing champ Jake La Motta, played with Oscar-winning heavyweight impact by Robert De Niro – smashes his fists against a cell wall and screams, 'I am not an animal!') As is often par for the course at the Oscars, the most powerful nominations lost out to a forgettable 'human interest' drama – in both cases, Robert Redford's *Ordinary People*.

Whatever the outcome of the awards, the event heralded that David Lynch, film-maker, was suddenly a recognised entity in the commercial cinema industry – an apparent overnight success after a decade of obscurity.

'I am really happy with *The Elephant Man*,' he emphasised at the time, though defence of his work was hardly necessary. 'I think I did the best job I could've done. And I didn't sell out – I may have sold out in a couple of moments,' he deferred, 'but I could've sold out in so many more.'

'Mel Brooks and Jonathan Sanger gave me tremendous freedom,' he asserted, not so unconsciously pinpointing the film's artistic success. 'I only had to please them. If I'd had to please twenty people, I would've been lost.'

In time, *The Elephant Man* – or, more specifically, its eponymous title character – would become a tragic pop-culture icon. As a measure of how much the film has since been assimilated into the culture, the viewer only has to consider the number of TV comedy sketches – blackly comic, or facile and ridiculous – which have parodied the shuffling figure in the cape and burlap hood.

Most poignant, and strangest of all, is the affection for the character developed by rock star Michael Jackson. Having viewed numerous private screenings of the film, he requested to view Joseph Merrick's skeleton at the Royal London Hospital museum, the curators only too happy to agree to visits this time around. They were suitably horrified, however, when Jackson sought to buy the Elephant Man's remains outright. Something in the story of the deformed Victorian who retained his child-like innocence – at least in its magical re-telling by Lynch – touched a resounding chord in the entertainer who cosmetically altered his own appearance many times, while fulfilling his stated ambition never to grow up.

Meanwhile, doors were opening for Lynch this time around, in a manner unimaginable back during the aftermath of *Eraserhead*. But, despite his optimism about future collaboration, this would have its unforeseen hazards.

Around the time of the Oscars ceremony, he was contacted by the office of Dino De Laurentiis, one of the last of the big European movie moguls. 'Dino was interested in me because of *The Elephant Man*,' Lynch recalled of a time when he was excited to become a number in Hollywood executives' phone books. 'He wanted to make a science fiction film that was about people and not about ray guns and space ships. He wanted to make everything very real and believable.'

The newly-arrived director was not even vaguely familiar with the literary property De Laurentiis was trying to cultivate: 'When Dino's office called me, they asked if I had read *Dune* and I thought they said "June".'

Such ignorance of the other party's pet project was at least consistent for both sides. 'When Dino and I first talked he had not seen *Eraserhead*,' admitted Lynch, 'so there were lots of things in my head that he didn't know about. When he finally saw that film, in fact, he hated it.'

The first grey taint of compromise was in the air.

PROD. DUNE
DIRECTOR DAVID LYNCH   CAMERAMAN F. FR
SLATE
1
TAKE
1
DATE

CHAPTER FOUR

Dune:

Detours to Other Worlds

In 1980, nonplussed by the offers he was receiving post-*Elephant Man*, Lynch had finally struck a deal to direct *Ronnie Rocket*, the script he had been writing and revising since the opening of *Eraserhead*.

The long-cherished, screwball-surrealist comedy script about 'a little three-foot-tall guy with red hair and a sixty-cycle alternating current' was finally scheduled for production by Francis Coppola's Zoetrope company. However, in early 1981, the over-budget musical *One From the Heart* started to push Zoetrope towards its now-inevitable bankruptcy, and *Ronnie Rocket* was no nearer take-off than he had been for the last two years.

In the light of such recurring disappointment, Lynch was more enthusiastic about the overtures received from Dino De Laurentiis on *Dune* than anything else on offer – including, perversely enough, the third of the *Star Wars* films, whose writer/producer, George Lucas, somehow shared the belief that Lynch – as a director of 'weird stuff' – would be a natural for science fiction. (As with the first of the series, it also ended up being directed by Lucas.)

'I'd been reading scripts for about a year after *The Elephant Man*, and never found anything that I wanted to do . . . I wouldn't have been able to influence *Return of the Jedi* because that's totally George's picture. I might've been a millionaire but I wouldn't have been too happy about it.

'*Dune* just had everything that I think a film should have. I love textures, and it has hundreds of different textures. It has mystery, mood, real people. It has an incredible adventure story, visions and dreams, and all sorts of symbols – areas that really can be cinema.'

Dune, science fiction writer Frank Herbert's hugely-popular 1965 novel, was a true phenomenon of its era. Having sold two million copies and translated into 14 languages, an estimated 40 to 50 million people worldwide had already read the SF-fantasy epic.

Dense with intricate plot background and interrelated incidents, it followed the emerging trend of the pseudo-history/fantasy novel. Not simply an action or 'quest' story, the author had gone to great pains to build a convincing group of alien (but clearly earthling-inspired) societies in conflict with each other, all with their own detailed histories, religions and languages.

So finely detailed was Herbert's epic vision – indeed, Koranic vision, given the self-consciously high number of Islamic allusions, and the messianic hero's spreading of 'the word', Mohammed-style, by leading his army into neighbouring desert territories – it seemed that, to all but the most blindly ambitious film-maker, *Dune* was clearly unfilmable.

Dune: a Basic Outline of the Novel

In the year 10,191, two ruling royal families, the Atreides of the planet Caladan and the Harkonnen of the industrial planet Geidi Prime, are at war over the spice produced on the desert planet Arrakis – 'he who controls the spice, controls the universe'.

Paul Atreides and his parents – the ruling Duke Leto Atreides and his concubine, the Lady Jessica – are sent forth by the Padishah Emperor, ruler of the universe, from their lush, green home planet to rule Arrakis, the 'Dune' of the title. Paul's very existence is an act of rebellion on the part of his mother, contrary to the command of the Bene Gesserit, the powerful psychic sisterhood of which she is part, who ordered her to please her husband by determining that her child be a girl. Now Paul is growing to a man, his mother is training him in the mental and physical disciplines of the Bene Gesserit. Secretly, she believes him to be the messiah the sisterhood has been trying to breed through ninety generations of genetic engineering – the super-being whose mental powers will bridge space and cleanse the universe of evil.

The Harkonnen are disturbed that the Atreides' relocation has given them direct domain over the holy spice. The spice, melange, the most precious substance in the universe, is fertilised by the giant sandworms of Arrakis. Essential in allowing the Guild of Navigators – controlled by evil Baron Harkonnen – to defy basic relativity by meshing two points in space and time and traversing the universe, the spice is essentially an addictive, psychotropic drug which expands consciousness to previously unimagined levels, produces prophetic dreams and turns the pupils of the Fremen – a tough, nomadic race who are its most regular users – deep metallic blue.

The tyrannical Emperor has ordered the Atreides' planetary migration to set them up for assassination by the Harkonnen. When Duke Leto is murdered, Paul and his mother escape into the desert. Their castle is seized by the Harkonnen and the Emperor's fanatical troops, the Sardaukar.

Paul and Jessica are accepted into the community of the spice-mining Fremen. Their holy woman, the Reverend Mother Ramallo, is dying. She asks Paul's young sister, Alia, who has been born with the full intelligence of an adult, to take her place. For a long time, the Reverend Mother has prophesied that 'One will come who will bring the Holy War, the Jihad, which will cleanse the universe and bring us out of darkness.' She believes that Paul may be 'the One'. In order to meet his apparent destiny, Paul takes a ritual overdose of melange, which produces certain supernatural – or messianic – powers, including the ability to read or even spiritually enter other people's minds.

The Fremen survive the intense desert conditions by conserving and recycling their own sweat and urine via the biologically designed 'stillsuits' they wear. They await the messiah who will lead them out of the desert, whose coming has been foretold. As Paul has fulfilled at least part of the prophecy by coming from a planet rich with water and exhibiting psychic powers, he is renamed by the Fremen 'Paul Muad'dib'.

In a final battle, the Fremen, riding giant sandworms and led by Paul, take the Great Houses of the Landsraad and destroy the leaders of the Harkonnen. Paul takes control of Arrakis, destroying the rule of the Emperor and his Spacing Guild by holding the sacred spice to ransom. He is acclaimed by the Fremen as their messiah, the 'Kwisatz Haderatch'.

The Sisters of the Bene Gesserit, with Sian Phillips, left, as the Reverend Mother Mohiam, in Lynch's film adaptation of **Dune** *(1984). What the film lacks in atmosphere, it almost makes up in visual inventiveness.*

As dauntingly near-impossible a task as it may have seemed to bring *Dune* to the screen, it was equally inevitable that a few film-makers would be intoxicated by its epic vision.

First was Arthur P. Jacobs, whose production company, APJAC, had proven proficient in creating an alien-yet-recognisable world out of stretches of American desert and rocky Canary Island terrain for *Planet of the Apes* (1968). However, the film was not to go beyond pre-production before Jacobs succumbed to a fatal heart attack in 1973. As the option died with him, there was a brief period of interest from B-movie king Roger Corman and his New World Pictures, who ultimately decided, wisely, that the scale of the narrative and their own budgetary restrictions made production impossible.

The second option was taken up by a wealthy Frenchman named Michel Seydoux, who channelled the project via Paris-based production company Camera One. Their director was a big admirer of the book: Russian-Chilean comic book illustrator/surrealist/film-maker/visionary Alejandro Jodorowsky.

Financed to the tune of $9 million, it seemed that Herbert's vision would finally be translated for the screen. Shooting in the Sahara region of Tassili, Jodorowsky's conception of *Dune* was that of a visually symbolic epic, with few restrictions placed on the imaginative input and not much thought given to the finite budget. Given the extremes of vision displayed in Jodorowsky's features thus far, *El Topo* (1969) and *The Holy Mountain* (1973), it was a pity, however, that no one would ever get to see what was likely to have been a vivid clash between elements of genius and undisciplined madness. With $2 million of American backers' money already sunk into pre-production, with no visible end in sight, *Dune* was already way over-budget before the first day of shooting had begun and, at the end of 1975, production stalled completely.

The next buyer of the option rights was Dino De Laurentiis, who purchased them in 1979, at the urging of his daughter Rafaella, a fan of the book since the early '70s. European movie mogul (producer of Fellini's *La Strada*, one of Lynch's favourite films) De Laurentiis had 35 years in the business and 600 production credits.

Ridley Scott was announced as director in October 1979, his production of *Alien* topping the box office on both sides of the Atlantic. Having been involved in Jodorowsky's stiffed, would-be epic, Swiss neo-surrealist and visionary H. R. Giger also entered into negotiations to helm the production design – his cinematic reputation now cemented by *Alien* (1979), for which the film's techno-biological visual appeal was at least part-inspired by *Eraserhead*: 'one of the greatest movies I have ever seen'.

Ironically, considering all the technical back-up and hardware utilised for the eventually-completed film, Scott's conception was regarded as 'too high-tech', according to Rafaella de Laurentiis – though such complaints were as nothing compared to the reaction to Scott's projected budget of $50 million. Scott abandoned the project and would go on to direct *Blade Runner* (1982).

Dino had by now handed over the daily production chores of *Dune* to Rafaella, deferring to her choice of latest director. Her objection to Scott's technological approach was that a film of Herbert's complex pseudo-history would require more 'heart' and 'dimension'. 'The book *Dune* had a depth,' she insisted. 'To try to do only worms and space would have been a mistake.'

The director she had in mind was David Lynch. Based on the success of *The Elephant Man*, it was felt he could bring spiritual and aesthetic elements to a fantasy of other worlds and techno-psychic cultures.

In May 1981 Lynch moved into the Universal studio lot to begin pre-production on the new project, having just familiarised himself with the source novel. Collaborating on the script with Christopher De Vore and Eric Bergren, the original screenwriters of *The Elephant Man*, he would pay a visit the following month to Frank Herbert's eco-farm (powered, as far as possible, by methane or solar energy) in Washington State.

Herbert had reservations when he first met Lynch at Dino's LA office: 'My first impression of David was that he was too young to tackle a project of this size. He's very boyish. He reminded me of a masters student going for his doctorate.'

Although there were initial problems with the script, development money existed for a further collaborative attempt by Lynch, De Vore and Bergren; according to Herbert, 'The script just didn't sing. It was all on the surface. During our discussions, I kept stressing the many levels of action in the story, and I could tell that David grasped the idea right away. Finally, he decided to write it himself.'

Back to the drawing board, Lynch got to work on the metaphysical and semi-mystical elements which were so important to Herbert. The director obsessively drafted and re-drafted until he finally produced a version on 9 December 1982, which he, Herbert and De Laurentiis felt fully represented the scope and imagery of the novel. (In retrospect, Lynch would change his screenplay credit to the pseudonym 'Judas Booth', giving a taste of how he now regards the project.) All in all, the screenwriting process had taken a full year and a half.

Meanwhile, Rafaella De Laurentiis began a worldwide scouting tour for studios and locations. Taking in North Africa, where Jodorowsky's ambitiously personal version of the project had come to grief, the Sahara Desert, India, Australia, Italy, even England, her eventual choice would be Churubusco Studios of Mexico City, the largest production sites in South America.

Shooting began on 30 March, 1983 – more than three years since Lynch had last been in the director's chair – and was expected to last until the end of September. It would ultimately see the year out, however.

The clapperboard on the first cut was held by Frank Herbert himself, who was so excited by the process of his best-seller finally becoming a live-action picture that he'd travel several times from his home in Washington State to watch production. Maximum use would be made of natural locations and the space offered up by both the surrounding countryside and the co-operative city authorities. At its most conventional, location shooting would include ten days in the burning Salamayuca Desert, just outside Juarez, and filming next to a 65-foot high lava rock wall in front of the Popcatepl and Ixtazihatal volcanoes.

At its most grandiosely creative, it would entail actually building a reservoir, 100 x 300 feet, in a warehouse just outside Mexico City, and a landing field in Aztec Stadium, the largest sports stadium in South America. No artificial set, it seemed, would be deemed too monumental, too time-consuming or too expensive. At final count, a total of 75 interior sets would be built by production designer Anthony Masters (renowned for *2001: A Space Odyssey*) on eight massive sound stages at Churubusco, under Lynch's creative direction.

Having replaced H. R. Giger from the abandoned Ridley Scott production, Masters had full access to the previous storyboards. However, he and Lynch agreed that Giger's designs, impressive – and sadly unrealised – as they were, would not fit the mid-Westerner's humanised concept of worlds beyond our own. 'We decided that we had to do something completely different,' explained Masters, '. . . in a way it was too powerful, too sci-fi-ish. Lynch wanted his *Dune* to be more believable because the people who are scattered throughout *Dune*'s galaxy have only left Earth, the mother planet, a few thousand years previous to the events in the story.'

In fact, Masters' set designs – alongside a few stray Lynchian touches – remain pretty much the highlights of the film, which, for all the intricacies of its source material, would be as resounding a triumph of style over substance as ever reached the screen. To echo Lynch, his greatest enticement in making *Dune* was the joy of travelling to – and creating – other worlds.

The boyishly-spellbound director would also find a new terrain for his fascinated eye to scan – the first of the 'other worlds' of *Dune* was Mexico City itself. Nearly eight thousand feet above sea level, Lynch found inspiration in the disorientating altitude, the hybrid Latin-Indian architecture, and the 'new things' all around him: 'It has a funny sort of mythical or surrealistic atmosphere. Strange things happen in Mexico, and I like it. I like the feeling of the place.'

For reasons which are prosaically apparent, the crew came to re-christen the Salamayuca Desert as the 'Dead Dog Dump' – appealing hugely to Lynch's love of the everyday bizarre, and, of course, to his appreciation of the aesthetic potential of dead animals.

The film-maker was not even bothered by the choking air pollution, by-product of his beloved factories. 'I come from LA,' he claimed, the mid-Western boy now appropriating the movie industry's motherland as his own hometown, 'so the smog really doesn't bother me too much.'

In his baggy pleated pants, black coat, white shirt buttoned to the top and aviator shades, it was as if he had found the perfect wardrobe combination to build his new professional persona. 'I never thought I'd ever be doing a real Hollywood movie,' he freely admitted to one of the many on-set interviewers who visited throughout the year. 'It's a lot of fun.'

Though the production history of *Dune* would be much smoother than the miraculously-completed *Eraserhead*, its helmsman would find there were different pressures inherent in being the captain of a big, expensive liner, as opposed to sailing his own small schooner through uncharted waters.

As for the technical expertise on what would become an increasingly technocratic film, the affable director's first choices were his old hands. Freddie Francis, director of cinematography and Oscar nominee on *The Elephant Man*, was back on board: 'Freddie is an incredible cinematographer,' Lynch would testify in post-production, 'and the look of the picture is very, very beautiful and really, really rich.'

Nonetheless, it was something of a wrench to renounce his preferred monochrome aesthetic: 'I would love to have made *Dune* in black and white,' he admitted, 'but it really is a colour film. I would love to have seen parts of it done in black and white, though. There are places where I might want to desaturate the colour and slip in that direction. It's not that I'm a negative person, really. It's just that I always like something dark in the frame, so that you don't see everything and you can sort of zoom out somewhere. It's a feeling. Of course, this caused some problems on *Dune*, but photographically it's important to me. A lot of times I'm not arguing with Freddie, I'm begging him to make something darker. Dino, on the other hand is begging him not to listen to me and make it lighter.'

At the same early point of production, Lynch also approvingly announced the participation of Alan Splet – the soundman and experimental partner on his previous two features and one college short.

'To me sound effects are like music. People call me a director,' Lynch rhapsodised with modest sincerity, 'but I really think of myself as a soundman. I want to bend and shape a sound, and I want to produce an album of this kind of music. I can't tell you how much I yearn to do this.'

One of the ironies of *Dune* is that the film itself could never live up to its aspirations, while one of its finer details – the sound recording – germinated a much smaller ambition in

Kyle MacLachlan making his screen debut in the role of Paul Atreides, a character he identified with ever since reading **Dune** *as a boy. Destiny had much more interesting roles in store, as screen detectives partly based upon the personality of David Lynch.*

Lynch's head, to be realised many years later.

In retrospect, the quietly creative sound designer, Alan Splet, remembered the aural concept of *Dune* as relating directly to the job at hand. 'They were just general ideas that we discussed rather than specific ones . . . A lot of what we talked about, like a strange system of echoes in the desert, never found their way into the film. On *The Elephant Man* and *Eraserhead* we worked a little closer than we did on *Dune*, actually. We were much more separated, because David had so many responsibilities with the optical effects and so on.'

The special effects team ran as a Who's Who of early '80s Hollywood technocrats:

Carlo Rambaldi (Oscars for De Laurentiis's remake of *King Kong*, 1976, *Alien* and *ET*, 1982) built and animated the giant sandworms. John Dkystra, of Apogee (visual effects/scientific technical achievements Oscars for *Star Wars*, 1977, Oscar nomination for *Star Trek – The Motion Picture*, 1979, and Emmy for the *Battlestar Galactica* TV series) was supervisor of special effects, though he would walk out on the production, dispirited, citing the classic 'mutual creative differences'. Barry Nolan, of Van der Veer Photo Effects (composition of laser sword fights on *Star Wars*, optical effects on the De Laurentiis remakes of *King Kong* and *Flash Gordon*, 1980) took over special effects supervision. Albert Whitlock (Oscars for *The Birds*, 1963, *Earthquake* and *The Hindenburg*, both 1975, and the nightmarish cardiac arrest sequence for *The Thing*, 1983), did additional special effects. The conceptual art behind the effects was created by Mentor Huebner (who did likewise for *Blade Runner*) and George Jensen (*Return of the Jedi* 1983), while the physical effects were designed by Kit West (*Raiders of the Lost Ark*, 1981).

It was all many, many light years away from Lynch's animated storyboards on *The Grandmother*. Whether all the creative manpower and expense would make the film any more effective than that modest but haunting little short is a matter for further exploration.

While the size of cast and crew – 1,400 in total – remained a daunting prospect, Lynch – referred to as a 'British director' by several trade papers, due to the success of the Victorian-themed *Elephant Man*, and as 'Guv'nor' by the crew, encouraged by Freddie Francis – would take the abundance of almost-famous faces much more in his stride.

In the lead role, however, was a young actor fresh to the screen. Kyle MacLachlan was Lynch's own choice for the role of Paul Atreides, giving the same all-American, peanut-butter-cookies-and-milk impression as the director himself, albeit of a wiry, more athletic kind. Chiefly notable for good notices earned during seven months of stage acting with the Oregon Shakespeare Festival, he looked a fresh-faced five years younger than his full 24. Almost touchingly, he had a sentimental reverence for *Dune* which Lynch, a newcomer to the book, had missed.

'I first discovered *Dune* when I was 14, and I've read it about once a year ever since,' enthused MacLachlan. 'It's almost been my Bible. When I was growing up, I always thought of myself as Paul – "What would Paul do?" When my agent suggested me for the role, I couldn't believe it. But I can't imagine another character I feel closer to.'

In the schmaltziest old Hollywood tradition, it was a dream come true. 'There, we hope, is the new heart-throb of the Western World,' Universal's publicity director claimed at the time, tongue only part-imbedded in cheek.

For all his thick dark hair and jut-jawed conviction, MacLachlan had an almost antique American everyman quality about him that would be lost among the blow-dried and designer-stubbled male sex symbols of the '80s. But chance had a much stranger and more interesting role in store – in the ensuing years, he would become a screen surrogate for the personality of David Lynch himself.

The rest of the cast was solidly composed of thespian worthies and tip-of-the-tongue,

The strangely anti-climactic battle between Paul (Kyle MacLachlan) and Feyd-Rautha (Sting), the outcome never in doubt. Sting's motivation for appearing in the film was to work with Lynch, 'a madman in sheep's clothing', who had become a fashionable figure in the rock world since David Bowie's championing of **Eraserhead.**

second league stars: Francesca Annis, the British actress from the simplified, poor man's *Dune*, *Krull* (1981), as the Lady Jessica; Kenneth McMillan, as pustular grotesque the Baron Harkonnen; Jose Ferrer as the Padishah Emperor; Aldo Ray as Atreides court member Gurney Halleck (though the faded 1950s star was replaced during filming, by British actor Patrick Stewart); Freddie Jones, from *The Elephant Man*, as assassin Thufit Hawat (the names just get crazier, and more Islamic-sounding); Sian Phillips (Lavia in *I, Claudius*) as the Reverend Mother Gaius Helen Mohiam; Sean Young, who made her first strong impression in *Blade Runner*, as Chani, bride to the hero once he fulfils his destiny of becoming a desert messiah (their relationship is one of the film's severely underplayed elements due, ironically enough, to lack of time and space); Paul Smith (the brutal Turkish guard in *Midnight Express*, 1978) as the Beast Rabban, a brutish Harkonnen; plus British rock star Sting, as Harknonnen heir Feyd-Rautha.

Sting's appearance in the film is testament to Lynch's hip appeal filtering through to the mainstream rock industry. 'I'm only doing this film because of David,' the singer claimed, as if pre-empting the attack; 'he's a madman in sheep's clothing.' Though the gentlemanly Freddie Jones found Sting's acting 'surprisingly good', he was called only to wear his hair in Irish-looking red tufts (a characteristic ascribed by Herbert to Paul Atreides, transferred by

Lynch to the Harkonnen), flex his muscles, and mouth a few lines of lacklustre dialogue.

Other cast members included Max Von Sydow (Bergman stalwart, Father Merrin in *The Exorcist*, 1973, Ming the Merciless in De Laurentiis's *Flash Gordon*) as planetary ecologist Dr Kynes; Brad Dourif (the sexually-repressed young suicide in *One Flew Over the Cuckoo's Nest*, 1975, evangelical atheist preacher in John Huston's *Wise Blood*, 1979) as Piter, the Harkonnen Mentat; Dean Stockwell, making an almost-comeback as the duplicitous Dr Yueh; Jurgen Prochnow (formerly a U-boat commander in *Das Boot*, 1980, Oscar winner for Best Foreign Language film) as Duke Leto, Paul's father; diminutive actress Linda Hunt (who played male midget Billy Kwan in Peter Weir's *The Year of Living Dangerously*, 1981) as the Shadout Mapes, Lady Jessica's Fremen servant. And, for old time's sake, there was good ol' Jack Nance (Henry Spencer in *Eraserhead*), wandering around the peripheries as Nefud, the Harkonnen ordered to feed Paul and his mother to the worms.

'*Dune* was such an unbelievable project,' Nance would later recall, 'it was so huge and you know, so many people involved. I don't think Lynch could really believe he was in charge of all this. You know, 2,500 people in costume on this thing. We walked into this rehearsal, and it was the first time I'd seen this particular set and these people, and I just cracked up. I mean, sometimes Lynch and I would look at each other and crack up. Laughing.'

Early in production, the huge budget (estimated at $30–40 million, though, incredibly, no ceiling had yet been set) began to escalate in any number of ways. Rafaella De Laurentiis had to pay for six emergency generators to defeat Mexico City's random power cuts, and install air conditioning in the studio for gringos not used to working in up to 100 degrees of heat.

After about two weeks of shooting, at least half the cast and crew would be out with 'Montezuma's Revenge' at any given time. Kyle MacLachlan recalled that he lost twelve pounds in weight during filming from wearing the heat-trapping Fremen stillsuit, and from 'being in Mexico' – the squits, in plain American.

Rafaella decided it would be more economic to keep everybody off the rice and beans, building a stucco-and-brick commissary restaurant to be attended by Papa's personal pasta chef, flown straight from Monte Carlo. Total cost of the catering arrangements alone: $20,000 – equal to the total budget of *Eraserhead*.

As the year wore on, the production team swelled to even more massive size due to the arrival of cast and crew members' spouses and children, not wishing to be separated throughout the entire length of shooting. At one time this included Lynch's wife Mary and their young son Austin, born in 1982 and still under a year old when his father headed south of the border.

Almost endearingly, the De Laurentiises initially had so much faith in their super-budget production that they optioned all five of Herbert's *Dune* novels. MacLachlan had been signed up for the whole series, while Francesca Annis – 'I'm not in *Dune* 2. I come back and take over the planets in *Dune* 3,' she confidently confided – and Everett McGill, who played the leader of the Fremen warriors, were signed for three each.

When interviewed at his home, Frank Herbert pointed to a bound manuscript and explained, 'That's David's rough draft of *Dune Messiah*. Now that we speak the same "language", it's much easier for both of us to make progress, especially with the screenplays.' The minds of Lynch admirers may boggle to reflect that somewhere, on an alternative world in a parallel universe, David Lynch is squandering the rest of his career by making sequels to *Dune*.

Dune, the end product, is a film which seems strangely half-finished but, at the same time, overdone. It is only nominally 'A David Lynch Film', in that touches of its director's

Dr Kynes (Max Von Sydow) expires as the Beast Rabban (Paul Smith) punctures his 'stillsuit'. Such imaginative grotesqueries occur all too rarely in **Dune**.

obsessive imagination sporadically filter through before being neutralised by the dated, anonymous sweep of the traditional Hollywood epic.

'In some ways I know I've had to hold back,' Lynch fatally admitted, part-way through shooting. 'For one thing this film has got to be PG. [Parental Guidance suggested, but under-17s may attend without an adult.] You can think of some strange things to do, but as soon as they throw in PG, a lot of them go out the window.'

One particular shot that had to be excised indulged Lynch's fascination with animal parts and textures, where Rabban the Beast rips the tongue from a cow and eats it. Among the moments which actually manage to tickle the Lynch fan's palate are the emergence of the gigantic sandworm, whose triple-levelled open mouth threatens to (but never quite does) swallow the camera's point of view, in the manner of the spermazoid worm emerging from the tiny planet in *Eraserhead*, or the eyehole of John Merrick's hood.

Small but cute grotesqueries include the super-intelligent activity of Paul's little sister, Alia, in the womb, reflecting Lynch's fascination with childbirth. 'The foetus was the first thing I worked on,' recalled Carlo Rambaldi, who based the foetal visage on that of nine-year-old Alicia Roanne Witt, the child actress who played Alia, 'when it comes out of the mother its arm muscles contract, the eyes open and roll, and it actually says "mother" – except that the scene was trimmed to gain the producers' desired PG certificate, though Alia's birth is still heralded by a brief splatter of afterbirth on the floor.

Then there's the 'squood'; a Lynchian idea which doesn't appear in the novel – live food, in this case a mouse, which is crushed in a glass tube with a plunger by the Beast Rabban, then has its fluids sucked out with a straw. (Despite Lynch's aesthetic fondness for moribund little furry creatures, the mouse was a perishable prop made out of rice paper.)

Most crudely Lynchian are the Baron Harkonnen's red-haired, three-and-a-half foot slaves (little Ronnie Rockets, the director apparently wishing he was somewhere else), and the cartoonish, anti-gravitational – i.e. he floats around – Baron having his enflamed pustules drained by a fawning lackey. By this point, anyone with the faintest interest in Lynch's films is screaming inwardly, 'Make me gag, make me laugh, but make me feel *something*!' – in which case, the mining of the Baron's leprous face fluid and the folksily anachronistic command, 'Put the pick in there, Pete, and turn it round real neat!' comes just in the nick of time, reminding the viewer this is 'A David Lynch Film'. But only for one moment.

Most visually impressive, however, is the image Lynch borrowed from *Dune Messiah*, the novel's first sequel. As described by Frank Herbert, the spice melange would not only grant the ability to circumnavigate time and space to the addicted Guild Navigators, it would prolong their lives fourfold with the unfortunate side effect of gradually turning them into the worms which produce the substance.

Lynch appropriated the idea for his screenplay, co-designing with Anthony Masters a mutated navigator to be built by Carlo Rambaldi. This 'doughy grasshopper', as described by Lynch, appears largely reptilian (or perhaps amphibian, like the *Eraserhead* Baby), with squelching, shapeless head and vaginal mouth. When last seen, floating through space emitting electrical charges, the creature appears like a more anatomically-detailed, technically realised version of the spermazoid creatures in *Eraserhead* and *The Grandmother*. But the

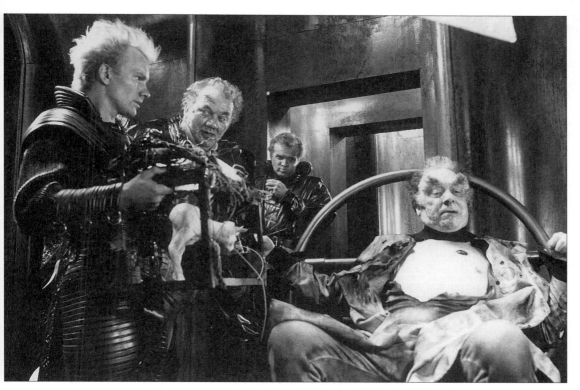

Feyd-Rautha (Sting) presents a life-preserving apparatus to Thufit Hawat (Freddie Jones, right); the pussycat was to be drained of its nutrients, but this footage ended on the cutting room floor, leaving the animal's appearance unexplained. (Background: Kenneth McMillan, left, as Baron Harkonnen, Lynch cast regular Jack Nance, right, as Nefud.)

creature's role is peripheral and, like all of the Lynchian touches, his appearance fleeting.

In the end, despite the many elements which went into the making of the film, despite the years of screenwriting, pre- and post-production, the efforts of the massive cast and crew, the only thing *Dune* would ever be noted for was its special effects. Even Lynch's normally essential elements of mood, atmosphere and texture were smothered by the necessity to put as many of Herbert's images on screen as possible.

The two-and-a-half-hour rough cut which would be shown as a preview to cast and crew was actually minus seven minutes of optical effects still to be added, ensuring roughly 25 minutes of expository narrative would be cut from the finished print and whizzed through in a voice-over narrative by Princess Irulan, the Emperor's daughter, cropping up at irregular intervals throughout.

Reassuring for Lynch – at least temporarily – was the positive reaction of Frank Herbert and the rest of the preview audience. 'My God, we've got it!' Herbert cried out loud at the screening, most of the cast and crew relieved that their long-term labours had paid off. 'I always knew *Dune* would make it to the screen – someday,' the author continued, 'but I just wouldn't believe it until I saw the credits roll.'

Whatever the final judgement of reviewers and public, the author had reached the apex of a dream nearly two decades long and was in no mood to equivocate. 'David's film is an artistic triumph, very visually beautiful,' he insisted. 'It begins as *Dune* begins, ends as *Dune* ends and I hear my dialogue all the way through.'

And, sad to say, there's the rub.

The 'final wrap' party for *Dune* took place on 27 January 1984 at Churubusco Studios.

Entrusting some final shots to the camera crew, David Lynch was ready to return home to LA. He had already spent nearly three years working on the film – including a full year in Mexico, much of the time separated from his wife and baby son – and post-production duties were still to be completed. He had lost weight during this time – not least due to the laxative benefits of Mexican food – and, though he remained as essentially youthful in appearance as ever, some crew members claimed his boyish features had aged.

In the autumn of 1984, Universal put him on the promotional treadmill. With his thick, floppy brown hair hacked and greased back, he reflected the decade's revival of the classic 1940s/early '50s look. Nervously diplomatic and wary of being verbally pinned down, he reiterated his good intentions to a series of interviewers he was only too awkwardly aware were not allowed to see a preview print of the film. To some critics, Lynch's equivocation was seen as an amusing bad omen, a reluctance to 'get behind the product'.

'The more familiar with the book you are, the more you'll like it,' he was able to admit, instantly alienating the greater part of both the mainstream and art-house movie audiences. 'You can't really tell what the mood of a thing will be until you see it – and you don't, at the time. You don't know if things are really gonna work till the end, and sometimes they don't and you can't always change things.

'That's frustrating. In *Eraserhead* I could do everything twice if I wanted to. With this film, even with the huge amount of time and money, there was not a lot of time for experimentation. Frustrating,' he echoed.

When the film eventually opened in early December 1984, it was the most eagerly awaited science fiction film yet put into production. The previous year, thousands of fans had packed a screening, at the World Science Fiction Convention, of cinema/SF writer Paul Sammon's *Destination Dune*, a video record of much of the film's shooting schedule. Frank

Baron Harkonnen (Kenneth McMillan, left) and the Beast Rabban (Paul Smith, right). 'Put the pick in there, Pete, and turn it round real neat!'– the Baron instructs a servant to drain the pus from his leprous visage, in a suspiciously earthly, Lynchian turn of phrase.

Herbert took the stage to totally endorse the adaptation – rather fearlessly, since at that point he'd only seen the shooting script (which continued to evolve on set), witnessed a few days of production and a few rushes. *The Making of Dune*, a glossy picture book celebrating the supposed magnitude of the event, was published to coincide with the opening.

Outside of the genre fan market, things were a little different. 'Huge, hollow, imaginative and cold', ran the *Variety* report for 5 December, in an unusually even-handed review which went out of its way to emphasise the film's positive points. Unfortunately for Lynch, for the De Laurentiises, and for everyone who gave at least a year of their life to the production, the report managed to set the tone for the film's reception. Reviews which unfairly savaged *Dune*, or failed to acknowledge its visual inventiveness, were rare – but neither did it elicit a passionate love-it-or-hate-it response. Instead, there was bemusement. And most of all, universal indifference.

As for Lynch fans, their general disappointment can be summed up in a comment from that first review: 'the enormity of the production pretty well crushes his artistic distinctiveness'. Most damning of all was the opinion: 'absent . . . is a real relish and delight in the fanciful creation of other worlds' – which, literally speaking, is inaccurate but still throws scorn on Lynch's whole *raison d'être* for the project.

No one involved with the film had stopped to wonder how cinema patrons – on the whole, a different animal from the readers of SF/fantasy sagas – were going to react to a film set on alien planets which makes references to 'the will of God' and constant Islamic allusions without any recognisable context for doing so; least of all, how numbed the viewer might feel by the ending, where an army of space nomads acclaim their leader with great fanfare as the 'Kwisatz Haderatch'. David Lynch, a film-maker since renowned for his genuinely quirky sense of humour, had made a ponderous, po-faced epic ending on a supreme note of bathos.

*One of the film's most effective visual touches: the spacing guild navigator who is mutating into a giant sandworm. Taken from one of the novel **Dune**'s sequels, the reptilian-insect hybrid is reminiscent of creatures in Lynch's early, more personal films.*

By the turn of the next decade, Lynch was to look back at the time spent on *Dune* as a hard lesson well learnt – but still hard enough to make it, by his own admission, 'extremely painful to talk about'.

'I sold out on *Dune*,' he admitted of the project which damn near sank him. 'I was making it for the producers, not for myself. That's why the right of final cut is crucial. One person has to be the filter for everything.'

What this fresh-faced fellow in his late thirties was not too proud to learn was that he shouldn't wander too far from his personal obsessions; that a story had to have some personal resonance for him to tell it successfully; but, most of all, just like fellow obsessive Jodorowsky before him, he'd learned the hard way that the novel *Dune* is basically unfilmable.

'I think that *Dune* was probably the first and last time that much money will be spent on a project around or by David,' Jennifer Lynch would later opine, having kept a close eye on her father's career as she grew up. 'After *Dune* was released, and the cut was what it was, he'll probably tell you this too, he died a thousand deaths. A *thousand* deaths, again and again and again.'

'I was, you know, beaten down badly after *Dune*,' concurred Lynch, 'and in my mind I had nowhere further to fall.'

As the year 1985 dawned, however, David Lynch was saved from his inner anxiety by the prospect of a project much closer to home.

In his own perversely innocent way, he was getting to grips with how you got things done in that crazy old movie-town. 'I finally realised that people didn't always know what I

70

meant,' he explained with the gauche charm of a tongue-tied teenager. 'Or they'd misinterpret what I meant, so I had to learn to say what it was that I wanted. On *Eraserhead*, it was a quiet process: going from inside me to the screen. I'd get something on film, get it paced a certain way, add the right sounds, and then I'd be able to say if it worked or not. Now, just to get to the point, there's a million times more talking. And in Hollywood, if you can't write your ideas down, or if you can't pitch them, or if they're so abstract that they can't be pitched properly, then they don't have a chance of surviving.

'Abstract things are important to a film. But very few people get the chance to really go all out with cinema.'

Fortunately for Lynch, whose career might otherwise have been destroyed by *Dune*, his contract with De Laurentiis had specified a *quid pro quo* arrangement that would allow him to make another, more personal project on a much lower budget. Despite the lengthy detour which diverted his energies up a creative blind alley, considerably reduced his stock in Hollywood, and introduced the pressure of long absences into his marriage, the celluloid painter was going to get the chance to go all out one more time.

Relieved to be free of the committee mentality, he had little doubt about the nature of his next project. It was to be about a little guy, 'three and a half feet tall, has physical problems, is bald and wears a red wig, and it's an absurd comedy and it has to do with electricity'. *Ronnie Rocket* was back on the launch-pad.

Or at least he was until Dino had second thoughts. Perhaps understanding that he'd previously set his director an impossible task, he was prepared to indulge him. But the *Ronnie Rocket* concept still smelled a little of science fiction, however way out of left-field his take on it – plus the fact that Lynch budgeted at nearly a quarter of what it took to produce *Dune*, from which the losses were currently giving De Laurentiis a huge pain in the pocket.

No, Papa Dino was not going to stamp on the idea – but it was for later, if the next film could turn a profit, if it could be done for less money.

For now, it was for Lynch to sit down, drink coffee, scratch his head. Get dreaming. After the strived-for but botched timelessness of the overblown effort he'd expended so much energy on, it was soothing, not to say evocative, to head back to those formative years when the little things of everyday life were charged with so much fascination and fear.

He decided that he yearned to set a film in the decade of his birth, the 1940s – 'a dark sort of film *noir* kind of thing' – or, even more nostalgic, the 1950s, the formative era when he grew to adolescence, full of stuff 'just like my woodpeckers and bobby socks and wild fins and plastic'. (Lynch, unsurprisingly, is a collector of kitsch, dime-store art and other evocative junk from that era. The woodpeckers he speaks of are five soft toys – individually named Chucko, Buster, Pete, Bob and Dan, Woody lookalikes to a man – who stood guard over his office at the Universal lot in the pre-production days of *Dune*.)

'I like diners,' he reflected aloud, keen to counter the already clichéd perception of himself. 'I don't like dark places. I like light places with Formica and metal and nice shiny silver-metal mugs, glasses, a good Coca-Cola machine. So I'm looking for stories or a script in the '50s, you know, detectives and that kind of thing – diner stuff.'

He could look, but he wouldn't find – unless he took the same route back into the worlds he wished to visit that he'd taken in order to arrive. If David Lynch wanted to work in some mythical 1950s world, he'd have to create it for himself.

CHAPTER FIVE

Blue Velvet:

America's Dark Underbelly

The first personal project David Lynch worked on for close to a decade had a long gestation period. After hoping, briefly, for someone to hand him the 1950s/*noir*/murder mystery project he desired, he looked back into his own files. In terms of foetal formation, there was one project that had laboured longer than a baby elephant.

'I started to get ideas for it in 1973,' recalled Lynch of the time when *Eraserhead* stalled, 'but it was all very vague. I only had a feeling and a title. Then, when I finished *The Elephant Man*, I met Richard Roth, the producer of *Julia* (1977). We had coffee and he told me he had read my script for *Ronnie Rocket*. He had liked it but, truly, he said it wasn't his cup of tea. He asked me if I had any other scripts. I said I had only ideas. I told him I had always wanted to sneak into a girl's room to watch her into the night and that, maybe, at one point or another, I would see something that would be the clue to a murder mystery. Roth loved the idea and asked me to write a treatment. I went home and thought of the ear in the field.'

Unsurprisingly, relations were a little cool between Dino De Laurentiis and his star director for nearly a year. While De Laurentiis Entertainment tried to make good losses on their failed epic, which had only recouped a fraction of its $45 million budget, Lynch was quietly but persistently reminding his producer that the terms of his contract gave him the option to direct a low-budget (in Hollywood terms) personal project.

Eventually, the Euro-mogul gave a few inches, offering a deal which, while his intent is not known, has been interpreted by a few Hollywood strategists as a deterrent. Chief among its stipulations was that Lynch would work for an unremunerative pay-day, his wages deferred, and with only a minimal share in whatever eventual profits there may have been.

'I could have total artistic freedom if I kept the budget down (to $6 million) and took a cut in my salary,' Lynch later confirmed. 'Of course, I took the deal.'

By default, De Laurentiis Entertainment had financed the second purely personal feature film of David Lynch's career.

In Blue Velvet *Jeffrey (Kyle MacLachan) finds a severed ear.*

David Lynch gesticulates on the mid-1980s set of **Blue Velvet,** *an artist whose time had come.*

Of the screenplay itself, Lynch explained, 'It's sort of a thriller and murder mystery – but it's also a 'psychological drama.'

For Frederick Elmes, veteran Lynch cinematographer from *Eraserhead*, the transition of *Blue Velvet* to the screen was almost as cherished an idea for him as it was for the man who dreamed it up. 'I'd read the script years ago,' confirmed Elmes, 'and we talked about it then: how we would go about it if it should happen, and what we did was to establish a point of view and a look for *Blue Velvet* even before *Dune*. We were dreaming, but it was always a fantasy of ours to go out and do it. '

Elmes' look for the film would be the antithesis of *Dune* – brightly lit, saturated, almost pastel colours. This even applies in the naturally darker night-time sequences where deep, dark browns and reds predominate.

'*Blue Velvet* is a very American movie,' stated Lynch. 'The look of it was inspired by my childhood in Spokane, Washington. Lumberton is a real name; there are many Lumbertons in America. I picked it because we could get police insignias and stuff, because it was an actual town. But then it took off in my mind and we started getting lumber trucks going through the frame and that jingle on the radio – "At the sound of the falling tree . . . " – that all came about because of the name.

'There is an autobiographical level to the movie. Kyle (MacLachlan), is dressed like me. My father was a research scientist for the Department of Agriculture in Washington. We were in the woods all the time. I'd sorta had enough of the woods by the time I left, but still, lumber and lumberjacks, all this kinda thing, that's America to me – like the picket fences and the roses in the opening shot. It's so burned in, that image, and it makes me feel so happy. That was in a lot of our childhoods.'

The story, while ostensibly *noir*-ish and influenced by the edgy, implicitly violent thrillers of the late '40s and early '50s, was little but a vehicle for Lynch to hang impressionistic moods on. The murders themselves are just about the least mysterious element of the story – while the surreal conclusion left loose ends unresolved, only the most pedantically literal viewer would complain about coherence.

There are so many red herrings that what lingers are the *mise-en-scène*s: the layering of cinematic technique to arrive at one desired atmosphere, feeling, or sense of predicament; the imagery of a young man's hunky-dory existence meshing with a strange world not more than a few blocks from his home; images of America's dark underbelly – a term that became clichéd from overuse, after the pundits identified the Lynchian genre of 'Weird Americana'. Its curiously anachronistic, 1950s-based scenario would suggest, to many, a hybrid of the style of American sentimentalist painter Norman Rockwell and shadowy, *noir*-ish crime movies. And the springboard for all this was an innocuous and, as originally sung, strangely sexless ballad: 'Blue Velvet', a song of longing for an exotic, sensuous woman.

While the story may have been a twisted plot device to hang the real ideas on, the characters at the centre were more crucial than the narrative itself:

Jeffrey Beaumont, an upright young man in his late teens, intoxicated by the dark mystery he finds swathing his small hometown – as played by Lynch protégé MacLachlan (whose fresh-faced, darkly-fixated appeal in *Blue Velvet* would go a long way towards dispelling the memory of *Dune*), the boy would appear at times to be a young David Lynch *manqué*.

Just as crucial were the roles of the adults who suck Jeffrey into their twilight world: Dorothy Vallens, a beautiful, other-worldly nightclub singer intimidated into entering a violent sexual relationship with a vicious gangster; and, not least, the gangster himself: Frank Booth, a man who is no more than the sum of his consuming obsessions, and all the deadlier for it.

'I don't know where Frank Booth came from,' expounded Lynch of his classic every-psycho. 'He just appeared one day. There's nobody that I based anything on. For me, he's like an archetype. He's a guy I somehow know from small towns. He's an American heavy. He has to be American, and he has to come from either a desert small town or a Midwestern small town.

'Frank, to me, is a guy Americans know very well. I'm sure most everybody growing up has met someone like Frank. They might not have shook his hand and gone out for a drink with him, but all you've got to do is exchange eye contact with someone like that and you know that you've met him.'

'The way agents and managers put it,' said Dennis Hopper, who won the part of Frank despite his self-professed reputation as a 'drinker-drugger', 'this part has no redeemable character. It's beyond redemption.'

'Dennis had been on earlier lists,' remembered Lynch, 'but because of his reputation I never even thought twice about him. Because if I'd thought about him, I'd freak out and want to work with him no matter what he was doing. But when I heard that he was totally on the wagon and had cleaned up his act, I got real excited. His manager said, "David, look, please talk to the producers who've worked with him recently, they'll tell you he's fantastic. I wouldn't tell you this if it weren't true. Dennis is in love with life, he's really got it together and he really loves this part and can we have Dennis call you?" I said, sure. Dennis called up and said, "I've got to play this part, David, because I *am* Frank." And that almost killed it right there.

'Dennis is the only guy who could have played that part,' Lynch conceded. 'What he offered was the life of Frank Booth. You see a much more complicated Frank and a guy who definitely has so much love and complicated emotions going on inside the guy. So you say, this is not a one-note person, this is a person who is very complete, although very dangerous at the same time.

'A punch in the nose is one thing. But a thought introduced into the mind lasts so long, it doesn't seem to shake loose. And Frank seems to understand these things.'

As a director himself (end-of-hippie-era cult flick *Easy Rider*, 1969, chaotic, commercially disastrous *The Last Movie*, 1971, grimly seedy and underrated *Out of the Blue*, 1980), Hopper was amused at first by how Gentleman Dave expected to draw out intense performances with the minimum of coercion or intimidation. Soon, like the rest of the cast, he came to appreciate it. 'He might say, "A little more,"' Hopper mused, 'then, "Peachy keen," but that's it. '

While casting the part of Dorothy Vallens, Lynch was introduced to a particularly striking fashion model by a mutual friend. Taken by her quietly imposing mix of icy cool and Mediterranean voluptuousness, he gazed across their restaurant table and told her, 'You could be Ingrid Bergman's daughter.'

'"You idiot," my friend said to me,' remembered Lynch of the magical moment, '"she *is* Ingrid Bergman's daughter."'

Isabella Rossellini was indeed the daughter of the celebrated Miss Bergman and Italian neo-realist film director Roberto Rossellini. Her birth had been the subject of a scandal which barred her mother from Hollywood productions for some years – during the days when adultery was okay so long as it wasn't conducted openly.

By the early 1980s, as an established model, Miss Bergman's grown-up love-child had landed a $2 million contract to be the public face of Lancôme cosmetics. In 1986, contemporaneous to the production of *Blue Velvet*, her contract with Lancôme would be renewed at the ripe old age of 34. 'Once you become the image of a company,' she later explained, with a refreshing lack of conceit, 'it's very hard for a company to change its image, so they keep you for a long time.'

La Rossellini, a relatively inexperienced actress, won out the part of Dorothy via those qualities Lynch had immediately recognised: her dark-complexioned beauty – her mother's features made deeper, more fiery, by her father's Latin lineage; her European 'otherness' and mystery; her inner strength and external vulnerability. Whereas the script called for 'a very beautiful woman in her late thirties', Ms R possessed the pulchritude but seemed about ten years younger. Looking every inch the *femme fatale*, the aloof-but-tragic Dorothy would try to influence her circumstances not by spinning a spider web of seduction, but by taking the part of a victim.

Both parties quickly became fascinated with each other; both were divorced (Rossellini's brief marriage had been to Martin Scorsese). Lynch's second marriage, to the former Mary Fisk, had been dissolved by the courts earlier in 1985. Whatever pressures the marriage had faced were not helped by his obsessive devotion to the *Dune* project for three and a half years, including one solid year on location. As in his first marriage, however, the split would remain amicable, with regular access to his small son, Austin.

With shooting set to begin in the autumn of 1985, the optimum location – in terms of both mood and economics – was found to be in the backwoods of North Carolina.

'It's a neighbourhood picture,' Lynch would announce at the time of release, far happier to promote a personal vision than his previous piece of corporate committee work.

'But in a way, *Eraserhead* is a neighbourhood picture as well; it's just a different neighbourhood. They don't ever connect with the government or Washington DC or world problems. Their problems are problems within a small area of the world, and a lot of the problems are inside the people themselves, so in that way, both films deal with sort of similar things. I think that *Eraserhead* was unsettling to some people because it might trigger things that were in their subconscious, somehow it would get under people's skin, but that's what it's all about. *Blue Velvet* could have the same effect on people, but it is, on the other hand, quite different. It's more of a surface picture than *Eraserhead* – and it's in colour and it's got cars in it!'

BLUE VELVET [1986]

The ornate credits roll against a backdrop of crushed blue velvet. Angelo Badalamenti's theme is a florid, dramatic string arrangement.

In a deferred opening glowing with unnaturally bright colours, the song 'Blue Velvet' by early '60s crooner Bobby Vinton plays against a wide-screen tableaux of life in an idyllic American small-town: Lumberton, USA. Aqua-blue skies overhead; deep red roses and yellow tulips grow against a bright white picket fence; in slow motion, a fire engine turns a corner, and a big old fireman stands on board with a docile dog, waving hospitably; a school traffic lady holds a 'Stop' sign for children to cross the road; a paunchy, middle-aged guy leisurely hoses his greener-than-green front lawn.

This is the surface memory of Lynch's childhood, which he associates closely with the town of Spokane, Washington: 'Blue skies, red flowers, white picket fences and green grass with birds chirping in the trees . . . But, on the cherry tree, there's this pitch oozing out – some black, some yellow.'

The lady of the house watches an old film noir *thriller on TV, where a top-coated gunman points his pistol at the screen; the connecting end of her husband's hosepipe starts leaking water. He struggles, holds the back of his neck in agonising pain and falls to the floor, stricken by a stroke. A little dog jumps about on his chest.*

The camera descends to the grass on his front lawn. Two animated beetles are engaged in a fight to the death; ominous noises drown out the rest of the soundtrack.

America's dark underbelly: the classic opening scene of **Blue Velvet***, where all is not well in the garden. Jeffrey's father (Jack Harvey) undergoes a stroke, while his curious dog and a toddler look on.*

'I had lots of friends,' Lynch remembers of his boyhood, 'but I loved being alone and looking at insects swarming in the garden.

'There's always the surface of something and something altogether different going on beneath the surface. Just like electrons busily moving about, but we can't see them. That's one of the things films do, is show you that conflict.'

'David's very in love with the cleanliness and patriotism of America,' his daughter Jennifer later remarked. 'How stable it appears on the outside, and how behind every door there is something off-kilter.

'I know *Blue Velvet* came out of the light and dark extremes that are so much David. His home life as a child, which was very white picket fence and lovely, with parents who were wonderful. I don't think David bought it, that there was only peace going on inside those doors. I think he knew better, and because he didn't think anybody believed him he exaggerated what might be going on inside those homes. And I'm sure that segued into *Blue Velvet*, a lot of it. And those things are going on in those houses, we just don't know those people. *Fortunately.*'

The local radio station announcer speaks to Lumberton, USA, telling the locals, 'It's a sunny day, so get out those chain-saws.' Casual-but-smart young college boy Jeffrey wanders across rural wasteland to see his father at the hospital. Jeffrey is deeply distressed at the sight of Dad lying strapped to an elaborate oxygen mask.

Walking moodily back along the same route, Jeffrey's foraging for stones leads him to pick up something shocking and mysterious: a severed human ear. The camera tracks slowly into the ear, the soundtrack drowned by droning noise.

As many have suggested, the descent into the disembodied ear seems to signify Jeffrey's journey into his own subconscious, or even a literal dream. Even the camera motion itself is not strictly realistic, tracking down into a middle ear which would not, of course, still be attached to a severed outer ear.

Jeffrey has returned home to help out in the Beaumont family hardware store, now that Dad is in hospital. There's no communication between him and Mom – she doesn't talk to him, too locked into her domestic nightmare. At the store, Jeffrey is welcomed back by his Dad's assistants, two 'credit-to-their-race'-type black men. One of them is blind, but has a photographic memory, remembering where every item sits and the cost of everything in the store; he also has a secret method of deducing the number of fingers Jeffrey holds in the air.

Intrigued by his anatomical find, Jeffrey visits the home of a local police detective. The cop is tolerant towards the young man, giving him a stiff talk on the confidentiality of the case. 'One day when it's all sewed up,' he promises, 'I'll let you know in detail. Right now though, I can't.' 'I understand,' says Jeffrey, unable to contain his boyish enthusiasm, 'I'm just real curious, like you said.' 'I was the same myself when I was your age,' confides the fatherly cop, 'that's why I went into this business.' 'Must be great,' smiles Jeffrey. 'It's horrible too,' corrects the stern adult.

Every clichéd word of this dialogue is read straight, without camp overacting, pointing back to when such prosaic banter was considered 'hardboiled'.

Leaving Detective Williams' home, he hears the policeman's daughter, Sandy, calling to him out of the darkness. She tells him that a woman named Dorothy Vallens, who works as a singer at the Slow Club, is believed to be connected with the case somehow. She is as keen as he is to investigate, but at the same time her conscience tries to keep the brakes on his enthusiasm – 'actually it's too weird'.

'You're a neat girl': Jeffrey (Kyle MacLachlan) is urged to investigate the mystery by Sandy (Laura Dern), the squeaky-clean kid who's the antithesis of the woman he becomes obsessed with, but ends up marrying him. Laura Dern was the latest recruit to the faithful Lynch mob.

Sandy is played by Laura Dern, young daughter of Bruce Dern and Diane Ladd. Blonde, healthy, clean-scrubbed and fair-skinned, she is the WASPish anti-Dorothy, lacking the older woman's enchanting other-worldliness and pouting allure. She is, however, the one who urges Jeffrey forward into the mystery, without whom he would never come into contact with Dorothy. As Lynch said, 'Sandy's the girl next door, but she's not just one-note, because she's the one who gets Jeffrey into it . . . there's something about her that's strange, too.'

The world which Jeffrey and Sandy inhabit appears to be that of the Eisenhower era, the mid-to-late 1950s – a time of cleanliness and conformity, a consumer paradise, as evoked by production designer Patricia Norris. However, Lynch throws anachronisms all around the screen to let us know that it's only the ethos of the era which he's stolen, and will ultimately corrupt: Jeffrey's ear stud and black leather box jacket – distinctly early '80s; the songs, 'Blue Velvet' and 'In Dreams', both implicitly meaningful to psychotic gangster Frank Booth – early '60s; the cars and fashions seen in Sandy's schoolyard seem of an indeterminate period when the '50s and '80s collide, while the large Montgomery Clift poster on her wall is distinctly '50s.

'In a way,' acknowledged Lynch, 'it's like a myth. All the characters are American archetypes from the '50s.'

Jeffrey impresses sweet young thing Sandy with his quirky charm: he shows her how he does the 'chicken walk', and tells her 'I used to know a kid who lived there [across the street] and who had the biggest tongue in the world.' She laughs and asks what happened to him. 'He moved away,' Jeffrey replies, which is pretty much the way life is at times – strange but trivial.

'It's a strange world, isn't it?' Jeffrey asks rhetorically, the banal statement becoming a recurring motif throughout the film.

'I understand when people say that the things in the films are strange or grotesque,' affirmed Lynch, 'but our world is strange and grotesque, right? They say that truth is stranger than fiction. All the strange things in the films are triggered by this world, so it can't be all that strange. I love things that are absurd. It's really real to me.'

Jeffrey hatches a plot whereby he will enter Dorothy Vallens' apartment posing as a bug exterminator. The Deep River Apartments could easily be the same block where Henry lives in Eraserhead *— the hum of a neon sign announcing 'elevator out of order' is a constant accompaniment. However, instead of living in a world of monochrome, Dorothy's place is rich with deep, dirty browns and dark, crimson reds.*

Jeffrey's first glimpse of her is through the crack of her chained door — beautiful as a sultry Renaissance muse, full glossy lips and dark eyes shining with aqua-marine shadow.

Inside her apartment, the feminine clutter of cosmetics, perfume bottles and green houseplants is offset by one child's toy: a pointed party hat with a propeller top.

The hat has been identified by more than one reviewer as a *Wizard of Oz* reference; other points of reference are said to be the intensely bright roses and tulips in the opening sequence, reminiscent of the scene change in the Judy Garland film which moves from dark monochrome Kansas to bright Technicolor Oz.

Soon after, when Jeffrey returns to the apartment to spy on Dorothy in her boudoir, she alluringly, and fetishistically, walks about in black underwear and a pair of red high-heeled shoes. Connections have been drawn — in an essay, by James Lindroth — between Dorothy's footwear and the magic ruby slippers of Dorothy in *The Wizard of Oz*. Later in the film, when Jeffrey is taken on a wild car ride by Frank Booth and his hoods, the camera cuts twice from the car's occupants to a yellow line running down the centre of the road — following the Yellow Brick Road?

If all this seems a little strained, it's worth taking Lynch's own testimony into account: 'Dennis [Hopper] was the perfect Frank because he's from Kansas. It's perfect that Frank would be from Kansas — because Kansas has something to do with *The Wizard of Oz* and Dorothy.'

Distracted by his bladder, Jeffrey fails to notice Dorothy answering her door to a hefty man in a yellow suit. He hears Dorothy return and hides in her wardrobe closet. Peering through the slats, he sees her disrobe and remove her wig to reveal her own hair underneath.

Dorothy finds Jeffrey, forcing him out of the wardrobe at knifepoint and making him strip down to his socks —in a reversal of the male voyeur role. 'Don't look at me . . . Don't touch me!' she warns him, foreshadowing the behaviour of her own perverted sex partner. Then she fellates Jeffrey, who's aroused by the tension.

They're interrupted by the arrival of someone she clearly fears. She makes Jeffrey hide in the wardrobe again. Seeing only their dark, broken images between the slats, Jeffrey is forced to listen to the new arrival's violent treatment of Dorothy and the gasping and sucking as he inhales helium from an elaborate gas mask.

At least, the gas is helium according to Lynch's script — though it would make Frank speak like Chip 'n' Dale. Other suggestions have been ether — large hits of which would knock him out — or nitrous oxide (laughing gas), which is more likely.

'She wore blue velvet': Dorothy, Jeffrey's obsession, played by Isabella Rossellini, David Lynch's muse. An inexperienced actress, **Blue Velvet** *elevated her to iconic status, with a dark allure born of painted sensuality and twisted perversion.*

'Hello, Frank,' Dorothy flatly intones. 'It's Daddy, you shithead!' he immediately reprimands her. He soon changes roles, yelling 'Baby wants to fuck!' like some demonic, retarded brat. 'Don't you fuckin' look at me!' he warns Dorothy, then slaps her face. A small, pained smile comes upon her, as if his blow has defused tension.

Jeffrey hears the snip of Frank's scissors as they cut the underwear from Dorothy's crotch. 'Baby wants blue velvet,' he whines menacingly. She feeds one end of the strap of her velvet robe into Frank's mouth. He chews, driving himself upwards into a greater frenzy. Maniacally inhaling gas, Frank throws himself into a brief, brutal fuck with Dorothy, shouting 'Daddy's coming home!', while keeping his unbuckled pants on.

Frank extinguishes the candle which burns in Dorothy's wall lantern. 'Now it's dark,' he says. This will be his motif statement throughout the film.

'Frank is totally in love,' insisted Lynch of the character and his rather abrasive method of seduction. 'He just doesn't know how to show it. He may have gotten into some strange things, but he's still motivated by positive things.'

Lynch was taken to task by some interviewers for his reported crack-up (with hilarity) on set, when Dennis Hopper, as Frank, was going bat-shit crazy on Dorothy. 'I'm pretty sure near every psychiatrist could tell me right now why I was laughing,' he defended, 'but I

Love hurts: Frank (Dennis Hopper) snorts laughing gas and shows the strength of his feeling to Dorothy (Isabella Rossellini). Manic, frightening, perversely comical, this sexually violent scene is unique in the cinema.

don't know. It was hysterically funny to me. Frank was completely obsessed. He was like a dog in a chocolate store. He could not help himself. He was completely into it . . . It has something to do with the fact that it was so horrible and so frightening and so intense and violent, that there was also this layer of humour. It has to do with the degree of obsession where people cannot help themselves.'

Frank re-covers Dorothy with her blue velvet robes and leaves. Fragmented, she turns to Jeffrey for comfort, calling him Don – the name of her missing husband. 'Hit me,' she implores him. Horrified, he refuses. 'Hit me! Hit me! Hit me!' she implores again, banging her fist on the wall, but he gets up to leave. 'Help me,' Dorothy begs her own reflection in the bathroom mirror.

Jeffrey can't leave Dorothy alone, visiting the Slow Club where she sings. There he spots Frank in the audience, chewing on a piece of the eponymous fabric while she sings 'Blue Velvet'.

Unable to stay away, Jeffrey visits Dorothy's apartment once more. Dorothy seductively begs him to 'Feel me. Hit me. Hurt me!' He recoils, but eventually she goads him into striking her in the mouth. Both of them are driven into erotic passion. 'Now I have your disease in me,' she tells him afterwards.

Jeffrey and Sandy sit outside a church in their car. The anguished young man asks her, 'Why are there people like Frank?' As organ music swells on the soundtrack Sandy tells Jeffrey about a dream she had.

'In the dream there was our world and the world was dark because there weren't any robins. And the robins represented love, and for the longest time there was just this darkness, and all of a sudden thousands of robins were set free and they flew down and brought this blinding light of love, and it seemed like that love would be the only thing that would make any difference. And it did. So I guess that means there's trouble till the robins come.'

'Like a dog in a chocolate store': according to Lynch, Frank just can't help himself. Compulsively profane, frenzied, obsessed with textured fabrics, Dennis Hopper's bravura performance suggests an exaggerated version of Tourette's syndrome.

'I like to have contrasts in a film,' explained Lynch, 'because there are so many horrific things and so many beautiful things in life . . . Right or wrong, the Dennis Hopper character is, to most people, the coolest character in *Blue Velvet*, and yet there's another side to that picture. The scene in which Sandy tells Jeffrey about the robins is real important to me.

'That scene is kind of embarrassing,' he admitted. 'Sandy is this emotional kind of girl who gets into this euphoric state which is quite beautiful . . . It's a feeling of what can happen when two people are sitting in a car and falling in love when they're all alone and no one else is listening. They say things like this in a safe environment, goofy things. And I think films should be embarrassing in some places.'

Jeffrey meets Dorothy at her apartment the following evening. 'I'm not crazy,' she says to him, 'I know the difference between right and wrong.' Frank and his gang of misfits arrive. 'You're like me, you fucker!' Frank insists to Jeffrey, instinctively sensing the boy frequents Dorothy's apartment for similar purposes.

Frank's contention that Jeffrey is like him is reinforced by the clothes he wears – on first appearance, he has a slicker version of Jeffrey's leather jacket, with the white shirt underneath buttoned up to the neck. Despite Freudian theorising about Frank as a father figure, the obvious inference is that, to Jeffrey, Frank is the dark side of himself he'd never normally wish to meet.

Their next stop is a cheap joint owned by Ben, a slap-painted fag-pimp-pusher. Frank acclaims him as a 'suave fucker', telling his henchmen to take Dorothy to see her small son, Donnie – 'Let Tits see her kid' – who is held prisoner behind a bedroom door while her husband, Don, is kept captive elsewhere. He boasts to Ben about a robbery-murder in which a 'drug dealer was shot to death and this woman had her legs broken'. Jeffrey is mocked as a 'pussy' by Frank, who punches him hard in the belly then playfully invites Ben to do the same. Ben sends Frank into rapture by miming to a tape of Roy Orbison singing 'In Dreams', using a table-light shining in his ghoulishly made-up face as a microphone.

> *'A candy-coloured clown they call the sandman*
> *Tiptoes to my room every night . . .'*

Hearing the opening lines of the song, Frank goes into a pained, semi-erotic ecstasy.

'What's interesting about this scene,' commented Fred Elmes, 'is that we have this group of very strange characters in one room . . . it's a very unreal situation.

'The lamp that Ben holds as a microphone grew out of a rehearsal that we did one afternoon . . . Basically, we went to see the location, and Dean Stockwell picked up a work light to mimic a microphone because we had talked about having him sing a song . . . Then we got the idea of having him sing with a work light instead of ever having the microphone, and all he ever does is mouth the words to the tape that Frank carries instead of really singing. It became something of a routine that the Dennis Hopper character and Dean did, and we wanted it to seem as though they'd done this before, which makes it a bit stranger.'

Psyched up on pills given to him by Ben, Frank and company head back off to the car. 'Now it's dark,' he warns. 'Let's fuck! I'll fuck anything that moves!' They roar off into the countryside at high speed, the inside of the car a maelstrom of psychosis.

Frank savagely squeezes Dorothy's breasts in the front seat of the car. Jeffrey lashes out and punches Frank in the mouth. Furious, Frank orders the car taken to a deserted timber mill at Meadow Lane, the industrial site where Dorothy's husband is held prisoner. With the song 'Love Letters Straight From Your Heart' playing in the background, Frank distorts the metaphor of the lyric. 'I'll send you a love letter. Straight from my heart, fucker. You know what a love letter is?' he asks Jeffrey. 'It's a bullet from a fucking gun, fucker. You receive a love letter from me, you're fucked forever. You understand, fucker? I'll send you straight to hell, fucker!'

Standard as the unholy F-word is to Hollywood crime movies these days, Frank's emphatic use of 'fuck' and all its derivations, in virtually every sentence he blurts out, is comically obsessive.

'David never said that word,' Dennis Hopper later claimed. 'He didn't say, "Say fuck," he said, "When you say *that word*." He seems to be able to write "fuck" and not say it. He's a very curious man,' the actor deadpanned, aware he was embroidering a myth.

'I had many, many of them written in the script, but he always added more,' came Lynch's genial retort. 'I didn't want to charge the atmosphere any more than it was already.'

Instead of killing Jeffrey, Frank enacts another ritual. To the tune of 'In Dreams', he applies thick red lipstick to his mouth, snorts helium, sucks velvet, kisses Jeffrey and smears it over his face, groaning 'pretty, pretty . . .' He invites Jeffrey to feel his muscles, flirting overtly and sadistically with the boy, then starts beating him up with near-orgasmic excitement.

Jeffrey has been beaten to within a few inches of his life. 'Things got a little out of hand,' he tells Sandy when she sees his face covered with bruises.

He goes to report Frank's activities to the police, but finds a big man in a yellow suit occupying an office. Later, when he visits Sandy's house, he finds the same Yellow Man locked in conversation with Detective Williams. Sandy's father takes him to one side. 'Easy does it, Jeffrey,' he warns him. 'Behave yourself. Don't blow it.' Jeffrey is shaken to think that Lumberton could be rotten at the core.

Jeffrey finds that Lumberton, USA, has its very own low-life: left to right, Frank's misfit cronies, Hunter (J. Michael Hunter), Paul (Jack Nance) and Raymond (Brad Dourif), intimidate the clean-cut student.

Sandy and Jeffrey go to a teenage prom together, dancing to the sincere, semi-devotional love song 'The Mysteries of Love' (lyrics by Lynch, music by Angelo Badalamenti), sung by the angelic Julee Cruise.

The formative partnership with soundtrack composer Badalamenti was forged in his collaboration with Lynch on 'The Mysteries of Love'. Originally, Lynch was simply looking for a musical director to coach Rossellini on her musically flat, but intoxicatingly sensuous version of 'Blue Velvet', but soon became enamoured of Badalamenti's emotion-fuelled mode of composition. The amiable Brooklynite, in his late forties at the time of production, explained his non-musician director's input.

'David presented me with what was essentially a few lines on paper, no metre, no rhyme, and he would come to my office and I'd sit at the piano and he'd describe the mood of a particular scene or, in the case of this poem, the themes he had in mind; he wanted something which conjured up the wind, very cosmic and angelic, all that from just six lines.'

For the haunting female voice, the composer sought advice from 28-year-old Julee Cruise, a singer he'd formerly worked with in a country and western show when he was musical director of a theatre in Manhattan's East Village.

As an off-Broadway 'belter', who played Janis Joplin in a musical, she was a perverse final choice for Badalamenti, who decided she was as well equipped to sustain clear notes in the upper registers as any singer he knew. (Though this meant giving up cigarettes and training her voice to iron out the huskiness.) With her new vocal style, as the ethereal 'floating lady', Ms Cruise found herself becoming part of an occasional but ultimately unique musical partnership.

On the way home, they're pursued by Mike, Sandy's former football-player boyfriend, with a

*Author J. G. Ballard describes the painterly vision of **Blue Velvet** as a clash between the styles of Norman Rockwell and Edward Hopper. In this scene, Rockwell's smalltown sentimentalism gives way to Hopper's noir-toned night-life: Ben (Dean Stockwell) mimes the 'candy-coloured clown' for entranced Frank (Dennis Hopper), as a hooker looks on.*

carload of buddies. 'Who's that, Jeffrey? That your mother?' sneers Mike, as the naked, tottering Dorothy comes stumbling out of the dark. As she draws nearer, they can see the many bruises and abrasions over her pale, untoned skin – Mike, obviously a good, all-American boy at heart, apologises and makes off. 'My secret love,' Dorothy murmurs to Jeffrey as he helps her stagger inside.

'When I was little,' reminisced Lynch, 'I think it was in Boise, Idaho, I was with my younger brother, and we saw a grown woman walking naked on the street. And that was Dorothy, right there.' Like the man says, it's a strange world. And, for schizophrenics and nervous breakdowns, a sad one too.

'Mom, we're home,' calls Sandy, bewildered, asking her mother to phone for an ambulance. 'He put his disease in me!' Dorothy screams, then makes a desperate plea: 'You're my special friend. I still have you inside me . . . I love you. Love me.' On hearing this, Sandy slaps Jeffrey's face. As she is driven away, Dorothy cries, 'I'm falling. I'm falling. Help me!' (Alongside the dream image of floating, falling would become another personal Lynch motif.)

Jeffrey resolves to visit Dorothy's apartment one more time, to look for clues. He finds a gory tableau of death: two men have been murdered, artfully juxtaposed and colour co-ordinated. The first is tied to a chair with strips of blue velvet, his mouth stuffed with Dorothy's velvet belt. The severed left ear identifies him as her husband, Don. The second is the Yellow Man, the corrupt policeman: his brain exposed, he floats listlessly on his feet like some helium-filled objet d'art.

'Well, the lab called,' remembered Lynch with amusement. 'Five different people called the producer that morning and said: "There's no problem, but what is that guy doing? Is he supposed to be dead? We see him moving." And the producer came to me on the set and said, "David, this must be a good scene. The lab never calls otherwise. They don't care about anything."' If anyone had so far failed to appreciate how *Blue Velvet* wasn't operating as a literal crime thriller, this is the point at which their bearings were totally lost.

Jeffrey hears Frank ascending the stairs and tries to hide. Frank is wearing what Jeffrey described to Detective Williams as his 'well-dressed man disguise': light jacket, false moustache, wig; an outfit already worn twice in the film for no apparent reason. Jeffrey uses the Yellow Man's walkie-talkie to contact Sandy's father, telling him he's hiding in the back bedroom. In the living room, Frank, who keeps his radio tuned to police frequencies, overhears the message; in a mad frenzy he shoots both corpses again, finally knocking down the Yellow Man. 'I hear you, fucker! One well-dressed fucking man knows where your fucking cute little butt's hiding!' he warns, a strip of blue velvet hanging from his handgun. Unable to find Jeffrey, he opens the wardrobe door. Jeffrey shoots him point blank through the head with the Yellow Man's gun. As Frank falls backwards, the wall light fuses. Now it's really dark.

The camera slowly pans out from a close-up of a human ear – this time it belongs to Jeffrey. Awaking in a hammock, he finds himself in his own backyard as Sandy – now apparently his wife – and both sets of parents prepare a barbecue. 'You okay, Dad?' Jeffrey asks. 'Fine, son,' comes the reply from Dad, who's locked in amiable conversation with Detective Williams.

The psychological sojourn, through the severed ear and out again, has been a journey through Jeffrey's strangest desires and fears. To read the story dead literally, it may also have been one long dream, signalled by the fact that his critically ill father seems in fine health on his awakening, and Sandy's policeman father – who formerly showed his true colours as a corrupt cop in league with the Yellow Man and Frank – is now a member of the happy, extended family. Other obvious dream factors include the sudden materialisation of the naked, wounded Dorothy on Jeffrey's front porch, and the free-standing corpse of the Yellow Man which keeps hanging around.

Sandy points out some (very obviously mechanical) robins sitting on a tree branch. The robin is munching on one of the predatory insects seen at the beginning of the film. 'Maybe the robins are here,' Jeffrey reflects aloud on Sandy's dream. 'It is a strange world, isn't it? agrees Sandy.

The purposely phoney robins are Sandy's messengers of love and the harmonious rightness of her world. They're also testament to Lynch's ambiguous attitude towards the artificial – playing up the superficiality of small-town life while celebrating its sentimentality – and to his love of low-budget animation technique.

As for the use of robins – albeit clockwork ones – as harbingers of gladness, Lynch reflects that 'everyone likes robins'. But not enough, it seems, to stop the young boy David, living then in Boise, Idaho, from throwing a clod of petrified mud at a robin and killing it. Then, remorseful, he and his equally young friend Willard gave it a proper send-off, setting it alight and floating it down the ditch 'like a Viking funeral'.

Accompanied by the semi-devotional love song, 'The Mysteries of Love', the film's first few images replay in reverse order. The final image is Dorothy's reunion with her young son, now free from captivity – indicating that events have not merely been a figment of Jeffrey's imagination.

'It's not a happy ending in *Blue Velvet*,' Lynch testified. 'It's the same images as at the start but you know so much more about them. It's like if two people walk into a room. One of them, you know, has just had his family machine-gunned and the other has just won a prize or something. If you didn't know that, they'd just look like normal people or something. There's light and varying degrees of darkness.'

To many, *Blue Velvet* was the first 'real' David Lynch film since *Eraserhead*. Lynch himself confirmed that the movie was 'the best film experience for me since *Eraserhead*, for sure.' For many other attendees of art-house and first run cinemas, it was the first time they could take seriously Lynch's personal version – a much more palatable slice of modern, all-American surrealism than his debut feature.

Blue Velvet quickly made waves in an industry that – like young Jeffrey – considered itself worldly and sophisticated, but really had much to see and much to learn.

'*Blue Velvet* is not a film for everybody,' admitted Lynch. 'Some people are going to really dig it, but we've experienced some really negative reactions, too. We had a sneak preview in the [San Fernando] Valley that was a disaster. People thought it was disgusting and sick. And of course it is, but it has two sides.'

Predictable accusations abounded: of misanthropy, misogyny, and heartless irony. The film's admirers, however, realised Lynch had done something much riskier than offending Christian, conservative or left-wing sensibilities – he'd laid many of his most precious memories and his darkest daydreams bare, side by side. Whatever the pastiche nature of its framework, *Blue Velvet* is as honest a piece of cinema as has come out of America in the last 30 years.

Every screening contained a number of audience walk-outs – particularly during the scenes between Frank and Dorothy. To less prissy types, it was the most compulsive personal vision witnessed in years. *Newsweek* reported on one heart patient who fainted at a Chicago screening. Rushed to hospital to have his pacemaker urgently adjusted, he made straight back to his local theatre afterwards to catch the film's ending at the next show. Pauline Kael, in her *New Yorker* review, quoted an overheard patron at the preview theatre as saying, 'Maybe I'm sick, but I want to see that again.'

Lizzie Borden, who conducted the definitive *Blue Velvet* interview for the *Village Voice*, locked in debate with the late feminist-fantasist Angela Carter in the pages of London's *City Limits* magazine. Carter, whose own work was alive with vivid archetypes, wrote Lynch off as a one-dimensional Freudian masturbator: 'It starts off with the father falling, watched by a small child and ends with the two fathers playing together like children, while the son who has returned to take over the tribe is waited on by three women. It's about fucking mummy (Dorothy) and marrying the girl next door (Sandy). '

Borden, on the other hand, was of the right mind-set, the right culture (its folklore acknowledged in her pseudonym) and the right generation, to empathise totally with Lynch. 'She's [Dorothy's] a fantasy, an image of desire with something nightmarish about her and her whole environment. She's like a photo or a memory of our mothers when they were young: a '50s woman with a '50s body. Her make-up is a parody of those times – too much of it, flabby bodies pinned into submission. Women put up on pedestals with the real woman underneath, never to be found. It links with my fantasies as a young girl. For me she represents the whole perversion of normative teen sexuality that Jeffrey and Sandy stand for, that I grew up with.'

There were a few detractors who went so far as to attribute Frank's sexual psychosis, or Jeffrey's implicit, reluctant sadism, to the director. Objections persisted to the character of Dorothy: Fred Elmes' rich cinematography paints her humiliation and beatings lovingly,

Lynch directs the scene where Frank has just had his brains blown out. Dennis Hopper was bemused by how his 'cool rube' director was able to draw such intense performances out of the cast; more disturbing to feminist commentators was Lynch's professed empathy with Frank's wild instincts, while recognising their vicious absurdity.

and Lynch, as a director, plays the most sadistic control games with his leading actress (and lover) since that great old misogynist Hitchcock terrorised the icy blonde starlets he so hopelessly desired.

But, as Jeffrey Beaumont would say, 'It's a strange world', and the strangest thing in it is the people. Dorothy is a victim, but accepts her victim-hood as the last vestige of control over her own life. This is clearly not the kind of 'empowerment' many feminists idealise. Her devotion to Frank's sick needs is a sacrifice on behalf of her kidnapped husband and son, who, in classic *noir* fashion, remain pivotal but dehumanised, unseen plot devices until the end. But the brief, ecstatic pleasure she gains from going beyond the moment of submission, her relieved smile as Frank's punch draws blood from her mouth, takes her character into a much deeper level of emotional-erotic masochism.

'The only thing to say about all the controversy,' Lynch commented later, 'is did I make all that up, or are there examples like that in real life? And there are countless examples like that in real life. So why do they get so upset when you put something like this in a film?'

'Because people have an idea that Dorothy was Everywoman,' he answered himself, 'instead of just being Dorothy. That's where the problem starts. If it's just Dorothy, and it's her story – which it is to me – then everything is fine. If Dorothy is Everywoman, it doesn't make any sense. It doesn't add up. It's completely false, and they'd be right to be upset.'

'Sex is such a fascinating thing,' he opined, wide-eyed and child-like in wonder. 'It's sorta like you can listen to one pop song just so many times, whereas jazz has so many variations. Sex should be like jazz. It can be the same tune, but there are many variations on it. And then when you start getting out there, it can be shocking to learn that something like that could be sexual. It would be kind of, you know, strange. But it's a real fact of life just the same. There's no real explaining in *Blue Velvet* because it's such an abstract thing inside a person.'

Most disarming of all Lynch's admissions is that, while he maintains his distance from the twisted obsessive Frank, he (like Jeffrey) has been tempted towards violence by women he believes possess the perverse self-destructiveness of Dorothy. 'There are certain women that you want to hit because you're getting a feeling from them that they want it, or maybe they upset you in a certain way. I see this happening, but I don't really understand it. But sometimes you can get into something and the next day feel very bad about it. So you decide you're never going to do that again, but you can never be sure.'

Against any odds the sharpest Hollywood bookie might have given, *Blue Velvet* gave Lynch resurrection, renewal and renaissance.

'Nobody ever thought it was going to be commercial,' he recalled. 'Now that it's made money, it goes down as an exception. It's fantastic when that happens.'

After all the overwrought controversy, those who wanted to join the debate still had to pay admission price. Added to the film's surprise commercial success would be Lynch's second nomination for a Best Director Oscar – which, strangely inevitably, he failed to win once more, an even greater injustice this time around.

Consequently, Lynch was bankable again. In fact, he had the unique status that *Blue Velvet* – added to the memory of one art-house and one semi-mainstream hit – had brought him: Hollywood's 'King of Weird', with a faithful cast and crew (regular actors by now included Kyle MacLachlan, Dean Stockwell, Brad Dourif and Jack Nance, La Rossellini and Laura Dern added to the coterie for future projects), and close as dammit to the only commercial movie-maker with the licence to be obsessive.

Lynch's long-desired total-concept ethos was also reflected in the soundtrack: realising a well-placed ballad had more evocative power to dredge up primal emotion and memory than Proust's tea-dipped madeleines, both the title song and 'In Dreams' gave power to and acquired a new lease of life from the film.

'Blue Velvet' would become a Top 10 chart song when revived in the late 1980s; Roy Orbison, who made two well-considered viewings of the film before giving permission to use 'In Dreams', became a hip figure all over again, after years of neglect on the cabaret circuit. However, Orbison's untimely death in 1989 made the concept of Lynch collaborating with him again, more closely, a sad impossibility.

Still, Lynch was coming closer to his avowed vision of himself as a 'sound man': Angelo Badalamenti had performed an exceptional task of pastiching styles and themes from '40s–'50s *noir* and TV detective shows, complimented by his own lush, melancholic romanticism. It was another new world opening up, and experimentation was far from over; with so many concepts waiting to be plucked out of the air, the Lynch mob were coming to town for sure.

CHAPTER SIX

Twin Peaks:

Weird Americana Goes Prime Time

By the late 1980s, David Lynch was on the verge of recognition as a small cinematic sub-genre all of his own. In the wake of *Blue Velvet*, he was recognised as the most all-American of artists – in a decidedly tilted manner.

As immediate reward, personal projects were pushed aside by the opportunity to film the biography of a genuine American icon: *Goddess*, by Anthony Summers, was the story of the last days of Marilyn Monroe, a balancing act between reverence and pure sleaze. The contractual obligation was that Lynch would direct from a screenplay by a third party, a TV screenwriter in his mid-30s who shared agents with Lynch.

Mark Frost had begun a productive career scripting episodes of *The Six Million Dollar Man* at age twenty, progressing to write and edit some of the most memorable episodes of the groundbreaking cop-opera, *Hill Street Blues*, for three years in the early 1980s. He won a Writer's Guild award and was nominated for an Emmy during this time.

'I had a strange premonition on seeing *The Elephant Man* that I would some day work with David Lynch,' said Frost, 'so I was eager to explore the possibility. We hit it off immediately.'

But *Goddess* was not to be, falling foul of the usual development and funding snags. In the meantime, however, a new creative friendship had been struck, even if it consisted purely of kicking mutual ideas around.

'I feel that David's probably the first surrealist director,' Frost would later appraise, correcting himself to add '*American* surrealist'.

'I think the American public is so surreal, and they understand surrealism,' concurred Lynch. 'And the idea they don't is so absurd. It's just that they've been told that they don't understand it. You go anywhere and old-timers will tell you very strange stories with surreal humour. And everyone has a friend who is totally surreal.'

Meanwhile, acknowledging his status as all-American surrealist, the BBC documentary series *Arena* gave Lynch his first foray into the TV medium.

Shot in the autumn of 1986, after the US release of *Blue Velvet*, *Ruth, Roses and Revolver* was a history of cinematic surrealism, narrated by Lynch. Taking its title from the Man Ray segment of the 1945 compendium film, *Dreams That Money Can Buy*, it charted the origin of surrealist film from *Un Chien Andalou* – though its origins lay further back, in the deranged expressionism of Wiene's *The Cabinet of Dr Caligari*, or even Melies' magical shorts – to the mavericks who picked up elements of the movement and ran with it to their own stylistic ends, like Ray, Hans Richter and Jean Cocteau.

Aired in February 1987, Lynch's TV debut (away from the subjective role of interviewee) was respectable if inauspicious, with little personal input and a scripted introduction/voice-over narrative. Whatever its impact, however, it marked the starting point of Lynch's entry into a new medium.

Meanwhile, Lynch's creativity began to proceed at a much more askew, almost self-consciously wacky angle.

His first collaboration with Mark Frost was the screenplay, *One Saliva Bubble*, written in 1987. Set in Newtonville, the 'lightning capital of the world', the script reads like a frenetic Marx Brothers or Preston Sturges movie updated for the technological age. Lynch's love of the everyday bizarre was taken on a wild detour by Frost's penchant for eccentric characterisation, the writer having lightened *Hill Street Blues*' urban nightmare with fruitcakes like the tights-wearing, would-be superhero Captain Freedom. It hinted at the same toytown-scale 'outer space' effects as the Man in the Planet scenes in *Eraserhead*, and imbued the small-town Weirdsville ethic of *Blue Velvet* with whimsical humour, while lacking the obsessiveness of that pivotal film (or any of Lynch's most personal work).

The comical characters of *One Saliva Bubble* were a foretaste of things to come, including a cartoonishly intimidating hitman who stares an elevator muzak machine into silence; a frizzy-haired mad scientist who carries his toothbrush and airline tickets down mismatched socks; a lineage of fathers and sons all reduced to imbecility after being struck by lightning; a sanatorium full of Jesus Christs; and a group of barbecue-loving Texans who double as a troupe of Chinese acrobats.

From the first draft of the script seen by this writer, dated May 1987, the basic scenario remained a mixture of screwball comedy and wish-fulfilment fantasy. As a plot device mutated from the similarly unmade *Ronnie Rocket*'s electricity fixation, one lunkhead's floating saliva bubble contaminates a computer-satellite system and causes electro-kinetic chaos: the scientific genius is genetically transposed with an institutionalised idiot; the hitman with a henpecked wimp; a blues singer with a prim Englishwoman. As one comic gangster testifies in a wincingly Lynchian phrase, this is surely an 'oh-gosh-by-golly world'.

In the scene where the mad professor and the corporation who have kidnapped him fraughtly await the explosion that will end the world, Lynch gives a shadow of things soon to come by having the professor declare, 'There's just about enough [time] for one more cup of good coffee.'

Ultimately, Lynchian sentimentality (which many critics would still only accept as irony) wins out: the wimp-turned-hitman reduces his son's school bully to tears by empathising with him; when the *Dr Strangelove*-style ending is averted by the apocalyptic device, a 'nuclear pig', producing barbecue sauce instead of sub-atomic fission, the script ends *Blue Velvet*-style, *sans* sinister undertones, with idyllic order come to Newtonville and Bing Crosby singing 'It's Beginning to Look a Lot Like Christmas'.

It may come as little surprise that Steve Martin was contracted to bring his trademark breathless clowning to *One Saliva Bubble*; in the short term, however, the project would suffer its first cancellation with the bankruptcy of its backers, De Laurentiis Entertainment, later in 1987 (a situation largely precipitated by the spectacular failure of *Dune*). With Lynch's film-making career once again on hold, the formative partnership found themselves looking towards Mark Frost's chosen medium in order to get any kind of project off the ground.

In the interim, Lynch took another sideways step – this time, in the summer of 1987, into mainstream art-cinema and his first acting role. Having previously limited his own screen appearances to the extended Hitchcockian cameo of a navigator pilot in *Dune*, he took the supporting role of Willie, the lover of a child's governess, in Tina Rathborne's debut feature, *Zelly and Me*.

Distinctly un-Lynchian in its portrayal of an alternately pampered (by her governess) and badly treated (by her guardian grandmother) child, the film dwells languidly on the surface world and bourgeois comforts of the moneyed Old South.

Hardly shown outside the USA, and little seen or remembered within it, *Zelly and Me* is chiefly notable for freezing a certain moment in time on screen, reflecting the love affair of Isabella Rossellini and David Lynch. In the lead role of Zelly, the girl's adoring nanny, Rossellini exhibited the emotional intensity which became her trademark in *Blue Velvet*;

Mark Frost, Lynch's co-writer/co-director/co-producer on the unmade **One Saliva Bubble** *as well as* **Twin Peaks, American Chronicles** *and* **On the Air**. *Note the Lynchian industrial tunnel backdrop.*

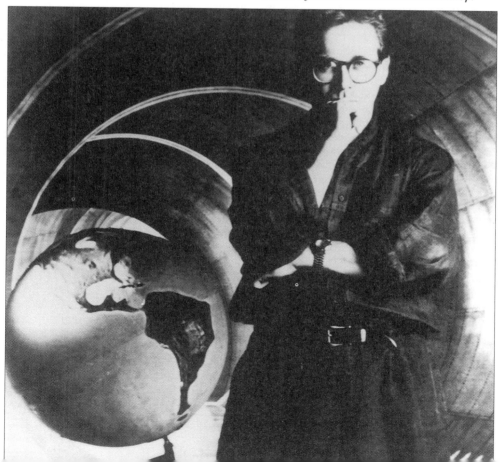

Lynch, too, is all sincerity as the boyfriend prepared to go along with the plan to kidnap her charge for her own good. Whether this was a genuine attempt to act, or simply an extension of his own wrapped-a-little-tight earnestness is difficult to judge, now that the film is virtually impossible to see.

After filming his scenes for *Zelly and Me*, Lynch would make an eccentric foray into video-making – as one of a group of film-makers commissioned by a Parisian publication, *Figaro* magazine, to produce a series of shorts commemorating its tenth anniversary, the only American among a prestigious roster including Werner Herzog and Jean-Luc Godard.

Le Cowboy et le Frenchman (1988) is a slight, little-noticed oddity in Lynch's canon. Basically a one-joke play on the collision between old-time American frontier values and European culture, it features Harry Dean Stanton as deaf ranch-hand Slim, whose affliction was regarded by Lynch as a comic device.

Slim sets out with a bunch of cowpokes and Red Indian buddies (in this cosy version of the Old West, everyone gets on just peachy keen) including Michael Horse, a Native American actor formerly seen as Tonto in *The Legend of the Lone Ranger*, soon to work with Lynch on something infinitely more substantial – to catch some wild bucks. Instead, they lasso a strange guy in a beret and striped blouse; this walking stereotype carries round a loaf of French bread, some stinking, overripe soft cheese and even models of the Eiffel Tower. The short film ends with a campfire sing-song, mixing country 'n' western with the can-can.

As merely an odd little piece of whimsy, its only interest lies in whether Lynch was trying (albeit not very successfully) to imitate the subtle, semi-silent humour of long-time influence Jacques Tati – or whether, more likely, it was a dry run for a project where humour and eccentric characterisation competed with dramatic intensity; where well-rounded figures would come into regular contact with walk-on oddballs.

Back at the drawing board with Mark Frost, Lynch and his new partner had an idea for working together in the latter's regular medium.

The celluloid painter – who had never expressed any great fondness for TV, watching very little even as a child – now found himself reminiscing over the desperate days back in Philadelphia, when he worked, Henry-like, as a printer to support new wife Peggy and baby Jennifer.

While inking printing plates, Lynch would let his attention wander to the in-plant TV, and the daily dramas which unfolded in the afternoon soap operas. Back then, he imagined the fun he could have with a long-running saga focused on one central locale. Years on, the daydreams remained. As Frost put it, he and Lynch decided they were going to take 'the next evolutionary step after *Dynasty*'.

As for the setting of the project, Frost recalled, 'We had worked on what was in Twin Peaks [the imaginary small-town location for the drama], what the town was like, for some months. But it wasn't until we said "a body washes up on shore" that we had a starting point not just for our first image, but for the whole mystery.

'We discovered that this is the body of a girl named Laura Palmer, who is the town's homecoming queen, a high school senior, the most popular and arguably the prettiest girl in town; involved in all sorts of charity work, a highly successful student, "most likely to succeed" kind of girl.

'In the investigation that ensues, we discover that there was all that to her life that was true, but we also discover there was this other kind of subterranean life she was living, that was much darker and much more dangerous and much more frightening. The show proceeds as a kind of exploration of that, through the eyes of the two detectives who are trying to solve the mystery. And, in doing so, gives us access to all the other subterranean lives which are going on in the town, because literally everybody has their own secret – as I believe they do in life.'

What they were talking about, Lynch was the first to admit, was 'a soap opera version of *Blue Velvet*'. For his part, he was only too thrilled to go further into the undergrowth of Everytown, USA. 'There are so many kinds of secrets,' he later enthused. 'Part of the thing about secrets is that they have a certain kind of mystery to me. A dark secret. Just the words "dark secret" are so beautiful . . . I love the process of going into a mystery.'

Laura Palmer was named after the eponymous heroine of a favourite Lynch movie, Otto Preminger's sublime 1944 *noir*, *Laura* – a missing girl believed to be murdered, seen mainly in flashback but placed at the centre of the story, for whom detective Dana Andrews develops a peculiarly necrophilic emotional attachment.

Having fleshed out their pitch, the formative Lynch–Frost Productions went for corporate backing. They soon found it with ABC Television, the third major network which, traditionally, has sought to pick up new viewers with novel series formats distinct from those of their predecessors, NBC and CBS.

Though the restrictions of TV would present Lynch with few problems, the small-town nightmare would obviously be visually circumscribed in a way *Blue Velvet* was not. What they gained was the space for characterisation, the slow build-up required to poison a homely, languorous atmosphere, and the feeling of a genuine community out there somewhere in TV-land. Despite the participation of the same production designer, Patricia Norris, Lynch's stipulations made it very clear that this was not to be a reprised '50s-pastiche locale.

'I like a town that's, y'know, small enough to not be overpowering,' Lynch reflected on the location. 'And yet large enough so you don't know everybody – there's some mysterious new people, some strangers that you can meet. I like towns near the woods, because to me the woods are mysterious.'

The original title for Lynch and Frost's pilot for their proposed series, as announced in the *Hollywood Reporter* of 13 February 1989, was *Northwest Passage*, and was to be shot in Snoqualmie, a small lumber town (or Lumberton, to recall *Blue Velvet*) located not in the north but mid-Western Washington State. Local landmarks would be immortalised in location scenes: Snoqualmie Falls – the waterfall shown over every set of pre-show credits; the small-town's Salish Lodge, standing in for the show's Great Northern Hotel; the pivotal Double R Diner, scene of many a personal drama and double-cross, represented by Snoqualmie's Mar T Cafe.

Confirmed among the cast was Kyle MacLachlan – mid-Western native of Yakima, Washington State, acting graduate of the nearby University of Seattle – who, as Frost confirmed, was taking his surrogate Lynch persona into wise adulthood as FBI Special Agent Dale Cooper, the character who would personify the show's trademark mix of tight-ass professionalism and absurdly acute perception, childlike wonder and quasi-mysticism.

The pilot was scheduled to begin shooting on 21 February 1989. Produced by David Latt, former producer of *Hill Street Blues*, Lynch and Frost were scheduled to act as executive producers on behalf of LA-based Propaganda Films for both the pilot and proposed series, while undertaking the respective roles of co-writer/director and co-writer for the pilot.

'David is somewhat inaccessible to other people and very solitary,' Frost later observed of their partnership, 'but there was some chemistry between us and we had a lot of fun together . . . The thing I remember the most is laughing ourselves ill from some of the things we would think of. I mean, we thought of some pretty odd things.'

The opening pilot – now entitled *Twin Peaks*, after its fictional locale – introduced 25 characters, all either involved in the investigation of, affected by, or implicated in the murder of Laura Palmer. As was traditional with any standard-budgeted, episodic series, Lynch, Frost and the casting producers had gone for almost-familiar names in need of work and newcomers looking for a break towards the big-time. MacLachlan aside, many of the adult (post-teen) members of the cast were just the right side of anonymity to provide a certain prime-time ambience, without either breaking the budget or diluting the atmosphere by association with more familiar roles.

TWIN PEAKS: Original Characters and Cast

Laura Palmer
Murdered homecoming queen who had a dark secret life. Seen as a bluing corpse at the opening of the pilot, and as a silent figure on home-made video footage, the dead girl remains one of the pivotal presences in the plot. In audacious soap opera style, Sheryl Lee, who played the dead Laura, was brought back a few episodes down the line as Madeleine Ferguson, Laura's near-identical cousin.

Leland Palmer
Laura's grief-torn father, business attorney to the Horne brothers; unhinged by his bereavement. Actor Ray Wise, who looked not unlike Ben Horne/Richard Beymer (see below), was formerly the male lead on the long-running daytime soap opera Love of Life, *the kind of cheesy production young David Lynch would take in back at the print plant.*

Sarah Palmer
Distraught mother; chain-smoking, edgy, the visions witnessed by her both before and after Laura's death reveal her as a psychic, with no way of averting her premonitions. Grace Zabriskie, who gave a tour de force *performance, had previously played Debra Winger's mother in* An Officer and a Gentleman *(1982) and Dennis Quaid's mother in* The Big Easy *(1986).*

FBI Special Agent Dale Cooper ('Coop')
As played by Kyle MacLachlan, Cooper is the embodiment of Lynch's attitude to small-town living: sentimentally-approving, full of affectionate homilies, but somehow mocking the provincial life with his

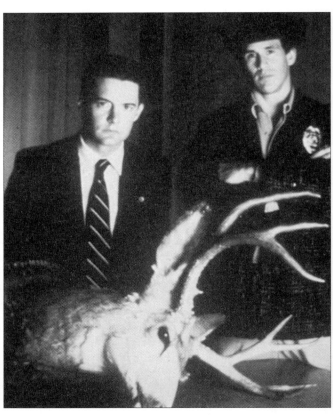

'Coop' (Kyle MacLachlan) and Harry (Michael Ontkean): the solid partnership of intellect, good humour, mysticism and small-town commonsense that kept most viewers watching **Twin Peaks**.

own sharp intellect and buddhist philosophy. The eccentric, young (early 30s) special agent has a keen taste for coffee ('Damn fine coffee – and hot!') and cherry pie ('This must be where pies go when they die!'). His quirky, stiff but amiable mannerisms, together with his regular, detailed memos to 'Diane' (who may be a woman receiving his Dictaphone tapes, an imaginary person, or even the Dictaphone itself) quickly immortalised him in pop culture.

Sheriff Harry S. Truman
The strong, silent type, as all-American and dependable as his name. Harry forms an instant rapport with Cooper, and, though often bemused, is never resentful of the outsider's authority. Locked in a secret romantic liaison with Josie Packard, the beautiful young Chinese widow and heir to the local lumber mill. Played by Michael Ontkean, who was Paul Newman's buddy in the hockey movie Slap Shot (1977), and almost destroyed his career with the gay 'relationship' film Making Love (1982).

Donna Hayward
Pretty teenage brunette with her heart in the right place, which the network banked on to attract the 15–21 audience. Best friend of Laura Palmer, but, as this is Twin Peaks, was also seeing Laura's boyfriend James since before the murder. Played by Lara Flynn Boyle, then going out in 'real life' with Kyle MacLachlan.

Dr William Hayward
Local GP and father of Donna; kindly old man with gammy leg; has the heartbreaking task of examining the corpse of Laura, his daughter's best friend, whom he delivered as a baby. Played by Warren Frost, father of co-writer/director/producer Mark.

Eileen Hayward
Paraplegic wife/mother to Dr Hayward/Donna; as with her husband, an epitome of decency and disciplined tolerance, sympathetic to their daughter and her troubled young boyfriend James. Played by Mary Jo Deschanel, wife of Caleb Deschanel, director of Episode 6.

Audrey Horne
Teenage wanna-be wildcat, daughter of local millionaire, corrupt businessman Ben. Keen to know who murdered Laura – who, she acknowledges, was far wilder than herself despite the apple-pie persona. Her appearance is often greeted by 'Audrey's Dance', a jazzy, finger-clicking theme by Angelo Badalamenti. Throughout the first season she nurtures a growing flame for Agent Cooper, who fends her off with friendly paternalism. Played by Sherilyn Fenn, formerly seen in Two Moon Junction (1988) and teen cop show 21 Jump Street; later starred in Boxing Helena (1993).

Benjamin Horne
Father of Audrey; local millionaire smoothie with business interests both legit and criminal; lover of Catherine Martell. Consistently duplicitous, with nothing he won't orchestrate and no one he won't betray in order to turn a buck. Played by Richard Beymer, who, since peaking as Tony, the lead character in West Side Story (1961), concentrated on his work as a cinematographer and film editor before being lured to Twin Peaks.

Jerry Horne
Kid brother played by David Patrick Kelly, off striking multi-national deals in Europe while Ben handles all the devious work at home: therefore not seen in the pilot episode. Full of crooked joie de vivre, effusing over brie-filled baguettes and tall Icelandic women, his brash confidence, vertical hair, wiry physique and muscular head, all out of proportion to his short stature, are pure comic relief.

James Hurley
Laura's bereaved boyfriend – also boyfriend of Donna; as played by James Marshall, James is a sensitive, brooding biker. Haunted by the death of Laura, willing to go to any bizarre lengths to trace Laura's final steps and find her killer.

Big Ed Hurley
Lanky cowpoke owner of local garage; even more laconic than Sheriff Truman. Lover of Norma, but refuses to desert his wife: the deranged, one-eyed Nadine. Has an unshakeable sense of right and wrong, giving his unhappy nephew James a home, and joins up as unpaid deputy to bust the cocaine ring selling to high-school kids. Played by character actor Everett McGill, previously seen as a man-horse in the Broadway production of Peter Shaafer's Equus, *and with Debbie Harry in* Union City *(1980). His numerous movie roles include a Fremen warrior in* Dune.

Nadine Hurley
As portrayed by Wendy Robie, Nadine is both grotesque and sympathetic. A bird-faced woman who insists on wearing a pirate-like patch to cover an eye injury, she can't see how her ambition to create the world's first fully-silent curtain drape has become an obsessive illness. Seemingly oblivious to her disintegrating marriage, she nonetheless inspires partial loyalty from Big Ed.

Bobby Briggs
Ex-boyfriend of Laura, middle-class wild boy from a good home, as played by Dana Ashbrook. Harbours homicidal feelings towards James Hurley, who he believes to be connected with Laura's death (though his main grievance is that James was seeing her behind his back). Somehow, it never occurs to Bobby he is doing the self-same thing with Shelly, Leo Johnson's wife. A lackey to Leo in the local illicit drugs trade.

Hank Jennings
Imprisoned local do-badder; not seen in the pilot episode, but his possible parole hangs like the switchblade of Damocles over his wife, Norma. Once released, he sets about his usual vocation of hired hand for anyone who needs an efficient thug. Played by Chris Mulkey, who, prior to Peaks, *is not known to have done very much bar the odd softcore porn movie.*

Norma Jennings
Late-thirtysomething beauty, manageress of the Double R diner; wife of bad guy Hank, lover of tormented cowboy Big Ed Hurley. Played by Peggy Lipton, former mini-skirted sex symbol from US TV series The Mod Squad *and ex-wife of big league record producer Quincy Jones.*

Leo Johnson
Pony-tailed young trucker; pathologically possessive of his pretty young wife; instrumental in running cocaine from racketeer Jacques Renault across the Canadian border. Heavily implicated in Laura's murder; the object of murderous plans by the long-suffering Shelly and lover Bobby. Played by Eric DaRe in a viciously effective acting debut.

Shelly Johnson
Waitress at the Double R; wife of local bad boy Leo; has a clandestine affair with Bobby Briggs, who treats her better than her brutal old man. Played by ultra-pretty Madchen Amick, who turned up in a variety of rock videos.

Dr Lawrence Jacoby
Wacko psychiatrist; with his one red/one blue spectacle lenses and his solitary gypsy earring, Jacoby

looks like a former attendee of Dr Timothy Leary's symposiums back in the 1960s. Confidant of Laura and loved her deeply, yet suspected by both the cops and the kids of involvement in her murder. Played by former musical star Russ Tamblyn – Seven Brides For Seven Brothers (1954), Tom Thumb (1958), West Side Story – who subsequently made a career out of exploitation movies like Satan's Sadists (1970). Starting to attend therapy himself during casting, Tamblyn believed the timing of the role 'very synchronistic'.

Jocelyn Packard
Young, glamorous, Oriental widow of former mill owner; lover of Sheriff Truman; while a victim of Catherine and Ben's plotting, Josie – whose unfamiliarity with common figures of speech suggests her first name was anglicised – also has something to hide. Played by Joan Chen, who was discovered in a parking lot by Lynch's old boss, Dino De Laurentiis, before going on to act in Bertolucci's The Last Emperor (1987).

Deputy Andy Brennan
Sheriff Truman's inept but good-hearted sidekick, who bursts into tears on seeing Laura Palmer's body and almost fatally fumbles his gun later in the series. Played by Harry Goaz, who was 'discovered by David Lynch on location in Texas', with few sightings of him since the end of the show.

Lucy Moran
Sheriff Truman's dizzy secretary, Deputy Andy's one-minute-hot-one-minute-cold girlfriend. Played by Kimmy Robertson in her acting debut, balances a maternal faithfulness towards the law office with comical Marilyn inflections and genuine girl-next-door appeal.

Deputy Hawk
Stolid, dependable Red Indian lawman; seemingly employed by the sheriff's office solely for tracking/following trails (something every surviving Native American must have on his CV!). Played by Michael Horse, who played Tonto in the last screen version of The Lone Ranger, and cropped up as a Red Indian in Le Cowboy et le Frenchman.

Catherine Martell
Wife of the put-upon Pete; lover of Ben Horne; sister of Andrew Packard, deceased owner of the lumber mill, locked in a bitter power struggle with his widow Josie. Played by the fine actress Piper Laurie, memorable as the sad bar-room dame who loved Paul Newman in The Hustler (1961), and as the grotesque, religious-fanatic mother in Carrie (1976).

Pete Martell
Unassuming mill foreman who takes refuge from his unhappy marriage to Catherine by 'goin' fishin''. Played by Jack Nance, who, after playing Henry in Eraserhead, went on to appear in every subsequent Lynch film bar The Elephant Man and the Twin Peaks tie-in. Nance also took small roles in Hammett (1982), Barfly (1987), and two Dennis Hopper-directed films, Colors (1988) and The Hot Spot (1990).

The Log Lady
Local eccentric who peers sagely over her coffee cup while holding a small log close to her chest; the log is a kind of pantheist's talisman which she believes communicates as her link to a departed husband. In many ways, the Log Lady, incidental character though she is, sums up what Twin Peaks was about – absurd but poignant, mundane but surreal, touching on the mystical. Played by Catherine Coulson, ex-wife of Jack Nance and Lynch's camerawoman on Eraserhead.

The Log Lady (Catherine Coulson), the minor character who best epitomised **Twin Peaks'** *surreal mundanity; longtime friend Catherine Coulson was told by Lynch, while making* **Eraserhead**, *that he imagined her hosting a game show called* **I'll Test My Log With Every Branch of Knowledge.**

Ms Coulson explains how an off-kilter comment back then foreshadowed the whole project: 'It was 1972, when we were doing Eraserhead . . . *at one time I put on my glasses, and David said: "One day you're going to play a girl with a log on a TV series." This was like so far-fetched . . . And I asked him recently, "Why did you say that at the time?", and he said, "Well, when you put on those glasses I just saw a log in your arms."'*

'Killer Bob'

The nightmare image first glimpsed by Sarah Palmer, whose role in the story becomes gradually both more explicit and more cryptic. Like a cross between an ageing heavy metal star and the beardless Charlie Manson, 'Bob' was actually prop man Frank Silva, whose sinister reflection was spotted by Lynch while he shifted the set around. Silva was signed up on the spot, and improvised alterations immediately made to the script.

Lynch and Frost's affection for the humble moniker 'Bob' is first apparent in the One Saliva Bubble *screenplay, where the scientific equation $ITXPIG2XC=[BOB]$ will either destroy the planet or produce the best barbecue sauce in the world.*

The reaction to the pilot's joint premieres at the Tellunde and Vancouver Film Festivals was overwhelmingly positive.

Back at the HQs of those who cater for the cathode-ray consumer, the response was a little more varied. As of December 1989, ABC had been sitting on the pilot since early autumn without scheduling a broadcast date. Eventually, the 110-minute introduction would be launched with extreme caution in the coming spring, just over a year after it was shot.

'Even the overcurrents have a spooky perversity,' enthused the *Washington Post*. '*Twin Peaks* is one of the most intoxicating combinations of grimness and giggles ever made for television, or for anything else . . . the show that reinvents the genre [soap] and gives it class.'

The *Village Voice* ran two articles on the show in a single issue devoted to the upcoming season's 'Rad TV'. *Connoisseur* magazine predicted that the ensuing series would change the face of prime-time TV: 'There is terror in sunlight, warmth in the darkness, and unspeakable murk just the other side of the white picket fence', their reviewer declared in a way which, while labouring the thematic variation on *Blue Velvet*, at least recognised Lynch was exploring a world he felt tremendously sentimental towards, warts and all.

By the time it played the Monte Carlo Television Festival in February 1990, a date had been set for transmission. Moreover, it now became apparent that Lynch and Frost (under the collective heading of Lynch–Frost Productions – company symbol: two lightning bolts adapted from the sign for Newtonville, 'lightning capital of the world', in the stalled *One Saliva Bubble* project) had shot one more episode of the series each, while farming out enough work to other scriptwriters and directors for a complete season. Both had conceived the storylines which were co-opted by the hired hands, while Lynch, who had other priorities (not least a new film – see Chapter Seven) left the role of day-to-day executive producer to Frost.

With the show every bit as much the latter's baby, the co-writer/producer came in for equal praise from his collaborators. Tina Rathborne, director of *Zelly and Me*, who also directed the episode where Laura Palmer's funeral quickly degenerates from a sad, dignified affair to grotesque farce, stressed, 'Mark is very straightforward and supportive. He is brilliant in his own right.'

Pre-broadcast, the odd dissenting doubt was raised about the non-resolution of the Palmer murder, the case seeming on the verge of resolution at the end of the season before all is thrown into chaos again. An unresolved storyline, however, is a basic mainstay of soap opera, carrying numerous tangential sub-plots. One other advance reservation about the show was whether it fitted into the soap opera category at all. One critic claimed that soap opera – by original definition, an ongoing set of interwoven storylines filmed on cheap sets to flesh out the sponsors' soap ads – was too insular a world to incorporate *Twin Peaks'* wide geo-psychological canvas (from morgue to sawmill to roadhouse, with progressively more outlandish stories of small-town myth, conspiracy theory, serial murder, the occult, weird belief and strange obsession, drug abuse, social hysteria, etc).

Lynch knew he was working in a long-established and formulaic medium, twisting all its conventions in the episodes he directed and/or co-wrote. Significant objects were held in extreme close-up, whether their relevance was immediately apparent or not; narrative developments were reinforced by holding shots much longer than the TV audience were used to, making dramatic use of the commercial break by fading with a slow dissolve. The colour photography was drenched in cinematic mood, rather than televisual gloss: yellow-brown woods and half-tone night-time greys.

The network had their fingers tightly crossed; mere cult success was a certainty, but they needed a wider audience in order not to make a loss on advertising revenue.

The pilot was finally aired on Sunday 8 April 1990, repeated the following Thursday, the day for which the regular one-hour (including ads) shows had been scheduled. By this time, ABC had spent $3.8 million on the pilot, including advertising – the relative equivalent of spending at least four times that amount on a theatrically-released motion picture.

'Like nothing else on prime time, or on God's earth,' enthused *Time* magazine; 'brilliant television' was *Variety*'s initial verdict on the pilot – although they echoed the standard doubts about whether 'cult TV', as an offshoot of the cult movie category, would attract enough viewers/consumers to make the series itself a commercial proposition. As Special Agent Cooper says to Sheriff Truman in the opening pilot, 'Have you ever been surprised?'

TWIN PEAKS — Season One (1989/90)

Pilot Film
Written by David Lynch and Mark Frost/Directed by David Lynch

Angelo Badalamenti's hauntingly ethereal theme music accompanies the establishing shots of a small North-Western town of the USA, population approximately 50,000. A robin turns its head to look at the camera; the sawmill turns; clean, pure water pours expansively down the falls. As the music winds down to a few ominous chords, a half-glimpsed naked body wrapped in plastic is washed ashore near the sawmill.

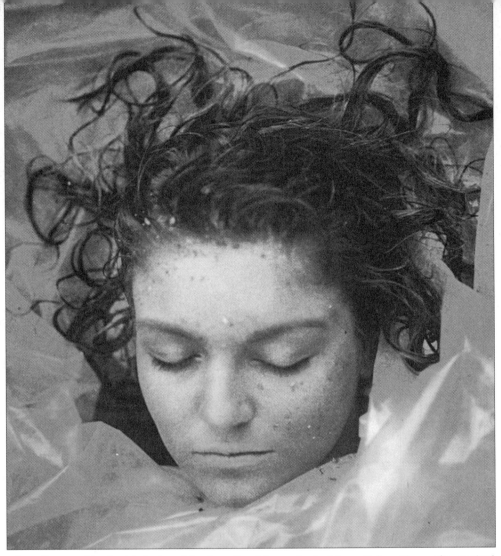

'She's all wrapped in plastic': the face of the show, Sheryl Lee, as the dead Laura Palmer. Her murder remained the core around which all the sub-plots revolved, until well into the second season.

'Gone fishin',' mild-mannered Pete Martell tells his indifferent wife as he sets off with his rods. But, down near the waterline, he discovers the body. Once the cops get there, they unwrap the body-bag and identify the grey-faced, blue-lipped young woman as 17-year-old Laura Palmer.

Meanwhile, an anguished Mrs Palmer finds her daughter is absent from the house that morning and contacts her husband, Leland, at the Horne office. As they speak on the telephone, Sheriff Harry S. Truman pulls up to tell her the bad news. Sarah drops the phone in shock and Leland hears her shrieks down the line. The camera tracks the twisted phone cord at the Palmer home till it reaches the receiver; Leland's anguished wails are then heard from the other end of the line.

Some critics felt this scene showed Lynch's supposed artistic heartlessness or emotional distance from his subject. Whereas Lynch succeeded in overplaying the classic soap 'dramatic moment' to the extent where the characters' inter-phone agony became palpable,

Naughty Audrey Horne, the show's schoolgirl sex symbol; played by Sherilyn Fenn, previously seen in the Zalman King softcore film **Two Moon Junction.** *The first season depicted her as a teenage temptress trying to do the right thing.*

the tracking shots and use of the telephone as a central device were taken as a distancing effect – he was supposedly being 'ironic' with his subject matter, as many felt was his approach to the whole series.

Grace Zabriskie, whose intense agony as the bereaved Sarah Palmer got uncomfortably under many viewers' skin, was in total disagreement: 'However grotesque or violent or weird one of David's scenes may be, the whole is coming from a place in his brain that I trust. It's that razor's edge of knowing and not knowing what he's doing.'

Meanwhile, Laura's boyfriend Bobby is driving Shelly Johnson, with whom he's having an affair, back to her home. He skids away as he sees her husband Leo's truck.

At school, Audrey Horne is changing into red stilettos. The finger-clicking 'Audrey's Dance' musical theme is introduced.

The creative partnership with Angelo Badalamenti, which had blossomed from the time of *Blue Velvet*, added an all-important extra dimension of aural atmosphere to the project. The composer, who had scored – among much other work – Bob Balaban's *Parents* (1988), a Lynch-inspired piece of weird American gothic, between *Velvet* and *Peaks*, was commissioned for the series as soon as it got the go-ahead.

'David likes to work from what he sees inside,' commented the composer. 'He isn't musical but he knows what he wants as soon as he recognises it . . . Take the *Twin Peaks* main theme: he wanted something in a minor mode – dark and ominous, but also beautiful, something which makes you ache with anticipation, builds so it rips your guts out and then falls away slowly.'

'We intend to become the Bernard Herrmann and Alfred Hitchcock of the 90s,' Badalamenti wistfully commented of his relationship with Lynch. The *Twin Peaks* soundtrack album would go on to sell two million copies, the first 40,000 within its first two weeks of American release.

103

At the sheriff's office: left-right, Deputy Andy (Harry Goaz, just out of shot), Doc Hayward (Warren Frost), Sheriff Harry S. Truman (Michael Ontkean), Donna Hayward (Lara Flynn Boyle), James Hurley (James Marshall), Special Agent Dale Cooper (Kyle MacLachlan).

Though no household name, Badalamenti was already a more commercially successful cinematic composer than the revered creator of the themes to *North By Northwest* and *Psycho*.

At school, Donna Hayward sees Sheriff Truman come in for a grim word in her teacher's ear, and begins sobbing in anticipation. Bobby is arrested and taken in for questioning, and the principal makes a dignified but tear-stained announcement over the school PA system.

Meanwhile, there's trouble up at the sawmill. Young, widowed owner Josie Packard gives orders to close for the day, in sympathy with Laura Palmer and mill worker Janek Pulaski's missing daughter, Ronnette. Catherine Martell – manageress, sister of the late Mr Packard and all-round hard bitch – immediately fires the man who pulls the plug.

Several miles away, a dazed, battered, bloodied, bedraggled girl is crossing a railway bridge. This is the missing Ronnette Pulaski.

Special Agent Dale Cooper is driving into town. This dapper, upright young man speaks to 'Diane' on his dictating machine. He gives the date as 24 February, making comparison to another murder downstate a year ago. 'I've never seen so many trees,' he records. He also describes his lunch: 'A tuna sandwich on whole-wheat, a slice of cherry pie and a cup of coffee. Damn good food!' As an FBI agent, he has been called in because the now catatonic Ronnette was raped and tortured across state lines.

In the mortuary, Coop slowly drags a letter 'R' from the bottom of Laura's fingernail, in a wincingly sustained shot.

The next associate of Laura's to be questioned is Dr Lawrence Jacoby, the psychiatrist. 'Her parents didn't know she was seeing me,' he confirms.

Bobby and his crony Mike blame a 'damn biker'. Examining a video of Laura and Donna clowning around on a picnic, Coop exhibits his extraordinary perception by claiming, 'Sure looks like *a hog' – then uses the video equipment to close in on Laura's eye, where he can see a motorcycle reflected. Harry confirms that Laura's other boyfriend, James Hurley, is a biker.*

Up at the abandoned rail car where Laura and Ronnette had been, the cops find bloodstains, Laura's diary, a necklace with half a golden heart attached, a deposit box key and a cryptic scrawled message: 'FIRE WALK WITH ME'. The identify of whoever holds the other piece of the heart is of paramount importance. 'My bet is it will test positive for cocaine,' says Coop of the key. 'Impossible. You didn't know this girl,' counters Harry. 'Have you ever been surprised?' Coop gently retorts.

At the Johnsons' place, Leo finds an unfamiliar brand of cigarettes around the house, threatening to break Shelly's jaw if it happens again.

Coop and Harry attend a public meeting on the tragedy. He spots an uptight-looking middle-aged woman, hugging a small section of a tree to her breast. 'Who's the lady with the log?' he enquires. 'We call her the Log Lady,' answers Harry.

Despite a curfew suggested by Agent Cooper, Donna visits the Roadhouse, with a clientele mainly consisting of bikers. The in-house entertainment is Julee Cruise, in leather cap, singing 'Falling' (which became the Twin Peaks *theme after stripping away its vocal) and 'The Nightingale'.*

'It's appropriate but ridiculous,' said Ms Cruise (with bright peroxide hair, like some physiognomically normal version of the Lady in the Radiator) of her first performance in the series. 'The bikers are sitting there politely, and the bikes are lined up neatly outside, and they're listening to *that* music?'

Contemporary to the shooting of the pilot and Episode 2, Lynch and Badalamenti had produced an album of songs with *Blue Velvet*/'Mysteries of Love' singer Ms Cruise, entitled *Floating into the Night*. With a Morricone-like fusion of light classical music styles by Badalamenti and minimalist, curiously impressionistic teen-dream lyrics by Lynch, its ethereal mix of hypnotic atmospherics and emotional longing led the vocalist to describe it as 'a cross between Wagner, Roy Orbison and the Cocteau Twins' – alternately 'blissfully romantic' and 'paranoid and depressed'.

As if anticipating how the TV series would briefly become a mini-industry, the album contained several songs that featured on the soundtrack: 'Falling', which turned Ms Cruise into the more interesting kind of one-hit wonder on both sides of the Atlantic, 'The Nightingale', and the mesmeric 'Into the Night', which begins with a whispered echo of Frank's call to chaos from *Blue Velvet*: 'Now it's dark.' With lyrics that are little more than fleeting sketches of emotions and images – love, loneliness, darkness, woods, birds – the album is an impressionistic collage of Lynch's adolescent memory.

'For *Twin Peaks*,' said Badalamenti, 'I was very aware that he [Lynch] wanted music that would be intensely evocative of pain and sadness but which was also quirky and playful, and so there are fusions; there are very '50s melodies such as 'The Nightingale' and things like jangling guitars and tenor saxes for the main themes.'

'David would say, "You're on a stage,"' recalls Ms Cruise, '"it's really dark, you can't see the house, you're all alone, and you're crying." He knows how to get a certain reaction.'

Bobby and Mike, his second banana and Donna's boyfriend, start a brawl at the Roadhouse after sounding off against bikers.

Donna is picked up by James on his cycle, out on the main highway. He tells her about the duality of Laura's personality: 'There was a darker side you didn't know.' James is picked up. Back at the station, Coop spells out 'He didn't do it' to Harry on his pocket computer. In the jail house, Bobby and Mike bait and threaten James; they turn strangely feral, barking and howling at him like wild dogs. Lucy, Harry's secretary, has left Coop and him a gluttonous table full of every kind of doughnut, plus coffee. Sweet-toothed Coop is thrilled.

Harry visits Josie Packard at the lumber mill: 'I hear you called for the sheriff,' he tells her, before they fall into each other's arms. Catherine watches, making a phone call to an unknown party, telling them, 'He's here again.'

Twenty-four hours since Laura was brutally murdered, the citizens of Twin Peaks settle down to rest. The tormented Sarah Palmer has a jolting, semi-conscious vision of an unidentified man reaching across to pick up the other half of Laura's heart pendant.

NB: the two-hour home video version of the pilot – released shortly before its airing and anticipating the rest of the series – featured an ending which stands as an entirely independent entity from the TV show, however perversely.

At the same time as Mrs Palmer has her vision of the long-haired 'Killer Bob' (seen in the series in Episode 1), Coop is awakened by a mysterious caller named Mike. Coop and Harry meet him at his stated venue, the hospital, where he identifies the police sketch as that of the mad visionary, Bob, for whom his search has led him to the hospital basement.

Sure enough, on searching the basement the cops detect the homicidally-crazed Bob, dancing ritualistically round a circle of candles; he just about has enough time to describe his rationale for placing letters of the alphabet under the fingernails of his victims – he is spelling out his name, R-O-B-E-R-T – before his obsessive hunter, Mike, shoots him dead. 'Make a wish,' suggests Coop, as the killer dies but the candles still flicker.

The video version ends with cryptically visual Lynch appeal – incorporating the dancing, speech-distorted dwarf from Episode 2 into a dream sequence.

Finally, an older Dale Cooper sits in a living room 25 years on, its velvet-curtained decor timeless but inspired by '50s kitsch. A glamorous young woman sits with him, who may have been a victim of the serial murders he came to *Twin Peaks* to investigate all those years ago – as Coop says, she's 'filled with secrets'.

Episode 1
Written by David Lynch and Mark Frost/Directed by Duwayne Dunham

Coop starts the day by reporting to Diane about his hotel room while hanging upside down from the roof beams by his ankles. 'There's something that bothers me,' he continues, 'not just as a federal agent, but as a human being: what was the relationship between Marilyn Monroe and the Kennedys, and who shot JFK?'

Audrey sidles up to Coop as he enjoys the 'damn fine coffee' at her father's Great Northern Hotel, during breakfast. Meanwhile, at the Johnsons' place, Shelly finds a blood-stained shirt in Leo's dirty laundry, stashing it away.

Back at the police station, James admits that he shot the Laura/Donna video, and that he knew Laura was taking cocaine though he tried to get her to stop. He tells the cops he last saw her on the day before her death.

In the cells, Bobby and Mike discuss $10,000 worth of cocaine money they owe to Leo, which Laura lost by dying on them.

Just released from hospital, Big Ed tells Coop and Harry he believes his beer was drugged at the Roadhouse the night before, before the bar-room brawl, and that Jacques Renault – a French-Canadian slob of local ill repute – was behind the bar. Coop phones Albert Rosenfield, federal forensic scientist, and strongly recommends the local cherry pie.

When the cops arrive to question Josie Packard, Coop immediately spots she and Harry are having an affair: 'Body language.' Harry admits they've been seeing each other for about six weeks, while Packard himself died a year-and-a-half ago.

Donna visits the distraught Mrs Palmer to try to comfort her. Sobbing, she holds Donna's hand and is momentarily comforted by a vision of her as Laura, which turns to a waking nightmare as she suddenly sees a sinister, long-haired man looming over a bloodstain.

Mr and Mrs Pulaski are interviewed about their traumatised daughter, Ronnette. They tell how she worked as a shop girl at Horne's Department Store, and helped with the meals-on-wheels program for elderly shut-ins which was implemented by Laura.

Ben Horne is in bed with Catherine Martell, his mistress. Conscious that her husband's loyalty to Josie may rumble the creative accounting that covers her embezzling, they agree a fire at the mill is overdue.

Shelly is quizzed by Leo about his missing shirt. He starts to beat her up with a bar of soap wrapped in a towel.

James goes to dinner at Donna's house. Outside, Bobby and Mike wait for a chance to kill James for stealing both of their girls.

Dr Jacoby plays back an audio tape that Laura recorded for him. She sounds happy, but talks of feeling lost out in the woods, and of a stranger she has met. Jacoby strokes the other half of her heart pendant, which he's hidden away, sobbing uncontrollably.

Episode 2
Written by Mark Frost and David Lynch/Directed by David Lynch

Ben and Jerry dine at the Hornes' residence, then visit One-Eyed Jack's, a casino and high-class cat-house. Jerry is introduced to the new girl, whom he and Ben toss a coin over.

Dead of night in the woods: Bobby and Mike retrieve a stash of money from a hollowed-out football. They have to meet with Leo, but can't get hold of half the cash which remains locked in Laura's safety deposit box. Leo is a mass of smouldering rage, not least because he suspects Shelly of 'giving it away' while he's out on the road.

Soap opera goes surrealistic: Coop meets the Man From Another Place (Michael J. Anderson) in a dream. The decor and the strange inhabitants will later identify the venue as the Black Lodge: a terrifying world-next-door.

At the police station, Hawk tells Coop about a one-armed man he spotted prowling around the hospital's intensive care facility. Brusque pathologist Albert Rosenfield arrives to undertake a complete autopsy. Coop takes Harry, Hawk, Andy and Lucy on a field trip; explaining how he's been influenced by Tibetan buddhism, he shows how he can detect the essence of a murder case within a dream, or via mind-body divination. To demonstrate, he chalks up on a board all the suspects whose names begin with 'J', then throws stones at a bottle to determine the extent of the suspect's guilt: he hits home on Dr Jacoby, but doesn't break the bottle; on the name of Leo Johnson, the bottle shatters. They also consider the name of 'Jack With One Eye', who has turned up in Laura's diary; they hit upon One-Eyed Jack's.

At the Palmer house, Leland, an increasingly fragmented figure, tries to exorcise his grief by dancing to Glenn Miller's 'Pennsylvania 6-5000' with Laura's photo clutched in his hand.

Coop dreams of the bearded, one-armed man, Mike – who pronounces a portentous piece of verse ending with the words, 'Fire Walk With Me' – and his ally Bob, the sinister long-haired man from Sarah Palmer's vision. In a red-velvet curtained room, he encounters Laura and a dwarf who talks cryptic trivia in a reversed, multi-tracked voice. The dwarf dances to a sleazy jazz theme, claiming Laura is his cousin. She kisses Coop, whispering in his ear. Coop wakes, his oiled hair quiffed into a massive wing, and phones Harry to tell him he knows who killed Laura Palmer. It can, he assures him, wait till the morning. The dwarf jazz-dances his way through the show's credits.

Episodes 3–7.

Writers: Harley Peyton (3 & 6)/Robert Engels/Mark Frost (5 & 7). Directors: Tina Rathborne/Tim Hunter/Lesli Linka Glatter/Caleb Deschanel/Mark Frost.

In an irritating anti-climax, Coop can't remember the name of Laura's killer. He receives a call from Gordon Cole, his immediate superior – whose twangy tones are those of David Lynch, the character's name first used for an unseen corporate agent in the One Saliva Bubble *screenplay – telling him Laura had sexual intercourse with three men in the 24 hours before her death, small pecking wounds on her shoulder were caused by a parakeet or mynah bird, and a broken gambling chip was found in her stomach. The cops go to stake out the hotel room of the one-armed man, who Coop believes, on the basis of his dream, will be named 'Mike' . His name is Gerard – though his middle name is Michael – but his best friend's name is* Bob Lydecker. *They visit Lydecker's veterinary surgery; as a curious pet lama stares him in the face, Coop orders them to check the records of all local bird owners. Renault is identified as the owner of a mynah. At Renault's place, the cops find a porn-contact magazine,* Flesh World, *containing a headless shot of a young woman seeking a 'generous older man'. Coop identifies her as Laura from the drapes in the background. Waldo, Renault's mynah bird, is left alone with a tape recorder in case he repeats anything heard at the cabin. Outside, Leo takes aim and blows the bird to hell. Listening to the playback, the cops hear him repeat Laura's name, pleading not to be hurt. At One-Eyed Jack's, Coop convinces Renault he's the man who bank-rolled Leo's drug deals; he shows him the broken gambling chip from Laura's stomach. Renault cheerfully admits that he and Leo bound Laura up – 'she really loved that' – and engaged in violent sex with her, laughing about how Leo kept her quiet by placing the chip in her mouth.*

Recalling Gentleman Dave's previous disarming candour about the temptation to hurt 'women who ask for it', at the time of *Blue Velvet*, a September 1990 interview with *Rolling Stone* posed the question of whether Laura's masochistic compulsions were implicitly to blame for her end.

'Everyone can picture in their mind a situation where the girl – for one reason or another – goes along with the situation,' Lynch reflected, 'and everyone can picture in their minds where the girl says, "I'm not into this one little bit!" and gets out. And then there's a borderline where it's right on the edge for a person: where it's interesting but it's sickening, or it's frightening, or it's too much, or almost, or not quite. There's every different combo in this world. When you start talking about "women" versus "women", then you're getting into this area of generalisations, and you can't win. There is no generalisation. There's a billion different stories and possibilities.'

Maddy, Laura's bespectacled, brunette, near-doppelganger cousin, quietly arrives to stay with her distraught aunt and uncle before the funeral, from her hometown of Missoula, Montana – birthplace of David Lynch.

'Maddy came along about six months after we had shot the pilot, when David flew me down to play the Good Witch in *Wild At Heart*,' recalled Sheryl Lee of her reward of a living, breathing, speaking role. 'He said, "I want to bring you back," I said, "How, I'm dead?" and he just said, "We'll figure something out."' In a further tribute to his influences in the detective movie genre, Lynch named Ms Lee's secondary character, Madeleine Ferguson, after Madeleine Elster (Kim Novak), the woman who appears to be a ghost in Hitchcock's *Vertigo* (1958), and Scottie Ferguson (Jimmy Stewart), the police detective who's obsessed with her.

Agent Cooper (Kyle MacLachlan) gunned down at the very end of the first season. Supposedly a conventional 'Who Shot JR?'-type cliffhanger, the mystery was quickly sidelined in the second season in favour of numerous other sub-plots.

Audrey tells Donna she wants to help catch the person who murdered Laura, insisting to her dad that she plays a part in running the family store – where Laura and Ronnette worked. She fantasises of Special Agent Cooper helping her escape to a new life outside Twin Peaks. Watching through the slats of a wardrobe closet – an exact simulation of Jeffrey watching Dorothy in Blue Velvet *– she sees Catherine accusing Ben of visiting One-Eyed Jack's, slapping his face till it drives him into a frenzy of desire. Coop retires to his room at the Great Northern and finds Audrey in his bed. He lets her down gently, offering friendship, fries and a chocolate malted. She goes to One-Eyed Jack's to ask for a job as a 'hostess', tying a knot in a cherry stalk with her tongue. Blackie, the madam, hires her instantly. Naughty Audrey is told to give the owner her special attention. Looking at the CCTV, she's horrified to see the honoured guest is her father.*

During the *Rolling Stone* interview, the tenacious reporter wondered aloud whether incestuously Freudian themes could be traced through Lynch's work: Mary's mother coming on like a lick-happy dog to Henry in *Eraserhead*; Jeffrey's supposed identification with Dorothy and Frank as Mom and Dad in *Blue Velvet*; Frank switching persona from

Daddy to Baby in his violent sex games with Dorothy, in the same; and now the cliffhanger with Audrey about to service Ben as a hooker in *Twin Peaks*. Lynch was politely evasive.

Harry, Hawk and Big Ed invite Coop to join their secret crime-fighting group, the Bookhouse Boys; they've arrested Renault's teenage brother, Bernard, for carrying a kilo of cocaine over the border. Out in the woods, Leo has the body of Bernie Renault at his feet, killed for talking to the cops. Ben tells him he wants the Packard mill torched. Leo arrives home to be ambushed by Hank, who beats hell out of him. Leo vents his frustration on Shelly; she shoots him, but he survives with an arm-wound. Leo strings Shelly up by her wrists at the Packard sawmill, with a timing device set to start a fire in one hour. At the hospital, wounded Renault tells Coop that Leo hit him with a whiskey bottle that fateful night at the cabin, before leaving with the girls. The evidence of the abandoned railcar bears him out. An arrest warrant goes out for Leo Johnson. Hank shoots Leo through the window of his house; as Leo slumps, he watches a character from Lynch's pastiche soap opera, Invitation To Love *(title cards framed in blue velvet), gunned down on the TV screen.*

At Laura's funeral, mortified Leland clambers onto the top of her coffin, jamming the automatic descent mechanism. At the Great Northern, he shuffles deliriously around the dancefloor to old swing records. Ben panics, ordering Catherine to dance with him; she jitterbugs about the floor, mimicking the anguished clutching of his temples until all the customers join in. When Leland hears a tip-off that the main suspect for Laura's murder is held at the hospital, he creeps in at night and smothers Renault with a pillow.

Hearing room service, Coop opens his door to find a handgun pointing at him; three shots fire point blank into his chest.
TO BE CONTINUED . . .

At Canada's Banff TV Festival, in early June 1990, *Twin Peaks* won the Rockie Award for best continuing series, but still came under attack from two US TV executives.

Barbara Corday, co-creator of *Cagney and Lacey,* claimed it had progressively lost its audience after the pilot, and that the second series was bound to fail in the 10 p.m. Saturday night graveyard slot now allotted to it by ABC. Linda Berman, vice president of original programmes at Turner Network TV, said, 'The network didn't want to lose face by being seen to drop *Twin Peaks.* That's why they put it in a slot it will fail in. It's too weird for the US.'

This pessimism-cum-sour-grapes was countered by the executive vice president of distributors WorldVision, Bert Cohen, who made demographic analogies with *Dallas.* 'In terms of hooking the viewer, in terms of momentum and the amount of press, *Twin Peaks* is the *Dallas* of the '90s,' he enthused. 'The press about who killed Laura Palmer is very reminiscent, in my mind, of "Who shot J.R.?"' (Though the question on everybody's lips at this moment, if momentum was genuinely being maintained, should have been 'Who shot Agent Cooper?')

In the UK, where the show's arrival was hyped by guide charts to all the characters and 'Who Killed Laura Palmer?' tabloid teasers, commentator Sean Day Lewis, in his column for the TV industry's *Broadcast* magazine, expressed a belief that the show's stock would progressively diminish throughout the second and, if commissioned, third seasons, as Lynch's other diverse commitments ate up his attention and hired-hand directors helmed a greater number of episodes.

'David is the keeper of the flame,' concurred Kyle MacLachlan, fervently pro-Lynch. 'This is his world. The show is unique because of the combination, the balance, of Mark and David. That uniqueness is not necessarily transferable. It may madden the staff when David directs a segment, because he throws the rules out. But to us actors that freedom is an elixir, a magic potion. It's hard to have it watered down once you've tasted it.'

Despite the catcalls from industry sceptics, *Peaks* somehow managed to touch a chord with middle-America. The nation could, it seems, recognise a little of their own lives and values in the show, whatever kind of absurdist mirror they had been reflected through.

James Marshall (James Hurley in the show) recalls: 'I sent a *Twin Peaks* tape to my grandparents as a joke. They live right outside of Boston, and they're really, really conservative. They hate everything . . . I thought it would be funny to get a phone call from them saying, "We just don't understand this. We found it very offensive. And this Log Lady thing – is that supposed to be funny?" But instead they called up and said, "Who's the killer? Who's the killer?" They said they were riveted to the screen the whole time. They can't wait for more episodes. *Twin Peaks* is unconventional, but it's not strange. I figure if my grandparents like it, it's got a chance.'

At *Twin Peaks'* peak, the first two airings of the pilot film and early episodes of the first season, an unanticipated 35 million Americans were either wondering who killed Laura Palmer, or just enjoying the myriad odd details of the locale where the mystery took place.

'We were in exactly the right place, at the right network, at the right time,' reflected Frost. 'The end of the Reagan era, a new decade – there were a lot of pointers.'

As testimony to the sudden pop-culture phenomenon that bore out the hype, the series was nominated for a notable 14 Primetime Emmy awards – the TV industry equivalent of the Oscars – in early August 1990. The nominations were: Best Drama Series: *Twin Peaks*, Best Lead Actor: Kyle MacLachlan, Best Lead Actress: Piper Laurie, Best Supporting Actress: Sherilyn Fenn, Best Writing in a Drama Series: David Lynch and Mark Frost for the *Twin Peaks* pilot, Best Writing in a Drama Series: David Lynch and Mark Frost for *Twin Peaks* episode 2, Best Drama Series Direction: David Lynch for the *Twin Peaks* pilot, Best Drama Series Direction: David Lynch for *Twin Peaks* episode 2, Best Music and Lyrics: Angelo Badalamenti and David Lynch, Best Main Title Theme Music: Angelo Badalamenti and David Lynch, Outstanding Music Composition: Angelo Badalamenti, Dramatic Underscore: Angelo Badalamenti, Editing: Duwayne Dunham, Costume Design: Patricia Norris.

'We're just delighted to be in the position we have suddenly found ourselves in,' bubbled Frost. 'Frankly, the whole thing has sort of been out of left field and this is the icing on the cake.' He may have been less effusive if he could have predicted the eventual outcome. Almost predictably, the show found itself in a relative *Elephant Man* situation: many nominations, few awards. (Editing and costume design only.)

'We kind of like the idea that we didn't get any Emmys,' protested Ray Wise (Leland Palmer in the show) defiantly. 'We're not about winning awards; we are about doing what we do. If the great American public accepts it, fine. If they don't we will still have our core audience. And even if we don't have our core audience, we know we have done it right.'

Meanwhile, Lynch–Frost Productions were not above a different kind of appeal to the great American public. 'Damn good coffee' and all-American cherry pie were to be sold in grocery stores, Agent Cooper-approved, under the *Twin Peaks* logo, with optimistic talks underway between the producers and Bloomingdales, the top Manhattan store, for an in-house promotion deal.

A paperback spin-off, *The Secret Diary of Laura Palmer*, was written by Lynch's 22-year-old daughter, Jennifer – her first entry into the family business. The book evoked the cheerleader's furtive world without too much detail about her sexual predilections, or, indeed, who murdered her. It was licensed to Simon & Schuster and hit the bookstores in the autumn. (Lynch and Frost toyed with the idea of restricting sales to supermarkets for the TV dinner set, but decided instead to treat it as a 'real' book.)

David Lynch at the peak of his media profile: the Emmy Awards, August 1990. As with his previous Oscar nominations, he lost out to more mainstream competition.

The show and its cast had become a phenomenon – but, like many who travel rapidly on the up-and-up, were propelled so fast by sudden popularity they couldn't tell when they reached their peak.

For Lynch, the show signified the peak of a personal renaissance that had begun with *Blue Velvet* and took in all his other areas of creative activity. As shallow an accolade as it is, considering the depth and range of those activities, David Lynch was now Hollywood's 'King of Weird' – the only avant-garde auteur whose deeply obsessive imagery was almost paradoxically accepted by the industry mainstream, because, hey, you know, that's what this guy Lynch *does*. And, for the first time, he had a project which was both a critical success and a major revenue earner for himself.

'I think that the freeing power of money is a very healing sort of thing,' he reflected aloud from his newly privileged position. 'Because all we want to do is to be able to do what we want to do. And if we can do that, we get the sense of freedom. One of my frustrations, one of the limiting things, was the lack of money. And I still don't have enough to do all the things I want to do yet. But least I have more than I had then.'

With money apparently buying more artistic freedom, there was the corresponding question of time: the commodity the newly successful never have enough of.

'The good side of failure is you've got plenty of time to work. A guy (artist Bushnell Keeler) told me that in order to get one good hour of painting done, you need four hours of uninterrupted time.'

Nothing had changed Lynch's primary perception of himself as a visual artist. Nothing was allowed to detract from art – not even the need for food and sustenance.

'No, ma'am!' confirmed Lynch, with the dogmatism of the born-again bachelor. 'I don't allow cooking in my house. The smell. The smell of cooking – when you have drawings, or even writings – that smell would go all over my work. So I eat things that you don't have to light a fire for. Or else I order a pizza. The speed at which I eat it, it doesn't smell up the place too bad . . .'

One of the quirkiest aspects by far of Lynch's Art Life is the regular cartoon that ran in the *LA Reader* from the mid-'80s to early '90s. *The Angriest Dog in the World* – minimalism at its most minimalist – was a four-frame drawing which remained unchanged every week, prefaced by the same scrawled introduction: 'The dog who is so angry he cannot move. He cannot eat. He cannot sleep. He can just barely growl . . . Bound so tightly with tension and anger, he approaches the state of rigor mortis.'

The following three frames were an identically primitive drawing of the small bundle of black fur and fangs, straining at the leash in his owner's backyard and growling low. The fourth was the same scene at night, illuminated only by a half moon and light from the living room. The only alteration came in terms of whatever maxim Lynch had emanating from a speech bubble in the house for the third frame, passed to his personal assistant each week to hand-deliver in an envelope. Example: 'It must be clear even to the non-mathematician that the things in this world just don't add up to beans.'

Assumed to be yet another implicit autobiographical statement, Lynch was asked what made him the angriest dog in the world. 'Well, I had tremendous anger,' he recalled, almost redundantly. 'When I began meditating (in 1973, before *Eraserhead* stalled), one of the first things that left was a great chunk of that. I don't know how – it just evaporated. '

Such anger had, presumably, long vanished into the ether by the time he was able to exhibit his own infantilely obsessive, brutalist art.

At the tail-end of the '80s, the Leo Castelli Gallery in New York City had put on the first of an occasional series of exhibitions of Lynch's primitivist paintings, priced between $5,000 and $13,500, with titles like *When I Returned There Were Bugs in My House and Fire and Blood in the Streets*. It must have seemed as if recognition had finally come for his 'real' career: the Art Life.

Lynch described one typical piece, inspired by another maladjusted canine – *Oww, God, Mom, the Dog He Bited Me*: 'There's a clump of Band-Aids in the bottom corner. A dark background. A stick figure whose head is a blur of blood. Then a very small dog, made out of glue. There is a house, a little black bump. It is pretty crude, pretty primitive and minimal. I like it a lot.'

Add to the Art Life a new movie due for release, plus a second season of *Twin Peaks* in the pipeline, and Lynch can be forgiven for feeling, despite all the attendant pressures, that the universe had opened itself up to him at last.

'Scientists are working right now, while we are having lunch,' he informed an interviewer from *Time*, overwhelmingly optimistic and only half tongue-in-cheek, 'to give us a better life. I hope they make some big breakthrough soon. If you could only reconcile the mental with the physical, then throw in the emotional! These growth hormones, where can I get a bunch of them? Is there some way that, with electricity, you could stimulate your own growth hormones? Plug yourself in for five minutes, there'd be a little jolt, but you'd get used to it. It wouldn't be bad at all; in fact, you'd get to enjoy it, probably. Then away you'd go, and youth wouldn't be wasted on the young any more. You'd be 25 with a 95-year-old mind. Grandad would start breaking into liquor stores and staying out late. Hope we have it soon!'

For the time being, at least, Lynch could reassure himself with the knowledge that he was buying into some kind of artistic immortality.

CHAPTER SEVEN

Wild At Heart:

Lynch Mob Rules

In the late summer of 1989, after post-production had finished on the *Twin Peaks* pilot, David Lynch felt just lucky enough to try returning to his regular vocation. Until then it hadn't been easy. Both *Ronnie Rocket* and *One Saliva Bubble* were buried in contractual complications surrounding the bankruptcy of De Laurentiis Entertainment, which had been bought out by Carolco Productions.

'I've had a bad time with obstacles,' admitted Lynch. 'It wasn't all Dino's fault, but when his company went down the tubes, I got swallowed up in that.'

After such a long period of stalled developments, a new project finally fell, almost effortlessly, into place. Independent production company Propaganda Films commissioned Lynch to develop an updated *noir* screenplay based on a 1940s crime novel. At the same time, his buddy at Propaganda, Monty Montgomery, had recently optioned a novel he'd read in pre-published galley form: *Wild At Heart: the Story of Sailor and Lula* by Barry Gifford.

'I read the book one day and bought it the next,' recalled Montgomery, who, as co-director of art-house biker picture *The Loveless* (1983), was instrumental in the debuts of *Near Dark / Strange Days* director Kathryn Bigelow and charismatic, reptilian character actor Willem Dafoe. Recommending the novel to Lynch, Montgomery hoped to get him on board as producer.

His friend was intrigued by the project as described to him. 'I said, "Monty, what happens if I read this book and really love it? It would make me crazy." And he said, "Well, if that happens, then you'll direct it."'

By page three of Gifford's novel, Lynch found himself in agreement. With the okay from Propaganda Films to switch projects, Lynch and Montgomery reversed their prospective producer-director roles. Taking the novel – split into a staccato 45 chapters over 159 short pages – as very basic raw material, Lynch was given a breathlessly tight deadline to switch screenplays and get the film into pre-production. 'One shouldn't be proud of writing fast,' he reflected after the event. 'But I wrote that draft in a week.'

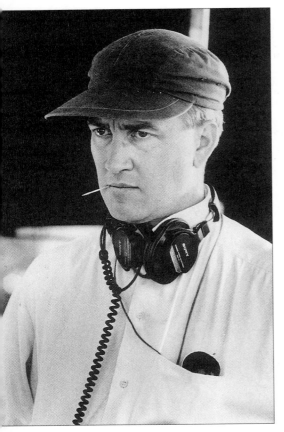

David Lynch directing **Wild At Heart** *(1990). The love-on-the-run fantasy made an easy transition from concept to screen; despite winning the Palme D'Or at the 1990 Cannes Film Festival, however, it met with much critical hostility in the USA.*

Within four months, he would be at the helm of cast and crew. Within six months of setting eyes on the book's galley proofs, he would put the wraps on the shoot. *Wild At Heart*, as Lynch abbreviated the title, was, he asserted with some relief, 'just a green light from the moment I said I wanted to do it'.

Gifford, the Chicago-born novelist and poet, had been hailed by some of his US cult readership as the inheritor of Jack Kerouac's restless-boho mantle. However, while his *Wild At Heart: the Story of Sailor and Lula* is definitely a road piece, it's less the studied or contrived cool of *On The Road* than an evocative grab-bag of snippets of life on the run through America's darklands.

Backed by Propaganda to the relatively modest tune of $10 million, *Wild At Heart* began shooting in and around LA (including the largely industrial area of San Fernando Valley) and New Orleans almost immediately.

For those who were looking for the big theme, *Wild At Heart* was, Lynch assured them '. . . about finding love in Hell. For me, it's just a compilation of ideas that come along. The darker ones and the lighter ones, the humorous ones, are all working together. You try to be as true as you can to those ideas and try to get them on film.'

As for the original source material, the odyssey of two naive kids through an unnerving but recognisably realistic America became merely the starting point for a series of ever more vivid set pieces.

'You know,' said author Gifford, close to the film's release date, 'they paid me a lot of money to keep my mouth shut and I'm pretty good at that. I understand what the terms of the deal are. And as I've said before, I can only reiterate that the novel is the novel and the film is the film.

'The best films are echoes of the books they're based on. That's all I was really looking for and I certainly haven't been disappointed as far as *Wild At Heart* is concerned. If you think it's wonderful, I don't take the credit.'

'It's not entirely my fault,' responded Lynch to the implication that he'd taken *Wild At Heart* to wilder extremes. 'His book suggested these ideas to me. I just made the brighter things a little brighter and darker things a little darker.'

WILD AT HEART (1990)

A match strikes, erupting into iridescent flames. Fire is the film's leitmotif. Throughout the film, any spark of fire is magnified to fill the screen – not least the sexually insinuating slow burn of a freshly lit cigarette.

Cape Fear – close to the North Carolina-South Carolina border.
First seen about to leave a hotel, Sailor Ripley and Lula Pace Fortune are lovers; he is a slow-talking, rockabillyish Southern dude, she is a bubbly, sassy piece of affluent white trash.

Nicolas Cage – the nephew of Francis Ford Coppola – had made a speciality out of incarnating wild innocents, as the small-town wanna-be doo-wop star of his uncle's *Peggy Sue Got Married* (1986), Cher's lover in *Moonstruck* (1987), and as the lady cop's law-breaking husband in *Raising Arizona* (1988). As Sailor Ripley, a gauche roughneck who takes as his ideal for living the Southern-gentleman mannerisms of Elvis (despite constant allusions, neither referred to by name nor eulogised in the film), Cage is both squirmingly corny and strangely endearing.

'All I kept thinking was he's not red wine, he's motor oil, ' said Cage, 'things like that. He's an old Corvette that needs a tune-up, wearing a snakeskin jacket. He can break down but when you drive him it feels good. Those ideas kept me into the character.'

'I'd say this world is maybe not the brightest place one could hope to be,' reflected Lynch. 'And I think that Sailor and Lula are trying to live properly. They're struggling in darkness and confusion, like everybody else. Sailor has this tender side – that's sort of like a rock 'n' roll concept. He sings and deals with emotion, but at the same time, a definite coolness and rebellious thing is running side by side it. The idea that there's some room for love in a really cool world is really interesting to me.'

Walking down the hotel steps a black guy, Bobby Ray Lemon, follows them, shouting, 'Hey Sailor, wait up! . . . Marietta tells me you been trying to fuck her in the toilet for the last ten minutes.' 'Oh man,' is all his target can say – aware his sense of Southern honour will demand he takes it all the way. Bobby Ray taunts that her mama promised him that 'cute little cunt Lula', but draws his blade too late to make a quick kill.
The outraged Sailor takes his would-be assassin by the lapels and spins him to the floor, battering Bobby Ray's head against a concrete step until his brains trickle out.
Sailor is convicted of manslaughter and sent to Pee Dee Correctional Institute.

Lynch's original shooting script was an altogether more oblique affair, closely resembling the anti-linear way in which the novel's episodes unfold. Cutting back and forth between present time and flashback, the 'truth' of the narrative was to unfold in a series of self-contradictory, *Rashomon*-type sequences.

Somewhere along the way, apparently before post-production, Lynch decided the film was too 'wild on top' to bear such a convoluted framework, and rearranged scenes in linear order. The first of these was the sequence in which Sailor bashes Bobby Ray Lemon's brains out – originally to have been held off until a flashback before the film's climactic bank robbery, it seems to have made little sense – dramatically, or in terms of character psychology – to keep secret the offence for which Sailor spent over two years in prison.

Instead of the fatal brawl, Lynch had originally intended to open the picture with a pre-narrative montage of everyday violence: a bloody motorcycle crash, a wild dog fight, and – shades of Peckinpah's *The Wild Bunch* – vicious young brats destroying a wasp's nest.

'22 months, 18 days later.'
As Sailor walks out the prison gates, his image is shown in a crystal ball over which passes a witch's long-taloned hand. 'If you even think about seeing Lula, you're dead,' warns her mama, Marietta, Wicked Witch of the West-style.

'This jacket symbolises my independence and belief in personal freedom': Sailor Ripley (Nicolas Cage) in **Wild At Heart.** *As portrayed by Cage, Sailor is a naive version of the drifter played by Marlon Brando in* **The Fugitive Kind** *(1960), even down to the same snakeskin jacket.*

The film's constant allusions to *The Wizard of Oz* are an elaborate sequel to that strand of sub-text from *Blue Velvet*. Reactions ranged from Gifford's own non-committal bemusement, to the fans who accepted it – inaccurately, according to Lynch – as wilful camp, and, more often than not, detractors who derided it as cheap whimsy – further proof, to them, *pace Velvet* and *Peaks*, that Lynch was too emotionally distanced from his subject matter to invest any serious intent, and that the *Wizard of Oz* fixation, along with the portrayal of Sailor as a passable Elvis impersonator, were kitsch devices allowing the director to celebrate his own insincerity.

Of course, the movie painter himself doesn't see it any of these ways: 'It was an awful tough world and there was something about Sailor being a rebel. But a rebel with a dream of *The Wizard of Oz* is kinda like a beautiful thing. And the characters of Sailor and Lula having this dream between them was pleasing.'

Lula arrives to greet Sailor at the gates; she's brought him his treasured snakeskin jacket. 'Did I ever tell you this jacket symbolises my independence and belief in personal freedom?' he asks her. 'About fifty thousand times,' she replies affectionately.

Enjoying a post-coital cigarette, Sailor lights two – as Paul Henreid once did for Bette Davis and himself – but keeps holding both in his mouth awhile. 'If we can stay in love for the rest of our lives,' reflects Lula, 'the future will be so simple and nice.'

The most remarkable near-characterisation in this frenetically over-acted film comes from Laura Dern. With her ultra-high heels, spray-on pants, studded bustier and luminous red lipstick, she's a sensual but worried bimbette, seeking to understand this world and all the evil in it – not unlike an uninhibited female version of Jeffrey in *Blue Velvet*, but hammed to the hilt.

Having established a rep for playing nice little white-bread girls, such as her embodiment of small town virtue in *Blue Velvet*, Laura Dern was just about the last actress anyone could picture as some hot, panting, hell-for-leather wild girl. Not so, Lynch. 'When I read Barry Gifford's book, I pictured Laura as Lula just as plainly as anything,' said the movie painter, revealing a psyche which, commonly enough, conjures up friends and acquaintances as the faces of fictional characters. 'There's a naive quality to her that is so sort of refreshing and thrilling and tender, so you just love her so much.' One slightly perverse enticement of Laura Dern into her role was the chance to work alongside her

Former goody two-shoes Laura Dern shows she has what it takes to be southern wildcat Lula Pace Fortune: 'She's kind of tall, but she's still a tidbit,' Lynch enthused of his 5'10" friend.

mother, Diane Ladd – herself the daughter of shortcake tough guy Alan Ladd.

'We've waited twenty years to work together,' said Ms Dern. 'I guess it isn't normal for parents to see their daughters have sex. That's probably why so many actors need therapy. But I think she did some things in that movie that aren't easy for a daughter to watch either. So I figure we're about equal.

'There's this anger I usually see in film that goes with sexuality that's very disturbing. It's, like, I turn you on, you turn me on, and fuck you. The thing that is so great about Sailor and Lula is that it's *so-oo* sexy because of the love. And that's the thing that's so beautiful about David. Here's this guy who's so weird and does things that are so terrifying to the psyche. And yet there's this purity in him and this belief in love that is almost cartoon-like and childlike.'

Lula talks about the pleasures of smoking, reminiscing on how she started by stealing her mother's brand. Sailor recalls how his mother smoked Marlboros, the same brand as himself, but died of lung cancer soon after her little boy got the habit at age four. 'I haven't had much parental guidance,' he laments, his negligent father dying of alcoholism soon after.

Lula recalls being raped by her 'Uncle Pooch' (a family friend) at age 13. 'Uncle Pooch died in a car crash three months later, when I was on holiday in Myrtle Beach,' she recounts, as a flashback shows Pooch dying in an arranged explosion.

Marietta schmoozes up to an old boyfriend, private detective Johnnie Farragut, in order to get him to give chase to the fleeing couple. She promises him that as soon as he catches up with Sailor and Lula, they can plan a future together. 'Do you mean it?' asks the too-innocent Johnnie. 'You bet your sweet ass I do!' blasts the brassy blonde. In a flashback sequence, drunken Marietta urges Sailor to fuck her in the men's toilet.

Harry Dean Stanton, whose inscrutable hangdog features hung over many a B-picture – as well as lending decoration and presence to big '70s features like *Pat Garrett and Billy the Kid* (1973), *The Godfather Part II* (1974) and *Alien* – had recently found leading-man status with Wim Wenders' *Paris, Texas* (1984) and Alex Cox's *Repo Man* (1986). Having turned down (according to Dennis Hopper) the role of Frank in *Blue Velvet*, due to a desire to continue with more sympathetic roles, the air of lowlife sleaze inhabited by characters such as his phoney blind beggar in John Huston's *Wise Blood* still hung over him.

In Gifford's novel, Johnnie Farragut is as central a figure as Sailor and Lula, an introspective bloodhound and aspiring author, providing the third first-person voice which informs the narrative. As incarnated by Stanton he's just another secondary role with a familiar air of soiled goods, yet he still has more integrity than any other male character (or cipher) apart from Sailor.

Sailor's 'peanut' promises she'll never leave him. 'That's rockin' good news!' yells the cornball Elvis-wannabe, and they put on their dancing shoes. At the concert hall, Sailor and Lula jump around going writhingly crazy to speed metal band Powermad. Some kid dances provocatively against Lula. Sailor steps in, to be told he dresses like an asshole. 'This is a snakeskin jacket,' Sailor instructs him. 'For me, it's a symbol of individuality and my belief in personal freedom.' He beats the kid senseless, forcing him to apologise to Lula. Ever the Southern gentleman, Sailor tells the chastised kid to go get himself a beer. He then breaks into the first bars of Leiber and Stoller's 'Love Me', as sung by Elvis, the be-studded, leathered, speed-metal crowd instantly turning into applauding nostalgicists.

Lula recalls how her beloved Daddy died: 'Mama says he covered himself in kerosene and put a match to himself, flailing around the house in flames.'

Marietta hedges her bets by contacting Marcello Santos to sweet-talk him into putting a contract out on Sailor. She makes the mistake of admitting she's already put Johnnie on his tail; Santos' conditions are that he'll also have the detective killed, before he has a chance to endanger them via connection with the mysterious Mr Reindeer.

Santos calls up Mr Reindeer, an elderly drug trafficker attended by bored, bare-breasted young women, who phones his hirelings and puts a contract out on both Sailor and Johnnie. He offers a single silver dollar for each (token symbol of accepting the hit); his first taker is a sinister, slender woman seen leaning on a crutch in silhouette.

Lula tells Sailor about her crazy cousin Dell. Dell is played by professional Californian eccentric Crispin Glover: nicknamed 'Jingle Dell' by Lula, a flashback sequence shows him blaming 'the men in black gloves' for 'destroying the spirit of Christmas'; he also becomes obsessed by preparing his lunch in advance, staying up all night building a huge pile of sandwiches, and keeps bugs in his undershorts. Lula recalls her aunt's disgust at finding Dell naked with a cockroach on the tip of his anus. 'Too bad Dell didn't visit that old Wizard of Oz,' comments Sailor on her cousin's mental health. 'Too bad we all can't,' responds Lula.

As the two lovers make for New Orleans along the night highway, Lula imagines she sees her mother in pursuit on a flying broomstick dressed as the Wicked Witch of the West. The jangling opening chords of Chris Isaak's song 'Wicked Game' become a recurring musical theme as they drive into the night.

'Wicked Game', chosen specifically by Lynch for the soundtrack, became a Top 20 hit on both sides of the Atlantic contemporary to the film's release. Although Isaak's haunting, Orbison-like voice is never heard in the film (the opening chords are merely repeated to form a motif), the photogenic ex-boxer swiftly became a new addition to the Lynch mob, with a character role in the *Twin Peaks* saga. Isaak's polished but timewarped style evokes the less kitschy, more atmospheric moments of 1950s pop-culture.

Marietta (Diane Ladd) puts Johnnie Farragut (Harry Dean Stanton) on the lovers' tail. According to Dennis Hopper, Stanton turned down Frank in **Blue Velvet** *for more sympathetic parts, but* **Wild At Heart** *contained the second of four roles he would take for Lynch.*

Lula listens to news reports of bizarre and depraved behaviour: a mother who murdered her three children; a murderer having sex with a corpse; turtles and crocodiles released into the River Ganges, to respectively reduce the amount of human waste and human corpses. Near hysterical, she pulls over. 'Ah can't take no more of this radio. Ah never heard so much shit in all mah life! Sailor Ripley, you get me some music this instant, ah mean it!' Sailor finds a station playing Powermad, and the two lovers go into their ecstatic speed-metal dance at the edge of the road.

Sailor and Lula head into New Orleans; the first street scene encountered is a cool black dude with a white guy trying to get his attention by walking alongside barking at him like a dog; in a bar, they're first unnerved, then amused, by a fruitcake (Freddie Jones – Bytes in The Elephant Man) who caws at them like a bird, then talks about pigeons in a heliumed voice: 'Pigeons spread diseases and mess up the place. You've seen that.'

Marietta catches up with Johnnie, feeling guilty, but Johnnie is knocked unconscious and goes missing from their hotel lobby. A card is retrieved by a prissy hotel clerk, who tells her it reads: 'Gone fishing. May go buffalo hunting later.' 'What the fuck does that mean?' she screams at him.

Bound and gagged, Johnnie is subjected to sadistic mind games by Juana, the 'voodoo woman' (Grace Zabriskie – Sarah Palmer in Twin Peaks). When first seen, this peroxide-haired, beetle-browed, cadaver-faced sex-slut is all the more menacing for resting on a crutch in silhouette. In this 'wild on top' world, deformity or disability are not markers for pity or respect but signifiers of a twisted soul. Accompanied by two black men, she terrorises Johnnie against a soundtrack of cacophony and drum rhythms; she howls to one of her accomplices, as their murderous ritual drives her into a frenzy: 'Fuck me, Reggie!' A shotgun is pointed at the back of Johnnie's head; it explodes, unseen, as the camera cuts to a road sign riddled with rifle shot.

On the road to Texas, our loving couple drive into a nightmare vision: scattered clothes are strewn

*From **Blue Velvet** icon to peroxide slut: Isabella Rossellini purportedly had a hand in creating Perdita Durango's black-browed sex appeal, but attributed it to Lynch's sense of visual surrealism.*

all over the road; a young male driver lies dead. Emerging from the wreck of the vehicle is an attractive young woman (Sherilyn Fenn – Audrey Horne in Twin Peaks*), delirious with injury and shock. Blood soaks one side of her brunette scalp; obsessed with finding her missing purse and credit cards, she dies in front of their eyes.*

As the most haunting scene of the film, the car crash sequence appears to emanate from the young Lynch's adolescent musing on death. During his high school years in Virginia, a close school friend was killed in a horrific traffic accident.

Arriving at their motel room in Big Tuna, Texas, a near-shanty town of drifters, misfits and criminals on the run, superstitious Lula crosses her fingers and hopes that 'seeing that girl die doesn't jinx us'.

Sailor confesses to Lula that he was sitting outside her house on the night her daddy burned to death, everyone connected with Santos (including her mama) wrongly believing he saw too much – implicit proof of his former employer's guilt.

At a bar, they encounter a local eccentric, O. O. Spool (Jack Nance), who is introduced to them as a 'rocket scientist'; he tells them of his dog, who he passionately insists is always with him – adding: 'Perhaps you might even picture Toto from The Wizard of Oz.'

In Gifford's original novel, the various misfits and madmen play a more direct role in the narrative. In fact, with the plot detail itself mainly consisting of entertaining but non-sequitorial diversions (as with the film), the characters, their personal recollections and fantasies, *are* the story. Perversely, given his penchant for all-American weirdness, lack of space forced Lynch to sideline them to a handful of brief cameo acts.

Sailor and Lula are sitting in a bar. A cop asks about the racket coming from outside, to be told that a porn movie is being made, 'Texas-style'. Curious, the patrons take a peek, amused to find another Lynchian addition to the narrative: three naked, obese porn starlets dancing in the street, none seemingly weighing less than 300 lbs. (Lynch says they were an overnight addition, inspired by a chubby-chaser porn mag called Hippos *the crew were passing around.) Distracted by the attention, Bobby Peru – pornographer in charge – comes walking over to greet the newcomers.*

Peru is thin and dirtily sun-tanned, with tombstone teeth and a sinister pencil moustache. Drinking with him back inside the bar, Sailor notices the USMC tattoo on his hand. (As with his decaying appearance, this is Lynch's invention.) A fellow Vietnam vet, who served in the navy, blurts out that Bobby was in Cao Ben when many women and children were massacred. 'Pretty hard to make contact with the people when you're out floatin' in the fuckin' Gulf of Tonkin,' snarls Peru, glowering.

Sailor enters the motel room to the odour of vomit. Lula admits that she barfed and didn't have the energy to clear it up, believing she's pregnant. She recalls being made pregnant by Uncle Pooch at age 13. The memory of her abortion conjures up the sudden, shocking image of a bloody foetus thrown straight in the pail.

Sailor takes a ride out to the shack of Perdita Durango, a local underworld contact who can tell him whether there's a contract on his head. Perdita is seen in a photo-portrait with Reggie and Juana, the voodoo woman, of whom, with her bleach-blonde hair and heavy dark eyebrows, she appears a younger version.

'David has developed his very personal brand of surrealism even more than in *Blue Velvet*,' commented Isabella Rossellini, who played Perdita towards the end of her relationship with Lynch.

'In *Blue Velvet*, I think you saw it strongest in the scene with Dean Stockwell. In *Wild At Heart*, that mood impregnates the whole film. It's about the reality of the unconscious, of your emotions, of how you remember things – and not the reality of a fact. When he puts a wig on me and makes my eyebrows very hairy, it's part of that perception of the brain.'

Knowing Lula's pregnant and Sailor only has $40 in his wallet, Bobby talks him into committing a minor bank robbery for slim pickings. With only $5,000 to split between the two of them, Sailor still believes 'that kinda money can get us a long way down the Yellow Brick Road'. Peru throws Sailor a sleazy metaphor for feeling horny as he leaves: 'One-eyed Jack's yearnin' to go a-peepin' in the seafood store.' Sailor is unaware that he intends to go visiting his girl.

Willem Dafoe had portrayed the title icon of Scorsese's *The Last Temptation of Christ* (1988) before signing up to play *Wild At Heart*'s main sleazebag, Bobby Peru. 'Dark angel, dark angel, remember, Willem – you're the dark angel,' Lynch would constantly remind him before a scene. Before a day's shooting, he was overheard by the director rehearsing a couple of lines relating to the heist in sing-song voice.

'Play with that on just those two lines,' Lynch suggested. 'Just keep that dark mood to it. Dark and strange, like a myth.'

'For a second you think, "This is nuts. He's asking me to sing these lines?"' reported Dafoe, who found his aimless babble incorporated into the action. 'But stylistically, I think the film has a lot of room for that – there aren't necessarily artistic dictates on what to do. So if some accident happens that David really responds to, he just accommodates it.'

Peru enters the motel room where Lula is alone. 'Fuck me,' he goads her in well-lit, claustrophobic close-up, then repeats his demand in every permutation – 'Fuck me! Fuck me! Ffuuck me!' – until she finally gives in. Then he's insultingly nonchalant: 'I will one day, honey – but right now I've got to run.'

Sailor (Nicolas Cage) meets the predatory Bobby Peru (Willem Dafoe). As to whether sleazy Peru's pencil-moustached look was based on 'Pope of Sleaze' John Waters, Eraserhead's *early champion, Lynch demurs, 'Waters is very upfront, sorta like a loud saxophone, and I want to back off into something a little different.'*

As he leaves her alone in the hotel room, disgusted with Peru for his tactics and with herself for her almost unfaithfulness to Sailor, Lula puts her red shoes on and frantically clicks the heels together – trying to quit the here-and-now like Dorothy using her ruby slippers to return home in The Wizard of Oz.

Perdita turns up to drive Peru and Sailor to the raid – Sailor's surprised to find they're involved with each other, but can't detect that Peru is Mr Reindeer's second assassin and the raid is a ruse to get him killed.

Inside the crumbling bank, Peru is given the excuse he's been waiting for by a would-be hero cashier. He fires through the steel bars on the counter, leaving a chaotic scene of carnage, then turns his gun towards Sailor, who makes a break.

Outside, Peru is shot six times before stumbling onto his own vertically-upturned rifle, which fires point blank through his throat. His head is blown off, flies through the air and bounces to a halt. 'That poor bastard,' laments Sailor, magnanimously.

Meanwhile, inside the bank, the mutilated clerk is distressed because he has lost his hand. 'They can stitch these things back on,' his frantic colleague tries to reassure him, while a little dog runs away with the lost body part held in his jaw.

Outside, Sailor is placed under arrest. 'We broke down along that Yellow Brick Road!' wails Lula, when she comes to visit him at the jail-house. But smug Mama is there to make sure everything's all right for her baby.

'5 years, 10 months, 21 days later.'

Sailor is about to be released, but drunken, hysterical Marietta's trying to forbid her daughter to see him again. In another Lynchian addition to the story, she layers her wrists with red lipstick, as if to simulate opening her veins.

Before making her way to Sailor, Lula throws water over a photo-portrait of her mother, which has a strange, corrosive effect: both her image and her influence fade, as if, like the Wicked Witch of the West, she's finally been disintegrated by fluid.

Driving to the prison gates with her little boy, Pace, she passes by a road accident – redolent of that with the dying girl nearly six years earlier – where a driver tries to reassure a motorcyclist lying comatose in a pool of blood, telling him: 'This happened to me last year, man.'

Sailor greets his woman and child (who he has never seen), but tells them there's no point in making their lives harder than they already are, and walks determinedly away. (It's at a similar point that Barry Gifford's novel ends.) Down a post-industrial backstreet, he's converged upon by a multi-racial street gang. 'What do you faggots want?' he sneers, but is only able to swing one punch before they break his nose. Knocked into delirium, Sailor has a vision heralding the happy ending that makes many viewers barf on their popcorn. Glinda, the Good Witch (Sheryl Lee – Laura/Maddy in Twin Peaks*) descends from the sky in a glass bubble to tell him: 'Don't turn away from love.'*

'I had a problem,' admitted Lynch, of the eight minutes he added to the original downbeat ending. 'It is much more commercial to make a happy ending. Yet if I had not done it, so that people wouldn't say it was commercial, I would have been untrue to what the material was saying. Sailor and Lula had to be together, the problem was figuring out how they could be together and still have the scene where they were apart. So that problem helped *The Wizard of Oz* come along.'

'Things get about as dark as they can in *Wild At Heart*,' affirmed Laura Dern, 'but I don't think we've seen a love story as pure as this for a long time. I think David realised that, if you're going to find love in Hell, you're going to make it out the other side.'

Sailor jumps over the bonnets of traffic-jammed cars to take Lula in his arms. As they embrace atop her Thunderbird convertible, their little boy smiles approvingly at his mom and dad. Sailor sings a heartfelt, pseudo-Elvis 'Love Me Tender'. As the screen fades, Lula sinks back into the classic Marilyn stance of submission – breasts forward, pelvis back, one arm above her head – and they embrace in a kiss.

In May 1990, Lynch was able to keep to his intended schedule for entering the completed *Wild At Heart* in competition at Cannes. Against the professed expectations of all concerned – and, apparently, a few disgruntled members of the jury – the panel, headed by Bernardo Bertolucci, presented the film with the coveted main prize: the Palme D'Or.

'I was very surprised that it won,' emphasised Lynch. 'Thrilled, but surprised.' Though the panel presented Lynch's film with the most prestigious prize of the festival, with Bertolucci giving the director a congratulatory hug, audible boos went up from those patriotic gauls who felt the award belonged to *Cyrano De Bergerac*.

Transatlantic industry responses to the Palme D'Or winner were divided. 'For those expecting *Blue Velvet 2*, or *Twin Peaks 8*,' commented an unimpressed *Screen International*, '*Wild At Heart* will come as something of a disappointment' – going on to bemoan the 'unstructured collection of intense and chilling snapshots', 'the rambling sprawl of plot', 'sugary anti-climax' and 'wilful dwelling on spilt guts and leaking brains [which] will have censors waving scissors worldwide'.

Though sex and violence were only implicitly combined in the film's most disturbing scene, where Johnnie Farragut is tortured and murdered by the 'voodoo woman', the ratings board still blanched at their close screen-time proximity in the same big-budget movie.

Despite its often slapstick style, however, Lynch's playfully gruesome violence retained its power to disturb. 'Some of these things were quite violent,' he recalled of his own handiwork. 'We had some test screenings in the States and at one of them 100 people got up and left. The next time we had a test screening 120 people got up and left. It was breaking the film.'

Research by the Goldwyn Organisation among US preview audiences was based around a mono-dimensional line that should have made Lynch blanch, given his dislike of 'one-

Diane Ladd, hamming it up to Grand Guignol extremes, as Marietta, Lula's witch-like mother. Personifying Lynch's **Wizard of Oz** *sub-plot, Marietta is also a psychopathic alcoholic. 'She did some things in that movie that aren't that easy for a daughter to watch,' laughed her real-life and screen daughter, Laura Dern.*

thing films': did they regard the picture as 'comedy', 'horror' or 'musical'? Apparently, too many affirmed in the middle category – Goldwyn, seeing the film's niche as a 'caper' comedy, urged Lynch to co-operate with their studio censors.

'We just had to cut it for the sake of the whole picture,' defended the director. 'This violence was just going over the line and ruining everything. The next time we just altered one tiny part and the audience was with the picture. I guess there is a magical line that you can go up against and if you cross it you're in big trouble.'

The 'one tiny part' trimmed from the original cut included the climax to the psychological torture of Johnnie Farragut/Harry Dean Stanton, which, as it now stands, ends with an unseen shotgun blast to the head. Prior to Johnnie's gory demise, the original script suggests the enigmatic term 'buffalo hunting' entailed a sadistic game involving masturbation, a gun and soda bottles.

Peru's/Dafoe's final shotgun decapitation was re-shot in less graphic detail with an obscuring smoke filter. His head is still seen to part company with his shoulders – but his exposed brain can no longer be glimpsed flying out of his skull.

Also trimmed considerably was the black comic aftermath of the raid, where the mutilated bank clerk searches for his severed hand; in its original form this scene was longer, even messier, involving a search for further missing body parts. The brief but shocking abortion sequence was also a bone of contention, while – inevitably, given the MPAA's strange intolerance of eroticism – some of the sex scenes between Sailor and Lula also had to be shortened for the film to be granted its 'R'.

Despite Lynch's willing concessions – there's 'no secret uncut masterpiece hidden in the closet,' he claims, though a scheduled 'director's cut' laser disc release may put that to the test – it seemed disingenuous in the extreme for Goldwyn's press office to insist of their final cut: 'We're proud to announce that this is the version as Lynch intended.'

With the censored cut's transatlantic release in August, the reviews were not so much divided as irreconcilably polarised.

'The movie equivalent of a hell-bent, fast-forward locomotive,' said an enthusiastic *Hollywood Reporter*. 'This handsome, volcanically-violent road movie is Lynch's first flat-out comedy; he and his ensemble . . . work at a high pitch and have a swell time at it,' praised *Time*.

'A malignant work,' accused *New York Magazine*, tapped right in to the general vein of hostility, 'full of self-mocking trash as well as perverted excitement . . . The trash is not redeemed by the joke.' The *New Yorker* claimed that the 'shocks have so little resonance; the weirdness here is inexpressive and trivial, even silly'.

Clearly, many pundits would only accept the idea of Lynch as the golly-gosh innocent in thrall to his wild imagination as a put-on, an insincere schtick. The final straw for many was his adoption by the right-wing *National Review*, who, with a dogmatic agenda of their own, acclaimed him for presenting 'weird America' without the ideological lens of a 'leftist avant-garde director'. What proved even more irksome was that many critics had once identified him as a satirist (which Lynch, as a Reagan-supporting nostalgicist for the Eisenhower area, had never claimed) with an ironic take on bourgeois middle-America, and looked increasingly less astute every time he reiterated his *Hey, golly-gee whillikers, I like all this stuff* line.

Now all the shouting's long over, *Wild At Heart* can be seen for what it is: a loosely-structured, garishly violent, sexually unrestrained cartoon, with characters at least one-and-a-half dimensional enough to inspire sympathy and encapsulate child-like innocence and adolescent yearning.

The film's major technical feat lay in the editing, with so many entertaining but disjointed set pieces, *mise-en-scènes* and cameos to join together. (Some critics felt this denoted big post-production problems; while the reduction of some of Gifford's characters to brief, eccentric walk-ons suggests much expository material ended on the cutting room floor, it's also true that the basic structure of the film follows the novel's fragmented, episodic nature.) Small wonder that the editor, Duwayne Dunham, was rewarded with directorial work on the *Twin Peaks* series.

Perversely, however, considering the disappointed critics who griped about how unlike *Blue Velvet* the movie was, Lynch was felt to be milking his 'weird Americana' stable – consisting solely of *Velvet* and several episodes of *Twin Peaks* – and giving the groundlings what they expected.

Despite essential differences in tone, the invariables of Lynch's current style (then only several years old, and originated solely by him) were felt to be becoming a clichéd stock in trade – compulsive obsession, eccentric characterisation, bizarre murder, the contrasts of folksy Americanism and contemporary sleaze, innocent nostalgia and bizarre sexuality were, as far as most critics were concerned, the be-all and end-all of Lynch, rather than the vehicles which carried his imagery.

In the ensuing years, Weird Americana had also become a sub-genre, not totally dominated by its most celebrated exponent. Around the same time *Blue Velvet* became a media sensation, *True Stories* (1986), the directorial feature by Talking Heads leader/musical polymath David Byrne, had celebrated small-town USA in a lighter but no less quirky manner. Bob Balaban's *Parents* (1988) married the Lynchian setting of a quiet, late '50s town with well-cut grass and picket fences to a gory, American gothic narrative. By the early

Sailor (Nicolas Cage) and Lula (Laura Dern): two lovers who come out the other side of hell. 'I didn't buy the ending in the book,' said Lynch, of Barry Gifford's original downbeat conclusion where Sailor walks away from the relationship after his release from prison. 'I think they've learned a lot more, and grown more, even through fantasy, this way.'

1990s, movies which were (a) essentially weird and (b) quintessentially American seemed the most amorphously omnipresent of sub-genres.

It was decided by critical consensus that David Lynch was milking his personally obsessive vision, and should somehow, paradoxically, find something else to bring to the screen. On an idiosyncratic level, it was as if John Ford had been deemed stale and repetitious for making more than one film with frontiersmen on horseback.

Strangest of all, for a movie which supposedly pandered to the expectations of a ready-made core audience, *Wild At Heart* did poorly at the American box office – one critic unkindly (and exaggeratedly) claiming it resembled *Dune* in its undisciplined sprawl.

'Not everybody loves what you've done,' Lynch conceded understatedly, 'and negativity is a very powerful thing. And even the positive things are upsetting in a way because then you want to please the next time again. You gotta kinda just think about the work but it's not always easy.

'I can't try to second-guess the critics. The world is changing, and we are changing within it. As soon as you think you've got something figured out, it's different. That is what I try to do. I don't try to do anything new, or weird, or David Lynch. But I'm real happy with the picture. See, I love 47 different genres in one film. I hate one-thing films. And I love B movies. But why not have three or four Bs running together? Like a little hive!'

While Lynch's enthusiasm for the film remained undimmed, Barry Gifford found himself becoming increasingly protective of the movie which bore only a passing resemblance to his original source material. 'The *faux* intelligentsia can jump on or off a bandwagon,' he pointed out, with a hint of vitriol. 'André Gide said that writers should expect to lose fifty percent of their audience with each new work, that the rest never understood it in the first place. Perhaps that has happened to David.'

Strangest of all, with hindsight, is the way in which Lynch was condemned in certain quarters for adopting a post-modern retro-chic approach to the aspects of pop culture which *Wild At Heart* eulogised – Elvis, Oz, cheesy melodramas (both cinematic and TV).

If such trash-fetish trainspotting doesn't seem so excessive these days, it's probably because, within three short years of the film's release, movies-as-referential-lists became a sub-genre of their own. While Lynch's film had an unforeseen influence on a brief new spate of violent road pictures, one early '90s release either played implicit tribute or ripped off Lynch's film, depending on your prejudices. Tony Scott's *True Romance* (1993) was shot from a screenplay by trash-culture *wunderkind* Quentin Tarantino; using the framework of two naive young lovers on the run, heavily out-of-their-depth in criminal activity, Tarantino wove a fabric of TV, movie and trash-oriented reference. The movie geek hero (Christian Slater), while too nerdish to carry the tongue-in-cheek physical presence of Nicolas Cage's Sailor, is an Elvis fanatic who communes with the ghost of his hero. There's also a series of cameo roles – neither as diverse nor as bizarre as in *Wild At Heart*, but with a definite parallel between the vicious gangster and noble murder victim played by Christopher Walken and Dennis Hopper respectively, and the powerful precedent of Willem Dafoe and Harry Dean Stanton.

This referential style would reach its apex in Tarantino's self-directed trash masterpiece, *Pulp Fiction* (1994), which featured a gangland figure, Marsellus Wallace, with a phonetically similar name to gangland figure Marcello Santos in *Wild At Heart*. As winner of the 1994 Palme D'Or at Cannes, the controversial impact of *Pulp Fiction* taking the award was, arguably, lessened by *Wild At Heart* having already paved the way.

Meanwhile, there was talk of Lynch collaborating with the English obsessive, disillusioned socialist and misanthropic TV playwright Dennis Potter (still riding high on acclaim for *The Singing Detective*). The idea was to collaborate on a film adaptation of D. M. Thomas's controversial novel, *The White Hotel*: a semi-fantasy which touched on the implicit relationship between concentration camp guards and their victims. It would soon come to nothing, however. As fascinating as it would have been to view the uneasy joining of two obsessive, creative forces, it has to be said that Lynch – with his inherently personal and all-American fixations – had few credentials for dealing with the darkest part of Europe's collective memory.

In the absence of any definite new film project after *Wild At Heart*, the all-American artist returned to unfinished business elsewhere. Back to an imaginary small town in the North-West, which, in the eyes of the average Joe or Jane, was more synonymous with the name 'David Lynch' than any puzzling, arty, exploitation movie.

CHAPTER EIGHT

Down the Far Side of the Peaks

In the autumn of 1989, the transformation of David Lynch, from film director to New Renaissance man, looked just about complete. The Brooklyn Academy of Music (to which musical sidekick Angelo Badalamenti had both professional and parochial connections) hosted a diverse but well-received 'New Wave festival', including Lynch and Badalamenti's baroque opera/revue, *Industrial Symphony No. 1*.

Titled after the conceptual hybrids of painting, drawing and animation Lynch first produced back in art school, *Industrial Symphony* was a measure of the licence he currently had to indulge his obsessions. While much of the music had its origin in the Julee Cruise album, *Floating into the Night*, released shortly after the *Twin Peaks* premiere and part-assimilated into the TV show itself, the visual echoes of dream imagery and industry came strictly from the psyche of the show's director.

As Ms Cruise recalls: 'We had huge jutting jagged edges of steel, a huge tower and planes, and babies with their eyes blowtorched out, all teeny tiny baby dolls hanging from the ceiling, and glitter flying, and I was hoisted up on wires, and I was, like, floating . . . It was almost like Tai Chi, but not quite so high art. Oh yeah, and we had a dwarf come on and furiously saw wood. David likes wood.'

The dwarf worked the saw for 'The Black Sea' – possibly the first piece of industrial *musique concrete* in Badalamenti's repertoire. Floating off into beautiful and dangerous realms of consciousness – as with the implicit concept of the Julee Cruise album, illustrated by Lynch's photograph of a floating fairy doll – the singer found herself magically and precariously airborne in a manner recalling the flying fairy of John Merrick's haunting theatre visit in *The Elephant Man*.

With steaming pipes – like the living viscera of organic factories – littering the stage, Ms Cruise's role was directly descended from the sweetly grotesque Lady in the Radiator in *Eraserhead*: the innocent muse of an industrial nightmare landscape, given more elaborate songs and a facial makeover. In this sense, *Industrial Symphony No. 1* (the video recording of the event released in 1990), is the most undiluted and overlooked of Lynch's works.

Given almost complete imaginative freedom by the lack of any coherent narrative, the show still managed a linear connection to Lynch's most recent commercial projects. Apart from a walking skinned deer, the most haunting image of the show was a young woman, seemingly naked but flesh-costumed, dragged from the wreck of an old Ford – the trunk of which is used by Julee Cruise as a performance pedestal. An obvious echo of the most horrific scene in *Wild At Heart* (though lost on the audience, as the film hadn't finished production), it was still more oblique than the revue's opening.

The prologue to the show actually featured TV images of Sailor (Nicolas Cage) giving Lula (Laura Dern) the kiss-off on the telephone: 'I can't do it anymore, baby,' he tells her. (In a piece called 'The Dream Conversation', dwarf actor Michael J. Anderson repeats the broken-hearted lovers' conversation word-for-word as a monologue, set to a clarinet accompaniment and the tormented writhings of a Lula lookalike.) Lynch denied this was his displaced recreation of Barry Gifford's original ending to the story. 'But I think it might have been if David had taken the movie further,' said Laura Dern, 'because its original ending (without the fantasy intervention of the Good Witch) was a little closer to that.'

Also riding high, on recognition of his own talent as well as connection with the mid-West's own artistic polymath, Badalamenti had no end of immediate projects in the pipeline: orchestrations for the Pet Shop Boys' *Behaviour* album, and the new album from melancholic rock 'n' roller Chris Isaak (whose connection with Lynch, via 'Wicked Game'/*Wild At Heart*, would develop into something surprisingly concrete at the end of the *Twin Peaks* saga); the second album from Julee Cruise; plus plans for an unrealised Broadway musical.

Lynch himself, at the declining end of the *Peaks* craze, would be signed up to direct the promotional film to the video for wanna-be Elephant Man/superstar Michael Jackson's hit single, 'Dangerous' (1991). The promo was a further homogenisation of Lynch's pop-surrealism, in aid of an artist whose showman bombast had little in common with the moods or tones of the Lynch Mob's musical contingent.

In between the hyper-active period which produced the *Twin Peaks* pilot and ensuing series, *Wild At Heart* and *Industrial Symphony No. 1,* and the second season of *Peaks*, Lynch–Frost Productions were contracted to produce two half-hour pilot documentaries for Fox TV in 1990.

Entitled *American Chronicles*, the proposed 'eclectic sight/sound journey across America' was a celebratory travelogue through the quirky side of the USA. With an emphasis on the wilder side of the mundane, rather than all-out human perversity, this was the new brand of Weird Americana Lite.

Debuting in September 1990, the first show – 'Farewell to the Flesh', an archaic literal translation of 'Mardi Gras' – had no directorial credit, all the creativity inherent in editor Bob Jenkins' use of real-life videotape footage (celluloid quality) shot at the New Orleans Mardi Gras. With a narrative written by Frost and read by Richard Dreyfuss, it gave a basic historical/anthropological account of the carnival, its pagan roots and history of rape and robbery, set against vividly colourful shots of all the participants (from garish drag queens to real McCoy bare-breasted women, with nipples carefully obscured), their costumes and masks.

Several more shows were commissioned on the basis of the pilot, with declining input from Frost and the occasional producer's credit for Lynch. With a computer graphics sequence – the planet Earth, a human eye, the Statue of Liberty, a golden mask, the natural landscape of the USA, skyscrapers and industry – that was vaguely redolent of the unsophisticated but showmanish 'Mondo' documentaries of the 1960s and early '70s, the series just about lived up to

Former Broadway musical singer Julee Cruise, in her reinvented guise as the 'floating lady' who vocalised Lynch and Badalamenti's musical atmospherics throughout **Twin Peaks.** *All the songs were captured on* **Floating into the Night,** *a 1989 album produced by Lynch; Ms Cruise is seen here in a promotional shot for* **Industrial Symphony No. 1,** *where the post-industrial* **chanteuse** *closely resembles a more sophisticated version of the Lady in the Radiator in* **Eraserhead.**

Variety's promise of 'part *National Geographic*, part *Psychology Today'*.

American Chronicles lasted two short seasons, without creating many waves. It may well be ripe for revival every now and then, to compare its gentle, sincere views of everyday quirkiness against the sensational prurience of vintage Mondo.

Meanwhile, the bosses of Lynch–Frost Productions had a bigger fish to fry.

Lynch was enthusiastic about the forthcoming second season of *Twin Peaks*, believing that, no matter how many first-season viewers were irritated by non-resolution of the Palmer mystery, its appeal lay somewhere else.

'You just sort of picture this kind of darkness and this wind going through the needles of these Douglas firs and you start getting a bit of a mood coming along. And if you hear footsteps and you see a light in the window, and you start moving towards it, little by little you are sucked in. And this fantastic mood and sense of place comes along, and hopefully you want to go back, and feel it each week.'

'I sort of think it was an accident, actually,' laughed Mark Frost of *Peaks'* continuing cult status. 'David and I kind of slipped in when nobody was looking. It proved a point in that you can do work like that and people will respond to it, although it certainly hasn't started any trends as far as I can see.'

While Frost's belief that few ripples were made seems modest with hindsight, those addicted to *Peaks* hadn't climbed aboard just for the story, but for the nicely off-kilter way it threw curved balls, the slightly artificial feeling of being 'in' on a cult, and its endearingly folksy range of characters. The essential cast and crew remained the same, with a few notable additions: the extra directors brought in to complement the core team on the much greater number of commissioned episodes (22), included, oddly enough, Diane Keaton.

Major Briggs would soon personify a pivotal plot device, while more frequent appearances by forensic scientist Albert (played by Miguel Ferrer, son of José) revealed him as not so much an acid-tongued pain-in-the-ass as a man walking a 'strange and difficult path'. The expanding number of sub-plots produced their share of flab, introducing disposable love interests for Audrey and James – as against the potentially tragic match of

Agent Cooper and new girl Annie Blackburn (Heather Graham), and the comic quirk of Nadine's tryst with Bobby's buddy, Mike Nelson. The character of Cooper's mentor/nemesis Windom Earle, meanwhile, was played by TV veteran Kenneth Welsh as a piece of bravura ham.

As the show re-opened in its supposed 'graveyard slot' of 10 p.m. on Saturdays, the main measure of its continued hipness was the interrupted business in trendy Manhattan bars and restaurants.

One establishment called Mike's American Bar hung logs and doughnuts from the ceiling, with the *coup de grâce* of a plastic-shrouded Laura Palmer mannequin; further upmarket, one NYC restaurant served *'Twin Peaks* oysters' – caught in Snoqualmie, Washington State, Lynch–Frost's main shooting location.

Downtown bars swayed to the finger-clicking rhythms of 'Audrey's Dance', Badalamenti becoming the first soundtrack composer hip enough for loft dwellers to collect on CD since Herrmann, Morricone and Elmer Bernstein. The fashionable Manhattan set was still wild about the show – but was Small-town, USA, keeping the faith?

TWIN PEAKS — Season Two (1990/91)

The photo-portrait of murdered prom queen Laura Palmer (Sheryl Lee), which ran with the end-credits of nearly every episode of **Twin Peaks**. Even after the Palmer mystery was resolved in Episode 16, the show continued to play out with the photo and the melancholy 'Laura's Theme' by Badalamenti.

Episode 8 (95 minutes without commercials) Written by Mark Frost/Story by David Lynch and Mark Frost (credit applies throughout)/Directed by David Lynch.

Special Agent Cooper lies on the floor, bleeding from his chest; Deputy Andy tries futilely to call him down the phone line, while a genial, imbecilic old waiter brings Coop his warm milk, too senile to organise an emergency phone call.

As Coop retreats into unconsciousness, the lanky figure of the dumb waiter fades, to be replaced by a bald giant who nearly touches the ceiling. 'We want to help you,' he tells Coop, and reveals three prophecies. 'There's a man with a smiling bag; the owls are not what they seem; without chemicals, he points.' For good measure, he adds, 'Leo inside a hungry horse – there's a clue at Leo's house.' He takes Coop's ring, which he will return once the agent has uncovered the truth of his statements.

*One of the **Twin Peaks** eternal triangles: duplicitous lovers Catherine Martell (Piper Laurie) and Ben Horne (Richard Beymer, right), flanked by Catherine's put-upon husband Pete (Jack Nance, left).*

At One-Eyed Jack's, Ben tries to force his way into the boudoir of 'Prudence', the new girl; Audrey, putting on a fragile voice, believes she's talked him into going away.

Coop is rescued, and, at the hospital, Doc Hayward shows him a bullet crowned by a squashed woodtick. Coop insists on getting back to work, despite his broken ribs and torn cartilage: 'Just give me two hours to get dressed.'

At the Palmer house, Sarah and Maddy are shocked to find Leland's hair has turned white overnight. As he leaves the room, terrified Maddy focuses on a carpet stain which grows into the ferocious face of Killer Bob.

The lawmen search Leo Johnson's place and find a stash of cocaine. Maddy meets Donna at the Double R, looking sultry in feline dark glasses that formerly belonged to Laura. Donna draws on a cigarette like a glamorous bad girl when she visits James in jail, coming on strong to him through the bars.

Under interrogation, James tells Harry – who believes in the kid's innocence – about a time in the woods when the coked-up Laura recited her 'scary poem' ('Fire Walk With Me'), and asked whether he wanted to play with fire; to play with 'Bob'. Coop interrupts the interview to tell James he knows the boy holds the other half of Laura's necklace; he hands it over, but tells how he found it hidden inside a coconut in Dr Jacoby's office.

Coop gives Andy and Lucy every issue of Flesh World to leaf through, to try to find a photo of Teresa Banks – the killer's downstate victim of one year previously – whose photo, he believes, will appear as did those of Laura and Ronnette.

In hospital, Dr Jacoby recovers from a mild heart attack. Under informal interrogation, Jacoby admits he spied on James and Donna when they went into the woods one night – digging up the necklace after the boy buried it. He also opines that, in the last days of her life, Laura brought herself peace by making a resolution to die. 'Laura didn't commit suicide,' retorts Coop, to which Jacoby replies she may have allowed herself to be killed.

Away from Jacoby's bed, Coop notices the unzipped body bag used to transport Jacques Renault's mortal remains – it looks as if it may be smiling, as in the clue given by the giant.

At a doughnuts-and-coffee session, Coop reiterates the known scenario for Laura's last night on earth, with the added factor of 'the third man' now believed to have raped and tortured her and Ronnette in the abandoned rail car – with Laura and Renault dead, Ronnette and Leo in comas, the third man is all that's left of the case.

At the Horne offices, Ben and Jerry complain to Hank that Leo wasn't killed; he's in a coma, with damage to the spinal column and nervous system – but congratulate him on the fire at the mill.

At One-Eyed Jack's, a heavy drags Audrey in to see Blackie who wants to know why she wouldn't go with the owner – Audrey answers that he wasn't her type. 'Who is your type?' growls Blackie. 'No offence, but not you,' she tells the glamorous, long-legged dyke, and is hoisted up by the heavy.

The Palmers are guests at a Hayward family musical evening. One of Donna's younger sisters recites a childishly moving poem about Laura, with images of the woods at night, and Laura lost in the midst of it all. Leland tells the Doc he believes the overnight whitening of his hair is a turning point, at which the sadness still remains but a weight has been lifted. On his feet, he sings 'Get Happy', going further and further up-tempo till he reaches fever pitch and blacks out. Revived with smelling salts, Leland tells the Doc he feels happy.

In her boudoir at One-Eyed Jack's, Audrey talks aloud to 'my special agent', wishing he could hear her. She imagines she's telling Coop that the link between her father's department store and One-Eyed Jack's (girls for the latter recruited from the former's perfume counter by Emery Bassett, store manager) is the key to Laura's murder. She believes Coop will have found the note she delivered under his door, unaware he was shot soon after.

In hospital, the comatose Ronnette is suddenly disturbed by a vision of the demonic Killer Bob, come to tear her to pieces. Her cerebral monitor reveals the intrusive phantom has woken her up.

The credits play out on a piece of boogie-woogie piano, played by a little girl in a fairy dress from the Hayward family get-together scene.

As much as the initial reviews were overwhelmingly favourable, *Variety*'s notice for 30 September, 1990 speculated that, 'Those not already addicted to the show could easily have decided not to bother.'

Slow fades in failing light; the recurring motif of a hanging traffic light when the teenagers try to flee some aspect of their lives; the camera's sustained fixation on some obscure object whose significance wouldn't be revealed till later. Where even a single shot or a seemingly throwaway line might have reverberations later in the episode, or even later in the series, such threads were not easily picked up once lost.

Episode 9
Written by Harley Peyton/Directed by David Lynch

Coop and Albert take breakfast at the Great Northern. Coop intends to show Ronnette sketches of 'Bob', now she's reached a form of semi-consciousness. Albert confides that his main reason for coming back to Twin Peaks is to inform Coop that his psychotic former partner, Windom Earle, has escaped from the laughing academy. All the time, the two agents are watched by a mysterious, pony-tailed Chinaman.

Donna has taken over Laura's meals-on-wheels round, to look for potential clues. She visits the home of old Mrs Tremond, who's watched by her little grandson in a dinner jacket and bow-tie. (This blond, miniature version of the director, with his customary brushed back crew-cut, is played by seven-year-old Austin Lynch.) The creamed corn in the pie and mash dinner disappears and reappears in the hands of the little boy, who's 'studying magic'. When Donna asks about Laura, the old lady tells her that 'Mr Smith next door' was a good friend of hers.

Lynch's party-piece: FBI controller Gordon Cole (David Lynch) briefs Agent Cooper (Kyle MacLachlan) in the sombre **Twin Peaks – Fire Walk With Me** . *In the TV show's more light-hearted scenes, Lynch got great comic mileage out of his role as Coop's ebullient, stone-deaf superior.*

In hospital Ronnette is shown sketches of Leo, Jacques and Bob. She responds hysterically to the latter, with a virtual seizure.

Coop and Harry arrive to find Hank waiting to report in, under his terms of parole; Coop detects they're former buddies. As he leaves, they're contacted by Ben Horne, who tells them that Audrey's been missing for at least two days.

At One-Eyed Jack's, Audrey grabs the job of pandering to a masochist. Making a ligature round the throat of her already-restrained john – Bassett, her former manager – she forces him to admit the connection between the store and One-Eyed Jack's, as well as revealing that her father owns the cathouse. He squeals that Ben Horne always made it his business to entertain all the girls, including Laura and Ronnette, and that Laura was thrown out of Jack's for her drug habit.

Bobby tells Shelly she can't be made to testify against her husband, Leo, in any Palmer case murder trial. Instead, he encourages her to move him home and claim the $5,000 per month insurance money she's entitled to as long as Leo doesn't go to prison.

Major Briggs calls Coop and gives an outline of his classified defence work for the government, which involves monitoring audio signals from the far reaches of outer space. On a computer print-out for the night of his shooting, Coop sees a break in the 'usual gibberish': the phrase 'the owls are not what they seem' appears, echoing the giant's words, as well as a constant repetition of the name 'Cooper'.

James sings a mutated, 50s-style love song, with Donna and Maddy on backing vocals. Donna receives a call from Harold Smith, Mrs Tremond's next-door neighbour and Laura's former friend, who agrees to meet her. Meanwhile, Maddy has a vision of Killer Bob clambering over the furniture to get to her.

Coop also has nightmare visions of Bob – his maniacal face transposed with that of an owl, the violated Ronnette and tormented Sarah Palmer. He's snapped back to consciousness by a phone call from Audrey; Coop expresses more paternal concern than her father, telling her to stop her childish *games and return home; she confides to him that she's in trouble. 'You've no idea how much trouble you're in, Miss Horne,' Blackie sneers while listening in to their telephone conversation.*

Episodes 10–13.

Writers: Robert Engels/Jerry Stahl, Harley Peyton, Mark Frost and Engels/Barry Pullman/Peyton and Engels. Directors: Lesli Linka Glatter (10 & 13)/Todd Holland/Graeme Clifford.

Gerard, the one-armed man, spots the wanted poster, recognising the menacing longhair as 'Bob'. Gordon Cole (played by Lynch), Coop's regional supervisor from the FBI, arrives noisily. Sporting a hearing aid from each ear, the deaf-but-ebullient Gordon shouts, at the top of his voice, that he always makes contact when there's a man down in the field. When Gerard is brought in he ignites Gordon's obvious prior knowledge: 'There's the one-armer now!' he hollers. (Much conjecture was spent at the time on whether Gordon Cole was an embodiment of some Lynchian obsession with sensory deprivation – which, if existent, had previously been confined to the severed ear and blind hardware store clerk of *Blue Velvet*. Lynch made the character a grotesque comic device, with stone-deaf Gordon repeating everyone's unheard statements as if they're his own suggestions.) *Gordon tells Coop he doesn't want him getting in too deep, 'like in Pittsburgh'.*

Donna visits Harold Smith, Laura's old meals-on-wheels customer, who turns out to be a nervous young agoraphobic. He reads her a passage from Laura's secret diary. She playfully snatches the diary, forcing him outside, but relents as he goes into psychosomatic convulsions. Harold discovers Maddy stealing the diary; in front of the two shocked girls, he mutilates his face with a garden hoe.

At One-Eyed Jack's, Audrey is bound and injected with heroin by Blackie and Jean Renault, sinister brother of the late Jacques. Ben receives a chilling message: Renault awaits him, with a ransom video of Audrey. Coop finds Audrey's long discarded note; it becomes clear she was heading for One-Eyed Jack's. Upon raiding the place, he can barely raise her from her opiated stupor. Harry finds the CCTV, watching Jean murder Blackie by stabbing her in the back.

Leland tells the cops the man in the wanted poster had a summer house alongside his grandparents at Pearl Lakes. Coop and Harry visit the convalescing Jacoby, putting him under hypnosis to recall the night Jacques Renault was suffocated in the adjacent hospital bed. The camera travels through a vortex of white fabric resembling an eye socket (as per the emergent camera in Eraserhead *and* The Elephant Man*), to reveal a stunned Leland. He admits he went to Calhoun Memorial Hospital to kill the man he believes killed his daughter. Gerard, the one-armed man, undergoes convulsions – a calmer, more dominant personality overtakes him. Asked if Bob inhabits our world, he replies that he currently resides in a huge wooden house with many people and many rooms all the same. 'The Great Northern Hotel,' deduces Coop.*

On 31 October, 1990, casting director Johanna Ray took the Casting Society of America's Artios award for dramatic episodic casting – recognition, at least, that the off-kilter storylines and numerous red herrings had been carried off with aplomb by the show's carefully chosen cast of wanna-bes and near has-beens. To a small degree at least, industry recognition had made apologies for the snubbing of Peaks' first season in that year's major Emmy awards.

Episode 14

Written by Mark Frost/Directed by David Lynch

Hawk is assigned to search Harold's home for Laura's diary. Gordon confirms torn pages were found down the track from the abandoned railcar where she was killed.

At the Great Northern, Gerard, the one-armed man, is presented with a seemingly endless stream of employees to identify (male and female), all dressed in sailors' suits. He undergoes a psychotic seizure, bringing an infuriated Ben to the lobby.

Hawk discovers Harold hanging in the greenhouse, with a suicide note: 'Je suis un homme solitaire.' The cops retrieve Laura's secret diary.

At the Johnson place, Shelly and Bobby work out her finances: when all medical and insurance costs are deducted, she's left with $42 a month. 'That's a good start,' her young brat lover tells her, unaware of what it costs to keep her and Leo (semi-) alive. While they argue over money, Leo makes a loud, animalistic grunting. 'He's alive!' screams Shelly. 'He's not alive,' claims Bobby, who's trying to work out what Leo did with his money.

Audrey confronts Ben with her knowledge about One-Eyed Jack's. An even greater blow comes with her bold admission she was 'Prudence', the masked sex kitten who evaded him. Undaunted, she forces him to confess he slept with Laura. When asked if he killed her, he can only whisper a response: 'I loved her.'

Coop memos his findings from the remains of Laura Palmer's secret diary to Diane. Laura seems to have suffered abuse and molestation by Bob – who, she intimates, is a friend of her father's – since her early teens.

It's at this point that Lynch and Frost stand accused of manipulation of the most hopelessly devoted Peakies, to a cunning commercial degree.

Published in late September, as a paperback compliment for the start of the new season, *The Secret Diary of Laura Palmer* was by this time selling in very respectable quantities. Written by Lynch's 22-year-old daughter, Jennifer, giving a feminine insight into Laura's mounting inner confusion, the limitations of the subject matter – what could and what could not be revealed – were dictated by her father and his fellow executive producer. What does *not* appear in the book at all, however, despite its supposed compatibility with the secret diary discovered in the series, is any direct insinuation that the omnipresent Bob is a friend of Leland – clearly, Lynch and Frost were happy to whet the appetite (and make a buck or two from licensing deals), but were holding back the juicier clues until Lynch could be persuaded to spill his well-kept secret.

Audrey tells Coop what she's gleaned from her father, eager for him to be arrested. He tells Harry to obtain a warrant; he believes the giant's prophecy – 'without chemicals, he points' – refers to the convulsive Gerard, who pointed to Ben as he stormed into the lobby of the Great Northern.

The cops tell Ben he's wanted for questioning in the murder of Laura Palmer. He flies into a blustering rage and is dragged away by Andy and Hawk.

At the Palmer house, a near-unconscious Sarah crawls down the stairs, dragging her lower half along the floor. She can't reach the phone and receives no help from her indifferent husband, while a played-out 78rpm record spins on its end-groove.

As Ben is hauled off to the holding cells, the Log Lady appears at the station: 'The owls are in the Roadhouse,' she tells Coop and Harry. 'It's happening again, isn't it?' asks Coop.

The delirious Sarah has a vision of a white horse appearing in her living room. As it fades, she slumps to the floor, unconscious. Over by the dressing mirror, Leland cheerfully tidies himself, despite his wife's plight. As he smiles, the demonic reflection which grins back is that of Killer Bob.

'I only found out the day that we shot Maddy's death scene,' said Sheryl Lee. 'David took Leland Palmer and Ben Horne and me into his office,' she continued, blurring actors and roles, 'and David doesn't have any furniture in his office, so we sat on the floor in the dark with just this one small light on and he said, "Okay, I'm now going to tell you who did it, what you've all been waiting for." And, you know, we'd already waited a year and a half for this. We were all guessing, and everybody held these lists of suspects and facts of who was where at what time. David said, "Ray Wise, Leland, *you* did it. And Sheryl Lee – *you're* gonna die again.'

'When David and I were working on *Twin Peaks*,' recalled Frost, 'our disagreements would mostly revolve around the fact that I wished for more clarity and David wanted to draw things out a little bit more – I mean, I think if David had had his way, we might *still* not know who killed Laura Palmer.'

Coop, Harry and the Log Lady attend the Roadhouse together. The singer (Julee Cruise) moves into the eerily romantic 'The World Spins'. (Which also served as the finale for Industrial Symphony No. 1.) *After the first couple of bars, Coop sees her fade from the stage. The giant takes her place, announcing, 'It's happening again.'*

Leland slips on white gloves. As Maddy enters the living room, she immediately sees Bob standing in Leland's place. She screams and runs, but Leland/Bob is quickly on top of her. He punches her fiercely in the face several times, leaving her dazed and bloodied. In a chillingly choreographed scene, Leland dances the wounded Maddy around in his arms, talking to her as if she was his dear, murdered Laura. In slow motion, with grinding sound effects, Maddy sees herself as under attack by the homicidal Bob. Leland/Bob shouts at her, 'You're going home . . . to Missoula . . . Montana!', then smashes her head with great force into a picture frame. (Note the macabre biographical references, to Lynch's birthplace and his former occupation of picture frame seller.) Maddy crumples into a bloody heap, dead. Her killer inserts a letter of his name at the bottom of one of her fingernails.

At the Roadhouse, the giant disappears from Coop's view, replaced by the band. To the atmospheric tones of 'The World Spins', everyone associated with the Palmers feels instinctively disturbed; Donna bursts into tears. The old waiter from the Great Northern, whose appearance is an echo of the giant, tells Coop: 'I'm very sorry.'

Final freeze on the red velvet curtains of the stage. Credits roll to the continuing sound of Julee Cruise.

Episodes 15–23.

Writers: Scott Frost (15 & 21)/Mark Frost, Harley Peyton and Robert Engels/Tricia Brock (17 & 23) /Barry Pullman/Peyton and Engels (20 & 22)/Peyton. Directors: Caleb Deschanel (15 & 19)/Tim Hunter/Tina Rathborne/Duwayne Dunham/Todd Holland/Uli Edel/Diane Keaton/Lesli Linka Glatter.

Inside Leland's golfing bag, he carries Maddy's body wrapped in plastic. He drives maniacally around narrow, bending roads with her dead weight in the trunk of the car. The lawmen retrieve Maddy's corpse, with the letter 'O' at the bottom of her fingernail.

Donna is given a letter mailed by Harold on the day he died. It's an extract from Laura's diary dated 22nd February, telling of her dream of a red-curtained room, a dwarf, and an old man (an aged Coop) she believed might be able to help her. Gerard refers to his former killing partnership with Bob as a 'circle of gold'; Coop associates this with the ring he gave the giant, which will be returned once he's solved the mystery. Leland is told the cops are gathering a number of suspects together. 'Señor Droolcup', the old waiter from the Great Northern, offers him a stick of gum, which he's delighted to find was his favourite brand as a kid. 'That gum you like is coming back,' the waiter tells him – an exact quote from the surreal dream in the first season, to which Coop is immediately returned, at last

The second season of **Twin Peaks** *delved further into the mysteries surrounding beautiful Oriental widow Josie Packard (Joan Chen), until she was revealed as the* **femme fatale** *who shot Agent Cooper after that particular sub-plot had been all but discarded.*

recollecting what Laura whispered in his ear: 'My father killed me.' The giant returns Coop's ring. At the holding cell, Ben is yanked out of the way and Leland pushed in. He goes berserk, charging the walls like some raging demon. Bob talks via Leland, promising that when he 'pulls the ripcord' Leland will remember everything. He launches himself/Leland against the iron door. Leland tells how Bob and other presences used his body; when they found Laura writing about Bob in her diary, she had to die. Dying, Leland says he can see the light, where his beautiful daughter waits for him.

Audrey comes to say goodbye to Coop: 'So you're going to save my life, break my heart and run?' He says that someone he loved was hurt because of him: 'She died in my arms . . . I was badly wounded. My partner, Windom Earle, lost his mind.' On a night-fishing expedition, Major Briggs asks Coop if he's heard of a place called the White Lodge; he hasn't, but wants to know more after he relieves his coffee-filled bladder. The Major disappears in a sudden eruption of white light. Hawk tells Coop about the mythical White Lodge, where the spirits who rule the world reside, and its opposite number, the Black Lodge, where the darker self dwells. Coop receives a postal message from Windom Earle, describing a chess move. USAF Colonel Riley tells Coop that, though their monitors are fixed on deep space, the warning Major Briggs gave him came from somewhere in the woods. Briggs re-appears in flashes of lightning – unaware he's been away for two days. He admits an involvement with Project Blue Book – the UFO-watching project which officially ended in 1969, when many of its participants trained their sights earthward towards the White Lodge. Doc Hayward shows Harry and Coop photos of three strangely-shaped scars beneath the Major's right ear.

In the darkened sheriff's office, the cops find the corpse of an unidentified, murdered man tied to Harry's chair. 'This is the first move in a very sick game of chess,' says Coop. He confides that his lover, Caroline, was Windom Earle's wife. Albert shows him the contents of packages sent to regional law enforcement agencies: pieces of Caroline Earle's wedding dress. At the head of his bed, Coop finds a life-mask of Caroline's face. Moving the mask activates a cassette recorder. Windom's voice reflects on how he still loves Caroline, despite what happened in Pittsburgh.

In the dead of night, Harry's woken by Josie outside the window – beaten, bruised, partly clothed, an echo of Dorothy in Blue Velvet. She tells Harry about Mr Eckahart, the businessman who became her father/master/lover. She's received an ultimatum that he will kill her if she doesn't return to him.

Catherine offers salvation: Josie can become her maid, obeying her every order, unless she wants her to 'find this Eckahart, and feed you to him piece by piece.' Josie falls away, to be overtaken by the shadow of her supposedly dead husband, Andrew. At the Great Northern, Eckahart (British character actor David Warner) books in. Coop meets good ol' Pete carrying two armfuls of Josie's drycleaning. As he helps him out, Coop excises a small patch of fabric from one garment. Albert matches the fibres found on Josie's coat with those found outside Coop's door after the shooting.

Leo attacks Shelly with an axe; as she stabs him with a steak knife, he takes off with an agonised scream. Brain-damaged 'Leo-stein' comes upon a shack where the occupant introduces himself as Windom Earle. He activates an electrode placed on Leo's neck.

Entering Eckahart's room with pistol drawn, Coop sees him drop dead. Josie claims self defence. 'Is that what you'll say about me, Josie?' seethes Coop, angry for the first time. By the time Harry cradles her in his arms, she's dead – without a mark on her body. Coop has a vision of Killer Bob, sneering, 'What happened to Josie, Coop?' He sees the dwarf dancing on the bed; Josie's face is trapped within a radio dial turned to flesh.

One day prior to the airing of Episode 23 on Saturday 16 February, 1991, the ABC network hastily announced the series was going 'on hiatus' – in other words, they were pulling the show.

The increasingly troubled production – which had already been hit by a crew strike in early November – had its final six segments postponed indefinitely on the network schedules. No notice was given of cancellation, no one at the network officially ruling out a third season – but by no account was it looking feasible, however, Lynch already taking the provision of making the final episode (29) into a near-apocalyptic climax.

At a press conference on 22 February, creators/executive producers/directors/co-writers Lynch–Frost implored all Peakies to come to the aid of the show. 'We feel that there's people out there that really love *Twin Peaks*,' appealed an earnest Lynch. 'We're in trouble and we need their help.'

Those who couldn't live without their weekly helping of cherry pie, cod-mysticism and murder were urged to write to the new Killer Bob – ABC Entertainment president Bob Iger – and demand the show's return to a prime time week night slot. Since the Saturday night relocation, *Peaks* had steadily and progressively plummeted down the ratings, threatening to make itself a major advertiser's no-man's land. 'Partying is very important to a great deal of people,' rationalised Lynch – referring both to the Saturday night partygoer's aversion to watching the show at transmission time, and to the student-ish ritual of throwing '*Peaks* parties', making the original week-night showings into an event, instead of just another hour in front of the tube. 'People had an excuse to have a party on a weeknight. It wouldn't be good on Mondays or Tuesdays because they're still recuperating from the weekend.'

'I'm sure it has something to do with what's happening in the show,' admitted Mark Frost, almost setting up a counter-argument to his partner. 'We can't lay all this at the feet of programming.'

Indeed they couldn't. Since the resolution of the Palmer case in Episode 16, *Twin Peaks* effectively lost half its audience – whereas more than half the original audience for the pilot film had already fallen off over the intervening six months, due to lack of patience with the plot. From hereon, the show was based around Special Agent Cooper, his tragic past, newfound love, and the homicidal contest with his former partner.

The amount of narrative information thrown at the viewer had already been much more than any soap opera junkie had ever been asked to assimilate: one recurring sub-plot either resolved or introduced every fourth or fifth episode. At its most elaborate point of the second season, *Twin Peaks* gave the viewer eleven separate narrative strands – as compared with between three and five per episode for the glossy *Dallas/Dynasty*-type soap. Against this, the 'previously on *Twin Peaks'* recap at the beginning of each show was an impressionistic smorgasbord of past events, not necessarily corresponding in any direct way with what was about to be shown.

Coupled with this, what constituted a major thread of the story, or a red herring, or random plot-device, was largely left to the viewer's discernment. Coop's shooting, back at the end of the first season, was supposedly the conventional cliffhanger to hold devotees of the show over from one season to the next. And yet, here in Episode 23, fifteen episodes later, was only the third point at which the shooting was explicitly referred to, let alone solved.

Continuing sub-plots concerning the secondary characters could still hold the interest – the mystery of Josie Packard, the fluctuating fortunes of Ben Horne, the Norma/Ed/Nadine love triangle, the whimsical comedy of Lynch's appearances as Gordon Cole, the deaf FBI supervisor – but, equally, as sub-plots began to multiply, some were, in true soap opera fashion, merely silly and banal: a *femme fatale* murder plot, which eased James Marshall out of the series, was hackneyed and failed to convince; a whirlwind love affair for Audrey – not yet seen before the series got yanked – was similarly pointless, except that it married, unconvincingly, voguish environmental concerns with an emotional, *Casablanca*-type airport farewell.

If anyone was to stay the course from here on, it was because they were enamoured with that mystic Eagle Scout, Coop, his war with the Luciferian Windom Earle, and the question of what was really out there in the woods and the Black Lodge. Subverting New Age wackiness into a strain of gothic horror, the pervading theme of the final episodes – with its paranoia about military cover-ups and unknown life forces – plays, with hindsight, very much like a less streamlined precursor of the hugely successful *X-Files*.

'Networks have to be responsible to their audience,' said Frost, lining up with Lynch on the question of Peakies being a sizeable-enough minority to wield influence. 'And we certainly hope that will be the case here.'

Backtracking fast from the original risks they took on the show (though it should be remembered the airing of the pilot was delayed for five months), ABC would eventually honour their reponsibility to the audience they created.

The last six episodes of *Twin Peaks* finally found a Monday night slot, running from 13 May onwards. By 25 May, however, the series was officially cancelled.

At the same time as ABC gave their vote of no confidence, Lynch's high standing in Europe was aiming him back toward his 'proper job' of film director.

On 13 February – two days before the network announced they were postponing the final *Peaks* episodes – the movie painter signed a film deal to the tune of $70 million, at the Paris home of construction tycoon and cineaste Francis Bouygues. Keen to channel much of his own capital into the film industry, the Frenchman had set up a production company, CiBy 2000, whose intial projects included three by Lynch. 'We're interested in long-term collaborations and so is Lynch,' said CiBy production head Pierre Edelman.

The first film, budgeted at $25 million, was to be, at last, *Ronnie Rocket*: fourteen years in the planning, as yet uncast, but scheduled to begin shooting in July 1991. Described by Edelman as typical Lynch, the surrealistic comedy, with elements of science fiction and rock 'n' roll, was much less vulnerable to a producer's interference than it would be if backed by a US production company.

After years of logjam, Lynch's film career was seemingly re-vitalised: next on the schedule, the delayed Lynch–Frost project, *One Saliva Bubble*, and one other, unspecified title, the nature of which would soon become apparent.

Despite *Twin Peaks'* shuddering to an admirably surreal end, Spelling Entertainment expressed interest in a possible movie spin-off Lynch had been planning since earlier that year – as did CiBy 2000. For the time being, the decision was left to Lynch and Frost, as joint copyright holders of the show, to choose whether the feature would ultimately work within similar restrictions to the TV series, but with a higher budget, or would have the relative freedom of an art movie, aimed towards the European Lynch mob.

Episodes 24–28.

Writers: Barry Pullman (24 & 28) / Harley Peyton and Robert Engels (25 & 27) / Mark Frost and Peyton. Directors: James Foley / Duwayne Dunham / Jonathan Sanger (producer of The Elephant Man*) / Stephen Gyllenhall / Tim Hunter.*

Harry drown his sorrows in Southern Comfort, reliving memories of Josie. 'Agent Dale Cooper!' rings out the dulcet tones of Gordon Cole: 'Brace yourself, Harry,' Coop warns the hungover sheriff. Earle is bugging Harry's office. Gordon tells Coop that Earle was loaned to the airforce for two years in the mid–'60s on Project Blue Book. Suddenly distracted by a bonsai plant, Gordon mistakes the word for the Japanese war cry ('Banzai!') in WWII movies: 'BONSAI!' he hollers, almost perforating the eardrums of eavesdropping Earle.

At the Double R, Norma's younger sister Annie arrives. She freely admits how strange life is outside the convent. Coop is visited by Major Briggs and the Log Lady; she shows him two large triangular shapes at the back of her leg, similar to the three marks on the Major's neck. Annie brings Coop his coffee. He tells her how he ended up sticking around in Twin Peaks, wondering if maybe she intends doing the same. He notices a scar across her wrist. Coop draws an intersecting pattern on a napkin – as Lynch had once planned Eraserhead, *back in the days of Bob's diner – based on Major Briggs' and the Log Lady's scars. Annie notes how his napkin drawing is a ringer for the wall art at Owl Cave. 'Harry, I don't know where this is leading us, but it's somewhere strange and wonderful,' he enthuses, Lynch-like.*

Donna tells Doc Hayward that his old friend, Gerald Craig, passed by on his way to a conference in Spokane. (Another of the small towns the young David Lynch grew up in.) The doc tells his daughter that Gerald was his room-mate when he was a student, and drowned in a canoe accident despite his attempts to save him. Earle shows zombified Leo some card tricks. He gives him three Queens: Shelly, Donna and Audrey, and produces a blank Queen of Hearts to match with the Miss Twin Peaks competition flyer. Earle descends into Owl Cave with a flashlight, as excited by the symbols as Coop.

In a boat on Pearl Lakes, Coop talks to Annie about her past. They kiss. Earle spies on them through binoculars. He leaves the cops a wooden crate with a rope-pull; inside, they find an entombed corpse, with a placard reading, 'Next time it will be someone you know.' Major Briggs shows Coop and Harry some black and white cinefilm: a young Earle talks of the Black Lodge, a place of limitless evil and power. Coop sees that Earle's pilgrimage to Twin Peaks and murder spree were red herrings, designed to lead him to the Black Lodge. He meets with Shelly, Donna and Audrey; they confirm they've all been approached by eccentric but personable old men over the last few days. Major Briggs is approached by a vaudeville horse – Earle's most elaborate disguise yet. Inviting him to the Project Blue Book reunion, the horse fires a large syringe into the Major's chest.

Coop and Annie dance cheek to cheek; she tells him she's entering the Miss Twin Peaks contest. Coop has a vision of the giant, waving and mouthing the word 'No'. Windom identifies the cave symbols as 'an invitation and a map of the Black Lodge'. Leo manages to break the Major's manacles, urging him to 'save Shelly'. Windom bids a fond farewell to Leo, who he ties to a cage full of tarantulas. Coop emerges from meditation in lieu of sleep – one more resemblance to David Lynch – to tell Diane about his feelings for Annie. He believes a period of intense astrological change will signify the opening of the Black Lodge. His next lateral deduction is that chess-playing Earle will seek to enter the Lodge via the Queen – targeting Miss Twin Peaks. Bobby, eyeing passing babes, spots the Log Lady both at the bar and in the lobby simultaneously; he's bludgeoned with a log by Windom Earle. Doc Hayward announces the winner of this year's Miss Twin Peaks award: Annie Blackburn. Suddenly, the auditorium is thrown into darkness; explosives and flares go off. Earle descends from the rafters in middle-aged lady drag.

Episode 29
Written by Mark Frost, Harley Peyton and Robert Engels/Directed by David Lynch

Andy comforts Lucy after the beauty pageant chaos; he reflects how she could have given birth to her baby in the elevator, 'in front of God and everyone'.

Harry tells Coop neither Windom Earle nor Annie can be found anywhere; Coop sees their only clue in the hieroglyphic map, one of the symbols of which he now recognises as a little man on fire: 'Fire Walk With Me,' he recalls Laura Palmer's poem.

Pete rushes into the sheriff's office, saying the Log Lady stole his truck. He tells how she took off in the direction of the woods, with 12 rainbow trout in the car. Lateral thinking and mystical connections are now in overdrive: Harry tells them about the circle of 12 sycamore trees at Glastonbury Grove, which Coop connects with the burial place of King Arthur.

The Log Lady arrives; Pete demands to know where his truck is, but Coop persuades him she's not the thief. She's brought along a jar of what appears to be engine oil – on the night before he died, her husband told her it was the key to another world. Coop takes it seriously, calling in Ronnette Pulaski to smell the dark gunk; when she recoils, telling him she smelled it the night Laura died, he knows they're on to something.

In the woods, Windom Earle drives Annie towards the circle of trees; she asks him why he doesn't kill her and get it over with, but he replies that he likes 'the fear'. She's manacled to him; as he strides towards the trees, she recites the 23rd Psalm. He tells her that he once 'took the little boy [Coop] to the edge', when he fell in love with his wife, and he intends to do it again. 'They are not dead,' he tells her enigmatically, 'they clasp your hand and mine.' Within the circle of trees, she suddenly becomes entranced. 'You will not leave me,' he promises her.

At the Hayward house, the doc arrives home; there's trouble when he realises Ben's told Donna he's her biological father; 'I only wanted to do good,' pleads Ben, 'to tell the truth.' 'You're my daddy, you're my daddy!' Donna wails to Doc Hayward. The doc, worked into a howling rage, punches Ben and sends him flying into the stone fireplace, leaving him motionless with a bloody forehead fracture – seemingly dead.

Coop and Harry find Pete's abandoned truck; Coop insists he has to go alone beyond this point. Under the owls' gaze, he finds the circle where Windom and Annie disappeared within the sycamore trees; watching from a distance, Harry sees him literally disappear into the night.

Coop recognises the familiar red velvet curtains of what must have been, all along, the Black Lodge; a saxophone chord vibrates, the dancing dwarf appears. A cadaverous crooner (Jimmy Scott) sings a dramatic torch song – with trademark, perversely innocent Lynch lyrics – called 'Sycamore Trees', then fades into the air with the last note.

Deputy Andy finds Sheriff Truman in the woods; ten hours later, in the daylight, Harry's still staring at the same circular pool of water within the sycamores.

Audrey enters the Twin Peaks Savings and Loan Bank; she tells the aged manager to phone the Twin Peaks Gazette, *letting them know Audrey Horne's chaining herself to the bank's vault in protest against the Ghostwood development project threatening the woodlands. Outside the vault, a guard scurries to the phone with the news that Lucy's given birth to a boy. Andrew Packard and Pete work their way through bank deposit boxes, eventually finding one rented by Eckahart. As the two brothers-in-law open it in excitement, they find a scrawled note from the South African: 'Got you now, Andrew!' Too late, they realise he's rigged a bomb which blows out the walls of the entire bank. Outside, Packard's spectacles land in the roadside foliage, along with raining dollar bills.*

At the Double R, different generations of couples – Major and Mrs Briggs, Bobby and Shelly – sit cooing sweetly to each other. Bobby tells Shelly not to worry about Leo: 'He's probably having the time of his life,' intercut with Leo's terrified face, joined by a tooth to the tarantula cage.

Dr Jacoby and a frazzled Sarah Palmer enter together; they sit with the Briggses, Jacoby telling the Major there's a message Sarah has to give him. In the distorted/reversed voice of the dwarf/Man From Another Place, she tells him: 'I'm in the Black Lodge with Annie and Cooper.'

'I'm waiting for you,' continues the dwarf's voice, among the red curtains and black-and-white zigzagged flooring. 'When you see me again, it won't be me,' the little guy says to Coop, telling him he's in a waiting room, and some of his friends are here. Laura Palmer appears before him, promising they'll meet again in 25 years' time – as per the dream in the first season when Coop was wrinkled and greying. 'Señor Droolcup', the old waiter from the Great Northern appears, taking forever to bring a cup of congealed, gunky coffee; as Coop tries to swallow it, the waiter becomes the giant, telling him things are not as they seem. 'Wow, Bob, wow,' says the dwarf, evoking the unseen demon. At the invoking words, 'Fire Walk With Me', infernal visions ignite. Coop makes a run for the corridor. Each frantic attempt to find a different part of the Black Lodge brings him back to the same identical room. Maddy appears briefly, telling him to watch out for her cousin; Laura reappears, screaming, possessed, with blank demonic eyes. As Coop makes for the corridor again, he finds himself bleeding from a stomach wound; as he re-enters the room, he finds himself lying on the floor, as in Pittsburgh, mortally wounded alongside the dying Caroline – who then turns into Annie. Annie returns to life, telling him she knows the name of the man who killed her, that she will live if he gives up his soul for her; he agrees that he will. Windom Earle appears, demanding he gives up his soul; suddenly, Windom is racked with terror and pain, as feral Killer Bob holds him by the shoulders. 'He was wrong,' Bob growls gleefully to Coop, 'he cannot ask for your soul; I will take his. You go.' Windom's pain is nullified by a bolt of flame Bob sends through his skull; he becomes motionless, zombified. Bob laughs maniacally. As Coop flees to the corridor once more, a different, demon-eyed, malevolent Coop waits in the wings. In the corridor, Leland Palmer makes pleading eye contact with him, asking him to believe he never killed anyone – but his eyes are as demonic as those of his screaming daughter. As Coop runs for the exit – or a different room – his dark doppelganger appears, laughing along with demonic Leland; Coop runs through sets of red curtains again and again, pursued all the time by his evil double.

In the dead of night, Harry finds Coop and Annie lying unconscious outside the sycamore circle.

Back at his hotel room, Coop awakes to find himself tended by Doc Hayward (having presumably colluded in the disposal of Ben Horne's body) and Harry. 'How's Annie?' he asks, to be told she's in hospital but she's going to be fine. He says he wants to clean his teeth, walking stiffly aloof to the bathroom; squeezing all the toothpaste out into the sink, he stares at the glimmer of a malevolent smile in the mirror. 'How's Annie?' he mocks his own question, repeating it as he headbutts the mirror. The doc and Harry hear the shattering, making for the bathroom; inside, the injured Coop's smile is gleefully demonic, the reflection grinning back at him that of Killer Bob.

The credits of this final episode play out over Laura Palmer's reflection in a coffee cup.

Twin Peaks reached a genuinely surrealistic climax on US TV, Monday 10 June 1991. Lynch's final episode is a little-recognised classic, bringing the supernatural world-beyond-the-woods theme into a haunting collision with the Palmer murder case, but there wasn't enough enthusiasm left in the entertainment press for any more rave reviews. The constant changes of schedule, near-cancellations and changing of thematic tack were enough to persuade the less attentive that the series completely lost its way at Episode 17 – when it was no longer about 'Who Killed Laura?' – and stayed lost to the very end.

The network didn't do anything to help the impression. Trying to give the series ending that same 'event' feel which characterised previous opening and closing segments, they edited programmes 28 and 29 into one feature-length episode. Following the competent but conventional direction of Tim Hunter with Lynch's final plunge into otherworldliness made little stylistic sense – still less when the editing lost some of the careful symmetry and mood, cutting commercial breaks into the wrong scenes.

If the show had run to another season, Leo may or may not have escaped from the hungry tarantulas; Ben may or may not have recovered from the frenzied beating dished out by Doc Hayward; most of all, it's hard not to believe some unforeseen mode of escape wouldn't have been engineered for sweet little Audrey, chained to the bomb-blasted vault of the Savings and Loan Bank – not to mention good ol' Pete.

But there the show ended, so there they all stayed. Faced with the show's demise, Lynch and Frost let the metaphysical side of *Twin Peaks* run wild, while dynamiting the tangible everyday – with a few back door escape routes, in case of change of plan. It's intriguing, however, to wonder how they might have continued with the black change of tone which replaced steady, reliable Coop with a doppelganger possessed by sicko Killer Bob.

Whatever the chequered history of *Twin Peaks'* transmission, it had, at least, effected the transformation of David Lynch, movie maverick with a small but dedicated cult audience, into David Lynch, mainstream pop culture's only respected artist of the perverse.

Prior to 1990, the Lynch cinematic catalogue amounted to four features released over 15 years – only eight hours of film, plus a couple of hard-to-see shorts; the two seasons of *Twin Peaks* alone amounted to two feature-length and four 45-minute episodes (minus commercial breaks) directed by Lynch himself, which, with the addition of *Wild At Heart*, more than doubled his available output in one 18-month period. (To which can be added four commercials for – appropriately enough – Obsession perfume, from the Calvin Klein stable.)

The long-term effects of *Twin Peaks* were unanticipated, but are still tangible today; as rapidly as the mainstream audiences diminished, so the legacy established itself. Some of the hardcore audience had organised into fanatical mini-societies, with names like the Cherry Pie Club, the Lynch Mob (naturally), the Laura Palmer Society and the Loggers, with a fanzine entitled *Wrapped in Plastic* to cater for them.

Despite the indifference of the average couch potato to the main post-'Who Killed Laura Palmer?' storyline, with its New Age/paranoid themes, and an FBI agent investigating the occult, UFOs and military cover-ups, it still found a ready-made audience. When these elements were later streamlined for an altogether different series – minus soap opera sub-plotting, diverse red herrings and broad humour – they would prove far more successful with a public which likes to know where it stands.

In the interim between the first season of *Twin Peaks* and the 1993 first airing of the highly successful *X-Files* (preshadowed by David Duchovny's wacky role as a transvestite DEA agent in a few late-*Peaks* episodes), television truly saw Weird Americana go prime time: *Eerie, Indiana* debuted on NBC in September 1991 – though short-lived, this junior *Twin Peaks*, where a young boy and his family moved to 'the centre of weirdness for the entire planet', with Bigfoot rifling the garbage cans, was well received. *Wild Palms* (1993), the postcyberpunk SF mini-series executively produced by Oliver Stone, showed a near-future where virtual reality technology was an everyday event, giving the main character (a detective, played by Jim Belushi) any number of Agent Cooper-type surreal experiences, earning the show the nickname *Twin Palms*. Post-*X-Files*, the 22-part 1995 series which became a minor hit on its tail, *American Gothic*, shared more of a common premise with *Peaks* – small-town, continuing characters, murderers and malign occult forces at work; *Dark Skies*, the 1996 series which expanded the *X-Files*-'truth is out there' maxim into a ufologist's rewrite of modern American history, used the legendary Project Blue Book as a reference point. The Lynch–Frost show which ended as a ratings failure, on a stop-start schedule, still left a continuing imprint on its medium.

Plans for the *Twin Peaks* film remained tentative throughout spring 1991. In July of that year, when Lynch had originally been scheduled to begin shooting *Ronnie Rocket*, Mark Frost announced there would be no *Peaks* movie spin-off, 'unless the actors become far more desperate than they are now'. The main obstacle was other movie commitments, plus the hope and desire to branch out from their TV roles by major cast members – principally Kyle MacLachlan and Sherilyn Fenn. Frost himself, at that time, was still tied up in post-production on his own directorial debut feature, *Storyville*.

At this stage, though there was still more in the pipeline from Lynch–Frost, the partnership had fragmented into two separate agendas. Not that it wasn't ever thus, to an extent.

'There were times when David was making *Wild At Heart*, when I was doing almost all the work on *Twin Peaks*,' asserted Frost, with the merest undertone of resentment. 'But everybody wants to believe in the *auteur* theory, that it all somehow springs from one person, and David had a much higher profile. I felt a little bit like Paul McCartney after Lennon had been shot – suddenly he was the one responsible for all the writing and all the work, whereas it was very much a collaboration.'

Despite Frost's assertions to the contrary, however, a deal on the *Twin Peaks* movie was finally struck with Francis Bouygues – Spelling Entertainment backing down on their claim after a financial arrangement was reached – that following month, to finance it ahead of other Lynch projects. Once again, *Ronnie Rocket* was off the launch pad. Though, as co-rights holder of the concept, Frost would be credited as executive producer, he had no direct creative input as Lynch collaborated with Robert Engels, one of the show's regular scriptwriters, on the screenplay.

The last remaining hurdle, an increasingly typecast Kyle MacLachlan's reluctance to play Agent Cooper one more time, was passed when Lynch and Engels decided the film would be an effective 'prequel' to the 1989 pilot, setting the scene in a manner both too Lynchian and too harrowing for prime-time TV, only requiring five days of shooting from MacLachlan.

'I think that Kyle is finally realising he can do anything else he wants,' said Lynch, 'and that people love him as Dale Cooper so much he should be very happy about that.

'In the very beginning, he was tired of doing the series, because we'd done 32 hours [US transmission time including commercials] and he didn't know if he wanted to go in and do it again. But then finally he decided that he would and off he went. He didn't want to do *Blue Velvet*, either. He turned it down, then thought about it and changed his mind a couple of times.'

Ironically, MacLachlan had pre-empted *Peaks* with the role of an FBI agent on the trail of alien life forms in *The Hidden* (1988). Besides the role of keyboard player Ray Manzarek in

Oliver Stone's *The Doors* (1991), post-*Peaks* he was most visible playing Agent Cooper in a UK potato crisp ad. Sadder still, a mid-'90s career lull has seen him in Coop mode – albeit with dark hair now distinctly greying – as one of a mixed-gender pair of FBI agents investigating unearthly phenomena, in a telecommunications ad for British TV: MacLachlan playing Coop playing Fox Mulder.

'I happened to be in love with the world of *Twin Peaks*,' Lynch would assert at the press conference accompanying the film's premiere, 'and the characters that exist there. I wanted to go back into the world before it started on the series and to see what was there, to actually see things that we had heard about.

'For me, and I think pretty much for everybody that's ever been, there's a feeling that there might be something like sub-atomic particles existing that we can't see and x-rays and maybe a few other things out there and that a little opening could exist and we could go somewhere else. And this kind of idea excites me.'

Shooting would begin soon after the announcement of production, on 5 September 1991, back in good ol' Snoqualmie, Washington State. Sheryl Lee, who laughingly confessed to typecasting as a 'dead girl', accepted the expanded role of Laura as a reward for appearing moribund in plastic and decorating the end-credits for so many weeks.

'I was incredibly excited,' Ms Lee girlishly recalled of her first major movie opportunity, 'not only to work with David again, whom I would work with any time, but also because it helped me give life to this character. David's brilliant to work with, he's very "in the moment", he's very intuitive, he's very specific, he's kind, he's humorous, he's just . . . he's *wonderful*.'

Such effusive praise, with the movie painter as some obsessive Superman or Santa Claus, was not universal among the *Peaks* cast. Of those roles required to be recreated for the film, one of the most crucial was that of Laura's best friend, Donna Hayward, as incarnated by Lara Flynn Boyle. Ms Flynn Boyle turned the picture down – her part taken by newcomer Moira Kelly, adequately (but less assuredly) filling shoes worn by someone else in over 20 hours of TV – citing other commitments, but also, reputedly, because she agreed with those feminist critics who labelled Lynch's treatment of female characters misogynistic.

As ever, Lynch's distrust in verbally communicating his ideas led to a plain and simple defence of art for art's sake – granting him absolution from the converted, increasing derision from the sceptical. 'If you have any sort of moral thing or boundaries you won't cross over, that's going to shape your story. But if you start worrying right away about the meanings of everything, chances are your poor intellect is only going to glean like a part of it.'

More pertinently, Lynch was accused of co-opting the highly-charged subject of incest: exploiting its transgressive *frisson* in the exposed abuse of Laura by Bob/Leland, then neatly side-stepping the issue by making Leland blameless, a victim himself (of demonic possession), absolved of all guilt and dying in forgiving young father-confessor Coop's arms. Ironically, by virtue of its more extreme nature, the *Twin Peaks* film – to be titled *Fire Walk With Me*, after Laura's ominous poem – would be far less liable to accusations of this kind of glibness, yet its willingness to confront the monstrous father as a psychological (rather than purely supernatural) creature gained few converts.

In the half-decade since *Blue Velvet*, the idea of 'violence against women' as an artistic taboo had intensified at either end of the social-political spectrum. While the contention that Lynch fills his films with nothing but female debasement is a ludicrous one, equally absurd is the idea that he should seek moral approval for every idea and image which comes, uncensored by analysis or verbal rationalisation, on a direct line from a strange but integral part of the American psyche.

Sheryl Lee as a living, breathing, vivacious Laura Palmer, in **Fire Walk With Me.** *The above shot was used on posters for the vastly underrated film.*

TWIN PEAKS — Fire Walk With Me (1992)

Opens to a downbeat sax theme and blue TV static. The TV is destroyed, as a scream is heard in the background.

The destruction signifies the rejection of TV's glossy aesthetics and restraint – in this *Twin Peaks*, there's no comic relief, no time given to likeable eccentrics, no heroic subplots involving the teenagers, no distracting soap opera strands. Only a relentless downward spiral shown in muted, grainy colours, a surreal descent into hell.

'There is less humour in this film,' conceded Lynch, 'because the story gets heavy after a while. Humour has a place in a picture, but you have to know sort of intuitively where that place is and where it isn't. But Bob [Engels] and I were laughing while we were writing many times, at various places,' he admitted disarmingly. 'I think humour is like electricity. You work with it but you don't understand how it works. It's an enigma.'

The scream comes from a murder victim, now, familiarly, wrapped in plastic and floating down a river. The murdered girl is Teresa Banks, a local waitress in this Washington State town.

Stone-deaf FBI chief Gordon Cole (Lynch, repeating his party piece) contacts Special Agent Chester Desmond, currently dealing with a school bus hijack. Chet Desmond, a laconically cool tough guy with sharp deductive powers, is partnered up with the more bookish Sam Stanley (respectively played by photogenic ex-boxer/singer/honorary Lynch mob member Chris Isaak, surprisingly good in his only major film role, and Kiefer Sutherland doing a nervous nerd routine).

Gordon introduces them to a geekish, red-haired, dancing mime: 'Her name is Lil – my mother's sister's girl!' Chet deciphers her actions: 'Lil's wearing a sour face. Both eyes blinking. Means there's going to be trouble up top: the authorities are not going to be co-operative. Her hand was in her pocket: they're hiding something. My mother's sister's girl . . . What's missing? The uncle. The sheriff's uncle is in federal prison.' Chet's deductive interpretation is both an acknowledgement of the cryptography routinely brought to bear on Lynch's work, and a precursor of the strange logic which informs Agent Cooper in his investigations.

The small Washington State town they investigate is the 'anti-Twin Peaks'. 'Get yourself some coffee,' they're told by the sour, cretinous deputy at the sheriff's office, 'it was fresh a week ago.' Chet Desmond is the 'anti-Coop', twisting the surly deputy's nose. Sheriff Cable is the corrupt, uncooperative 'anti-Harry'.

As the sheriff's office closes at 4.30 p.m., Chet and Sam run their own forensic tests on 17-year-old Teresa's body. There's a graphic, wince-making replay of the fingernail search from the pilot film, the nail lifted completely off to reveal the letter 'T'.

The Feds visit the local diner where she worked. The manageress, Irene, is a sluttish old hag with a cigarette butt hanging from her mouth – the 'anti-Norma'. Irene says Teresa had a cocaine problem and suffered from a weird medical condition wherein 'her left arm went dead about her time'.

The owner of the trailer park where Teresa lived, Carl Rodd (Harry Dean Stanton), has a sign scrawled on his door saying, 'Do not ever disturb before 9 a.m. . . . . EVER.' They knock him up anyway. 'That goddamn trailer was just about as popular as a whorehouse on Uncle's Day, know what I mean?' he tells them. He gives them a cup of 'Good Morning, America' (the film has a cheap and nasty version of the show's coffee fetish) as they examine the trailer. In a photo of Teresa, Chet detects a ring on her finger which was missing from the body. Outside, a grotesque old trailer park lady with an eye injury walks by. Chet finds the ring hidden at the park, in a trailer wheel.

Philadelphia: Special Agent Dale Cooper dictates to Diane. 'Ten a.m. February 16th. I was worried about today because of the dream I told you about.' (Like Laura, James, Leo and some of the other young characters who have walk-on parts, Coop inevitably appears a little older than when last seen on the TV show – despite the film supposedly taking place beforehand.)

Coop searches for apparitions in the FBI office hallway. One frantic, thin character in a sports jacket and Hawaiian shirt comes racing through to Gordon's office. Gordon introduces him as 'the long-lost Phillip Jeffries'. (He is, in fact, David Bowie in a mercifully brief cameo appearance, sporting the most embarrassing Southern accent ever heard.)

This is the cue for grainy dream images of a man in a long-nosed geek mask; the backwards-speaking dwarf; fearsome, long-haired Bob; the little boy magician from Episode 9 (not played by Lynch's son this time), and the red curtains of the Black Lodge.

Jeffries disappears again – 'Reception says he was never here,' says Cooper – as has Chester Desmond. Coop is assigned to take over the case.

Coop checks out the trailer park. He's courteous to Mr Rodd, telling him he's sorry to wake him. He finds a missing trailer space which he's told belonged to an old lady, Mrs Chalfont (Mrs Tremond in the TV series), and her grandson (the little magician and his grandmother now revealed as inhabitants of the Black Lodge), and Agent Desmond's – or perhaps Chris Isaak's – old Ford, with 'Let it rock!' screenprinted across the windshield. He tells Diane this is one of Gordon Cole's 'blue rose cases' – the latest in an apparently unconnected series of cryptic murders.

One year later: thirty-three minutes into the film, the scene changes to the town of Twin Peaks, announced by the chords of Angelo Badalamenti's theme. Laura Palmer prepares for her schoolday in the ladies' room with a line of cocaine.

Her two boyfriends are introduced – her regular guy, James Hurley, a sensitive biker, and Bobby Briggs, the kid who supplies her coke habit.

151

New boys in town: the murder which pre-dates that of Laura Palmer by a year, in **Fire Walk With Me**, *is investigated by FBI agents Sam Stanley (Kiefer Sutherland, left) and Chet Desmond (Chris Isaak, right). Initially recruited to the Lynch mob to lend his moody, Orbison-like sound to* **Wild At Heart**, *singer Isaak is surprisingly good in his only major film role.*

'Stop trying to hold on so tight – I'm gone, gone,' Laura tells James. They engage in a brief, barebreasted lovemaking scene.

Laura and Donna lie down in front of the fire together, seemingly stoned. 'Do you think that if you were falling through space,' Donna asks her friend, 'you'd eventually slow or get faster and faster?' 'Faster and faster,' imagines Laura, 'till you eventually burst into fire. And the angels wouldn't help you 'cos they've gone away.'

Laura panics when she finds a page from her secret diary is missing; she goes to see her friend Harold Smith, novelist and gardener. 'Who would do that?' he asks her. 'Bob!' she insists. 'Bob is real, he's been having me since I was twelve . . . He comes in my window . . . He says he wants to be in me or he'll kill me.' She speaks the title of her poem, 'Fire Walk With Me,' becoming momentarily possessed by demons, her teeth stained with blood. She leaves the diary with Harold where it will be safe. They kiss each other and cry. Laura has a vision of Bob's face glaring at her: 'I want to taste through your mouth,' he tells her.

Coop is at FBI headquarters. He's visualised the next murder victim, but doesn't know exactly who she is. 'When the next murder happens,' he tells forensics man Albert Rosenfield, 'I want you to help me solve it . . . She's young, sexually active, she takes drugs and she's crying out for help.' 'Damn it, Coop,' retorts cynical Albert, 'you're talking about half the high school girls in America.'

Laura is approached by Mrs Chalfont and her sinister little grandson. The little boy wears the geek mask. 'This would look nice on your wall,' the old lady tells her, giving her a painting of an empty room.

Bob enters Laura's bedroom; he rapes her, his tonsils jangling above her in his open mouth. Afterwards, she looks out her window and sees Leland leaving the house. Hysterical, Laura realises for the first time that Bob and her father are one and the same.

That evening, Leland makes Laura sit down to dinner with him. 'Those hands are dirty, look at this fingernail!' he scolds. Looking for more ways to attack her, he picks on the half-necklace she's wearing: 'Did you get this from your lover?' he demands, touching her lightly but with incestuous menace. 'Leland, leave her alone,' insists Sarah, 'she doesn't like it!' 'How do you know what she likes?' he intones clammily.

Leland is in tears as he kisses Laura: 'Goodnight, Princess,' he sobs. As the invading spirit affects his rational memory, this is the only indication of remorse at his actions.

Also sobbing, Laura takes the painting of an angel at a table of children from her wall. She replaces it with Mrs Chalfont's picture of an open door in an empty room. In her dreams, she passes through the door. The little boy magician conjures up the Black/White Lodge. She meets Coop and the dwarf: 'Do you know who I am?' the dwarf asks her. 'I am the arm,' he warbles, offering the ring belonging to Teresa, the girl with the dead arm. 'Don't take the ring, Laura,' warns Coop – implying he knew who was going to die all along, but could do nothing to stop it.

She has a nightmare/hallucination in bed, in which a blood-spattered young woman, identifying herself as Annie, tells her: 'The good Dale is in the lodge and he can't leave. Write it in your diary.' The picture on the wall now shows Laura passing through the door – but only in her dreams.

This effectively macabre scene makes absolutely zero narrative sense to anyone who hasn't seen the final episode of the TV series – which, in turn, isn't fully comprehensible to anyone who hasn't sat through the preceding, incident-packed 20-odd hours of TV.

Typically perverse, Lynch stressed the benefit of a little narrative incoherence: 'I think, although I have been wrong many times in the past, that someone could get very much from not having seen anything of the series.

Strange but familiar: Special Agent Dale Cooper (Kyle MacLachlan) takes over the case, seen here interviewing trailer site manager Carl Rodd (Harry Dean Stanton).

'There are things in there that they wouldn't understand as much as some others, who have seen the series. But abstractions are a good thing and they exist all around us anyway. They sometimes can conjure up a thrilling experience within the person.'

Leo Johnson, in his first short cameo scene, slaps Shelly around to encourage her to wash the floor properly. Bobby Briggs phones: Leo tells him he already owes $5,000; Bobby tries Jacques Renault at the Roadhouse instead. 'You desperate, baby?' gloats the French-Canadian. He tells Bobby to meet him in 'two days – midnight – to the sound of sawing wood'.

Donna finds Laura smoking a cigarette and pouring herself a drink at home. 'Where are you going?' Donna asks. 'Nowhere. Fast,' Laura replies, 'and you're not coming.' But the far less worldly Donna insists on following her friend out.

Donna follows Laura into a club on the Canadian border, run by fat sleazoid Renault. Jacques sends a couple of lowlifes over. 'So you wanna fuck the homecoming queen?' asks an aggressive Laura. Donna follows her around like a little lamb. 'She part of the deal?' asks the other lowlife. 'No, she isn't!' snaps Laura. But when Laura tongues the guy she's with, Donna follows likewise.

The nightclub scene opens to a grinding musical riff. The club is an empire of sensuality, with topless dancers and two groping lesbians stripped down to their lingerie. Everyone downs beers containing some unspecified drug; Laura strips topless, embracing a sexy, stoned brunette named Ronnette – who, like Laura, earns her cocaine money via prostitution at the club. Drugged Donna also starts losing her inhibitions. Laura clicks her fingers to make her 'boy' perform cunnilingus under the table; she stops abruptly, screaming, 'Donna, not you!' when she sees her friend giving it away. Partly snapping her out of her stupor, she grabs Donna and insists they leave.

The club scene, a descent into a sensual underworld, is treated by Lynch as pure auditory overload. As sound designer of the film, he used the methods inspired by Alan Splet, who he hadn't worked with since *Blue Velvet*, but somehow lacked his sense of balance; the numbing, repetitive music the club vibrates to is overwhelming, enveloping – but, Lynch would doubtless argue, as integral an ingredient as the scene's dialogue.

The inaudible dialogue was, in fact, subtitled for the home market, as well as for non-English speaking territories; disastrously, however, it was omitted from the British release print, leading to several minutes of half-comprehension. Essentially, what's missing is some lewd, sinister banter between Laura and Jacques; Ronnette and Laura talk about Teresa Banks, who's been dead for a year, Ronnette hearing a rumour she was trying to get rich by blackmailing somebody; Jacques tells them she even called up one day to ask what Laura's father looked like.

Donna has very little memory the next day. Leland walks in on them, visualising both girls getting intimate in their underwear. He takes Laura out to meet her mom for breakfast; Mike, the one-armed man, spots Leland in the street and immediately recognises Bob (another incomprehensible point to anyone who never watched the TV series).

Images of the one-armed man, the dwarf, Teresa and the ring intermingle in Laura's mind. White light flashes in her bedroom, indicating the arrival of Bob. 'Who are you?' she demands of him.

In flashback, Leland recalls bashing in the back of Teresa's head with a shovel.

Ever more dependent on coke, Laura goes with Bobby to make the night-time connection; both are stoned or drunk. They meet with the moronic deputy from downstate, who obstructed Special Agent Desmond in the Banks case; he takes Bobby's money in return for a shitload of cocaine, then tries to pull a fast one on him. Bobby shoots him first, shocking himself by blowing part of the bad cop's head away, exposing his brain. He panics, but Laura becomes hysterical with laughter.

Sarah has a vision of a white horse (as in Episode 14, when Maddy is murdered). The electrical

We're a happy family: the seeming domestic bliss of the Palmers hides horror, in **Fire Walk With Me.** *(Left to right: Grace Zabriskie as Sarah; Sheryl Lee as Laura; Ray Wise as Leland.)*

lights flicker; Laura is in a cocaine ecstasy when Bob creeps into her bed. Her reaction is halfway between that of a rape victim and burning passion, till Bob's face becomes Leland's and she screams.

Laura shows disgust and fear towards Leland the next morning; the minutes of the school clock tick by rapidly as she dreads going home.

Jennifer Lynch's tie-in paperback, *The Secret Diary of Laura Palmer*, may have given precious little away in terms of narrative, but at least, in its own unsophisticated way, it touched on the pitiful self-loathing of the incest/rape victim:

'I just wanted to be normal. I just want to be like everybody else. I don't like to have to be careful of who to talk to because someone might hate me if they knew the truth about me, about how dirty I am. And how somehow, I don't remember it, but, somehow every day I asked to be treated this way. It always happens, so it must be something I don't realise I say, or something I think . . . But I didn't deserve that. I deserved to stay here. I had done something wrong. My heart hurt so badly, but I knew I had to stay.'

Laura's final words are a negation of her psychic pain, and the pain of the extinction that she knows is coming: 'I have to be numb.' 'The preceding was Laura's last entry,' reads Ms Lynch's epitaph for the character. 'She was found dead just days later.'

In this cinematic prologue, the vices of Laura Palmer were traced back to their dark origin. Confused and insecure – despite her own unreserved popularity and beauty – due to a long history of sexual abuse, she seeks reassurance wherever she can: in cocaine, in promiscuity, increasingly violent sex with older men – a kind of one-upmanship to prove no man can really hurt her any more, only satisfying her with the wild extremes her rapacious daddy's already introduced her to.

The schizoid, demonically possessed Leland (Ray Wise) makes incestuous threats to his daughter Laura (Sheryl Lee). Leland's long reign of abuse is depicted as the root cause of Laura's secret, wildcat behaviour.

In this context, the emergence from her wall painting of a guardian angel (which, again, many believed to be offensively ironic) is not at all the camp stylisation of *Wild At Heart*'s good fairy, but a heartfelt gesture of mercy in a pitiless world – both towards Laura and the viewer.

Out on James's bike, Laura slaps his face to provoke him. 'You always hurt the one you love,' he rationalises. 'The one you pity,' she corrects, trying to alienate him for his own good.

Red traffic lights hang suspended in the air as they ride home; she jumps from his bike, telling him 'I love you, James!' before taking off. That night, Laura joins Ronnette, Jacques Renault and Leo Johnson in a cocaine-fuelled orgy up at Jacques' wood cabin; in a near-bestial coupling, she surrenders herself to the huge slob. His mynah bird watches closely as she pleads, 'Don't tie me up!' – but Jacques binds her up tight and hurts her, against her stoned protestations. Outside, Leland Palmer watches, possessed by Bob, unmoved by his daughter's plight. As Jacques comes to the door, Leland bludgeons him, then smashes a whiskey bottle over his head (for which Jacques blames Leo in the TV series) – but the last thing he has in mind is rescue. Leo realises they're under attack and runs, leaving the girls bound and helpless.

Both the girls are dragged by Leland to an abandoned rail car. Mike, the spirit who inhabits the one-armed man, gives chase but is too late to stop anything.

Demonic Bob is dominant, the camera cutting between his face and that of Leland. 'I always thought you knew it was me!' the crazed Leland tells his terrified daughter, casting the reflection of Bob in a mirror. In the most relentlessly terrifying scene Lynch had filmed thus far, lights flicker, first Leland then Bob are seen to bring the knife down repeatedly into Laura's bloodied body, as the choral 'Requiem in C Minor' plays on the soundtrack.

Predictably, the film's violence – or at least, that against women in general, and Laura in particular – drew wails of criticism. Those who were prepared to forgive Lynch his transgressions at the time of *Blue Velvet* mostly backed off from giving him the same support. His pre-emptive, common-sense response to the coming attacks, voiced at the film's premiere press conference, is worth noting, particularly in today's censorial climate.

'I don't know why there is violence in American films: it's probably because there is a lot of violence everywhere in the air. And I think that whenever people get stories they pick up on whatever is around them and the story starts unfolding in your mind.

'I believe in violence but I don't want to champion violence. I believe that a film should have contrasts, and I believe that a film is a place where you can go and have an experience, like reading a book.'

In **Fire Walk With Me**, *heinous murder has a perverse happy ending. Laura (Sheryl Lee) finds herself in the White Lodge, a sanctuary for departed souls, with the future shade of Agent Cooper (Kyle MacLachlan), the man who will bring her father/'Killer Bob' to justice. The scene is an echo of Coop's dream in Episode Two of the show, part of the vein of cryptic surrealism which runs throughout the saga.*

Laura's body floats in a plastic bag down the river. The pale face of Leland screams. Leland/Bob passes through the sycamore circle entrance to the Black Lodge. They appear before Mike, the one-armed man, and the dwarf for judgement. Helpless Leland floats listlessly, like a helium balloon.

After death, Laura is transported to the White Lodge (the visually-identical but positive mirror image of the Black Lodge – only comprehensible to devotees of the TV series), to meet with Agent Cooper. She laughs, then cries, at the vision of her guardian angel, emerged from the wall picture in her bedroom, hovering above her. The film ends with 'Requiem in C Minor' playing over the angelic image of Laura's face.

At the June 1992 Cannes premiere, the audience divided into factions – everybody apparently either cheering or booing, the latter group in a clear majority. In a dramatic turnabout of his European status (considering his controversial 1990 Palme D'Or win, *Wild At Heart*, a lesser film, was much more tolerantly regarded), Lynch, unaware of the negative reaction to his film which had just played in the Grand Palais, entered a press conference to boos and hisses.

(At one point, a typically prosaic Lynch reply did draw appreciative applause, when he responded to portentous questioning by a French critic: 'You are playing with the whole idea of family and social conscience. Are you trying to attack the American dream?'

'No,' responded Lynch. 'I was trying to make the story of Teresa Banks and the last seven days of Laura Palmer.')

Immediately post-Cannes, the first opening was in Japan – where the film did extremely well at the box office, becoming an instant hit. *Twin Peaks* was already a huge cult in Japan, which, while it didn't stop the film from failing elsewhere, at least hinted at the intensity of the likely response. Sheryl Lee recalls, with some bemusement, a ritualistic funeral for Laura Palmer attended by *Peaks* fans in the Land of the Rising Sun: 'They made a fake Laura, wrapped it in plastic, put it in a coffin, had a memorial service, and people came and cried and put flowers on the body and everything.'

On US release, however, the critical consensus was avidly against the film. Andy Warhol's *Interview* magazine pastiched the audio memoranda of Agent Cooper in their attack: 'I have to solve the mystery of why one of our most original talents should de-caffeinate his creativity on an ill-structured, lurid, shock-crazy prequel to a once popular saga. Believe me, Diane, this is torture.'

'Too weird and not very meaningful for general audiences,' was *Variety*'s verdict, also commenting that 'suspense is (inevitably) lacking in this story with a preordained outcome.'

The movie bombed at the US box office, and most other western markets bar France, with a leaden determination so far unprecedented in the movie painter's career. (*Eraserhead* may have been unsuccessful at first, but it had only a limited art-house release and picked up a large cult audience over the ensuing years; even *Dune*, which attracted the curious over the 1984 Christmas season, initially did better.)

Ever faithful, Sheryl Lee saw *Fire Walk With Me*'s commercial failure in terms of its inherent controversiality. 'All of David's films have got mixed reactions,' she defended. 'People love them or hate them, and you know Laura is a victim of incest and she has turned to drugs. In our country we are still denying that incest is a huge problem, and so in that sense it can be very confrontational to certain people. I have had many people, victims of incest, approach me since the film was released, so glad that it had been made because it helped them to release a lot. And so for me, it doesn't matter what the critics say – if one person walks away having released something, then it's worth seeing.'

More than this, however, the film transgressed against the pervading style of popular US cinema; whereas tackling such universal (not just American) taboos can always prove thorny, the TV series still managed to touch on such dark areas implicitly, layering them over with distracting characterisations and myriad sub-plots. *Fire Walk With Me* took the origins of *Twin Peaks*' progenitive murder case to ground zero. It was Lynchian, but it was also grim, with none of the whimsy associated with him in the post-*Blue Velvet* years; the trademark dream imagery was inherited from the TV show – but here it became inherently nightmarish, uncompromising modern *noir* at its blackest.

However, some critics – like the reviewer for Britain's *Monthly Film Bulletin* – went so far as to call for revision of opinion on Lynch's early masterpieces, *Eraserhead* and *Blue Velvet*, on the basis they now considered him nothing more than an exploitation director with an overblown reputation, trying to disguise basic sleaze with his trademark American surrealism.

'Fame is an unnatural thing,' Mark Frost had reflected at the beginning of his erstwhile partner's fall from media grace. 'There is no equivalent to it in the animal kingdom.' There was, however, an all-too human jungle where reputations were destroyed as casually as they were doled out.

With the tides of Western cultural opinion turned against him, only the small press and underground fanzines on both sides of the Atlantic – *Video Watchdog* calling the film 'a major event in the cinema of imagination', *Divinity* hailing it as Lynch's most uncompromising work since *Eraserhead* – appreciated how courageously sincere a move *Fire Walk With Me* was for a major film-maker.

From the peak of early 1990, with the first season of *Peaks*, to the summer of 1992, it had been a very sharp decline in Lynch's critical stock. Rock bottom was at hand. Plans were now uncertain, but still vaguely optimistic.

'I'm not going to do *Ronnie Rocket*,' conceded Lynch yet again, 'or at least I'm not going to do it right away. I think I may be doing *One Saliva Bubble*, but I'm not one hundred per cent on that. *One Saliva Bubble* is a very wacko, infantile, bad-humour kind of film.'

But plans, as fate and David Lynch can assure us, often take a thousand wrong turnings.

CHAPTER NINE

It's A Weird, Weird World Out There

In the summer of 1992, on a downhill race to the pits of his reputation, David Lynch still had several cinematic projects in development. Unfazed by the decline in his critical stock, the deal with the newly-formed CiBy 2000, inked in 1991, paradoxically seemed to open a wider range of options for Lynch than at the height of the *Twin Peaks* craze. And it remained a three-picture contract – the French production company had also financed *Fire Walk With Me*, but struck a special one-off deal for that particular project.

Preliminary pre-production had begun on the much-delayed *Ronnie Rocket* in the latter days of 1991, even before post-production started in earnest for *Fire Walk With Me*. As witness to his confidence in CiBy's backing, Lynch also started to design and build a giant cockroach over the Christmas period – intended to represent the transmogrified Gregor Samsa, man-into-insect of Franz Kafka's nightmarishly surreal allegory *The Metamorphosis*. Kafka, with his sense of alienated dislocation, remained the 20th century author with whose vision Lynch most strongly empathised; *Metamorphosis* would form the third of Lynch's French-backed triumvirate of films, after *Ronnie* and *One Saliva Bubble*.

Meanwhile, however, there was unfinished business on the tube – the medium that came close, almost by default, to becoming the former celluloid painter's primary career.

At the end of February 1991, after the ABC network took *Twin Peaks* into its pre-cancellation hiatus, the *Hollywood Reporter* announced production of the new show from Lynch–Frost Productions.

On the Air, a series of 30-minute comedies set during the early days of live TV, was the most atypical, un-Lynchian project (with the possible exception of *Dune*) its co-originator had so far been involved with. Devoid of the darkness which permeates all his most personal work, the programme showcased the wackier, largely Frost-influenced elements of *Twin Peaks* in undiluted form – as well as promoting secondary members of the cast into starring roles and working with essentially the same crew (including day-to-day *Peaks* producer Gregg Fienberg). Alongside the more controlled absurdity of *Peaks*, the show proved to be an outlet for that love of slapstick which distinguishes the still-unproduced *One Saliva Bubble*.

By the time it premiered on ABC, in June 1992 (within days of the hostile reception to *Fire Walk With Me*), *On the Air* was a project which managed to confound the expectations of pining Peakies while appearing very seriously out of time.

ON THE AIR (1992)

Pilot Episode (each episode 30 minutes including commercials)
Written by Mark Frost and David Lynch/Directed by David Lynch

1957: the era of live-broadcast TV, based in Manhattan's Broadway – recreated in rich, saturated pastel colours. Apart from the photography, the show's best feature is the dreamily evocative Angelo Badalamenti sax theme.

The cast of The Lester Guy Show are suffering first-night nerves – especially Betty 'What day is it?' Hudson, the show's cretinously cute, bubble-blonde starlet.

The show has a carnival atmosphere, illustrated by the Hurry-Up Twins – black Siamese twins who walk around exclaiming, 'Hurry up, hurry up!'

The show's regulars are introduced: Lester Guy, the star of the show, is an effete, washed-up British movie star making a living in TV (played by Ian Buchanan, who took the tertiary role of foppish menswear salesman Dick Tremayne in Twin Peaks).

The show's director is an East European émigré proficient in pidgin English – from which much of the pilot episode's unsophisticated humour derives. The producer is told how he 'really knows his way around a set', as the director hollers through the wrong end of a megaphone. Throughout the (short) series, he will be reliant on his endlessly patient PA/secretary, Ruthie, to keep everything on the rails and translate his utterances to the cast. 'Can you scram?' (as in scream), he asks Betty, who thinks he wants her to leave.

'Binky is not blind,' announces the old-style narrator, introducing a staring back-room boy: 'He has Boseman's Simplex and actually sees 25.62 times as much as we do.' The first of the regular surreal sight gags is introduced, with Binky seeing kaleidoscopic multiples of whatever he looks at, plus some childish cartoon image imposed over the top of it.

The show's producer is Buddy Budwaller (played by Miguel Ferrer) – a less witty but more uptight version of the same actor's acerbic Albert Rosenfield character in Twin Peaks.

The pilot episode crudely (and funnily) satirises the thin line between early commercial TV and the sponsor's commercials – in this case, Wellbee's Doggysnacks. Filled with rapid-fire jokes, many of which were dated even in the 1950s, the humour works on the A Night At The Opera/A Day At The Races basis that everyone that can go wrong will go wrong. The show's best visual gag shows an Italian family out there in TV land who turn their black and white set on its vertical edge to follow the skewiff camera.

By the end of the show, Lester ends up swinging upside down on set by his ankles. Predictably, ZTV boss Mr Zublotnik (another borsch eater) tells cast and crew: 'Ve haf a hit on our hands.'

Episodes 1—4/6

Writers: Mark Frost (1–3/6)/Robert Engels (co-author of Fire Walk With Me). Directors: Jack Fisk (cinematographer/long-time friend of David Lynch/the Man in the Planet in Eraserhead)/Jonathan Sanger (producer of The Elephant Man)/Lesli Linka Glatter (3/6)/Betty Thomas.

All the post-pilot shows continue with variations on the frantic 'show must go on' theme.

Episode 5
Written by David Lynch and Robert Engels/Directed by Jack Fisk

Lester insists the Woman With No Name appears on his show; he announces he's 'been downtown, where the avant-garde *leaves off'.*

Betty can't remember her mother's name – Ruthie calls her to try to confirm, to be told she's 'Mrs Noel Hudson'. 'Do you think it's possible for both my mother and father to have the same name?' asks bewildered Betty.

The wacky East European director enters a dance routine with the boho-existentialist Woman With No Name, creating confusion with questions about her shoes. (New subtitles for his heavy accent reveal 'beatnik' to be the way he pronounces 'bootmaker'.) A dear friend from the old country makes a joyful appearance, helping him put together the gift of a trolley-load of shoes for the beatnik dancer.

Lester hits on a plan to ruin Betty's lines by distorting her voice, using the high technology approach of a 45rpm record arm.

A beatnik sax player decides Betty is a 'crazy chick who digs the reefer', when she complains she can't remember her mother's name.

*The usual chaos comes in the shape of a boho-*avant-garde *jazz-dance mixed with a shoe fetishism routine, plus Lester accidentally distorting his own voice; Betty saves the day once more by remembering her mom's name, urging everyone in America to phone their mothers.*

That's all, folks, as they used to say on *Merry Melodies*.

A ratings disaster which made the final days of *Twin Peaks* seem a demographic triumph, *On the Air* was cancelled by the network during its seventh week, in early August 1992. With little sense of anticipation for even the opening pilot, Lynch's mainstream profile having declined steadily since the height of *Peaks* mania, its viewing figures reflected a new low in audience indifference each successive week.

Even Lynch-admiring commentators were aghast at the lightweight whimsy presented for their delectation: 'bottomlessly horrid' and 'mercifully ablated' are two typical retrospective comments. Conceived back in the early days of *Twin Peaks'* second season, when Lynch and Frost still confidently believed they had a licence to follow every creative whim, *On the Air* was confoundingly naive to the cult audience, incomprehensibly anachronistic to the average viewer.

Without any wiseacre Groucho or Bilko-esque lynchpin to identify with, the show paid tribute to a faded era and sense of humour the modern couch potato didn't recognise. Fated to be a late-night re-run curiosity, TV cultists may find a little fascination – and maybe a few genuine dumb laughs – in seeing how two major talents alienated their audience with pure nostalgic self-indulgence.

David Lynch had little to say about the total commercial failure of *On the Air* – it was to be the last Lynch–Frost production, all recent collaborations (except the modestly underrated *American Chronicles*, which attracted little in the way of either scorn or approbation) falling into an ever-widening, prime time black hole.

At the same time, in the wake of the extremely mixed international performance of *Fire Walk With Me*, even the faithful CiBy 2000 saw fit to lift *Ronnie Rocket* off the launch-pad once again – possibly forever, now the seminal concept had passed its fifteenth anniversary. Strangely, Lynch himself remains stoical about the smothering of his long-term brainchild.

In a June 1995 interview with *Screen International*, he later admitted how it would feel 'sort of cool' to finally launch *Ronnie* for the year 2000, but had still resigned himself to the film's pie-in-the-sky status.

'The people with the money just don't see it. And I can't really blame them, you know what I mean?'

As dispiriting as it may be to see such a genial acceptance of defeat in someone who occasionally touches visionary status, there were still other avenues away from stagnation. These led, perversely enough, back to TV Land.

At the time of *On the Air*'s monumental failure, Lynch was engaged in pre-production on an idea he'd been kicking around for a short time with buddy Monty Montgomery, head of Propaganda Films. It was based on the loosely-defined old framework of hotel rooms linking a series of otherwise independent vignettes or narratives (often attributed to Neil Simon's 1979 *California Suite*, but stretching back to MGM's star vehicle *Grand Hotel*, 1932).

Prosaically entitled *Hotel Room*, the central idea was for a TV series of separate stories to take place in the same New York City hotel room, where, as the opening voice-over informs, 'sometimes in passing through, they [the occupants] found themselves brushing up against the secret names of truth'. Which, like the concept itself, is atmospheric but very vaguely defined.

Produced by Propaganda Films and Lynch's Asymmetrical Productions for Home Box Office (HBO) pay TV, the pilot film for the intended series was shot during summer 1992. With the backing of the usual Lynch mob – music by Badalamenti, casting by Johanna Ray, production design by Patricia Norris – the project was chiefly remarkable for uniting Lynch with Barry Gifford, 'Weird Americana' novelist and author of *Wild At Heart: the Story of Sailor and Lula*.

Most significantly, this would be the first genuine creative collaboration between Lynch and Gifford – the latter merely having licensed his novel as the bedrock for Lynch's more wackily askew vision of *Wild At Heart*. Gifford contributed two stories, marrying basic themes from hardboiled fiction and southern gothic to the more 'respectable' style of mainstream 20th century American literature. (The pilot was composed of three independently-shot episodes, the middle segment written by Jay McInerney and directed by James Signorelli.)

Lynch's interpretation of such fertile source material was, however, hidebound by the 'hotel room' format, which was inherently stagey, concentrating on dialogue instead of visual imagery or action. Though it benefits from fluid camerawork, at least giving the impression of movement around a confined space, *Hotel Room* is far closer to a faithfully filmed play than an original movie screenplay or TV pilot. The least Lynchian, in a visual sense, of any of his directorial projects, *Hotel Room* has the feel of an unpredictable talent marking time, almost condescending towards the mundane. Its more intense moments do, however, give some hint of what the screenwriter's incisive plotting and characterisation might be able to achieve, were it eventually to be combined with undiluted Lynchian imagery.

Hotel Room [1992]

Pilot film for an unproduced TV series
Story One – Tricks
Written by Barry Gifford/Directed by David Lynch

September 1969. An awkward, middle-aged guy (Harry Dean Stanton) enters the hotel room with Darlene, a hooker he's hired. She makes him edgier still by lighting a joint while he's in the john.

A bearish, white-bearded old guy named Lou (Freddie Jones) bursts in on his buddy, Mo – the uptight trick in the hotel room. He warns Mo to watch his heart, drawing a few biographical details from Darlene. As he reminisces about passing through her home state of Iowa with his wife, Felicia, Mo complains he shouldn't talk about Felicia right now. Lou tells him about an article he's been reading on Martine Mustique – a movie star born on the same day as Felicia.

Darlene's stoned, letting Lou talk her into a cheerleader's chant; he lays her while Mo sits and mopes. When they come around after sex, Lou gets her talking about how she came to New York, following her boyfriend. He has an uncanny knowledge of how she stabbed him four times when he dumped her with child, only wounding him, but would have shot him if she had a gun.

Darlene's pretty shook up; Mo tries to talk her round, telling her Felicia was once a cheerleader too. At first, she's too disorientated to remember who he's talking about, but then remembers Felicia was Lou's wife. When Lou leaves the room, Mo flies into a rage: 'She wouldn't fuckin' look at a guy like Lou!' he insists. Felicia was *his* wife; the boy, who Lou described being born as they drove through the wheatfields of Iowa, his son. She's unnerved by the spooky set-up, telling them she's had some strange tricks before but no one ever played this kind of game. Mo's even more enraged, Lou joining the cat-call chorus as they berate her as a cheap little whore. As a hotel clerk calls at the door, she tells him to call the cops before these two guys hurt her.

Lou tells Mo to take it easy, leaving him alone to rest.

Mo's awoken by the cops banging at the door; once they're in, they identify him as Lou, via his credit cards, driver's licence and ID photo, arresting him for the murder of a woman named Felicia. 'I don't understand,' moans Mo – but Lou is a part of his personality who's taken the upper hand.

Story Two – Getting Rid of Robert
Written by Jay McInerney/Directed by James Signorelli

A comparatively lightweight piece set in June 1992, the time of production. Starring Deborah Unger as a spoiled rich bitch discussing how she'll hook the perfect husband, the climax comes when she finds that the boyfriend she wants to jilt, movie producer Robert (Griffin Dunne), plans to end the relationship himself. After she splits his skull with a golf-club, the harassed maid she previously abused tries to help keep his bloody head together. 'Do you mind?' she snaps at her. 'We're having a private moment here.'

Story Three – Blackout
Written by Barry Gifford/Directed by David Lynch

April 1936. In the midst of an electrical black-out, a pleasant young Okie (Crispin Glover) enters the hotel room.

His young wife, Di, sits with her eyes determinedly closed, covered by one hand – when she moves the hand, she claims being in the candle-lit city is 'like being inside a Christmas tree', covered in decorations.

As he tells Di about the Chinese restaurant where he's just collected their food, she reminds him he's not in China. Her strange, far-away, half-sightless gaze is fixed elsewhere; her voice is slow, child-like, distant. They both have an appointment to see a doctor in the morning. 'You still do like to fool around with your Danny, don't you honey?' her devoted young husband tries to reassure himself. In her faltering manner, Di reminds him of the time he was away 'in the sea of red'. He has to interpret everything she says: 'When I was in the navy, the Red Sea?' Danny reminds her about their little boy, Danny Junior – Dan-Bug. 'He drowned in the sea of red,' she remembers. 'He drowned in Lake Osace,' he corrects her.

As an electrical storm rages outside, they recall their little Dan-Bug: she claims he was scared of the lightning, but Danny remembers how he loved those big old Okie storms.

Childishly, Di claims she has a good idea – what if, when they go to see Dr Herschel Smith, the specialist, they don't tell him about Dan-Bug? Danny replies that they have to, as he's on her medical records from the clinic.

Di is burning up with fever; she tells Danny the names of her imaginary five children who she calls after her fingers: 'Pinkie, Thumb, Index . . . ' She makes Danny talk through how they lost little Dan-Bug when he wandered into the river while they were 'in an intimate way'. Di overheard a woman saying 'some people are unfit for having children', meaning her. Danny reassures his feverish young wife that she's as fit as anyone; she tells him she wouldn't be able to live without him. They kiss; she starts to regain some of her bodily strength. As the lights begin to flicker back on, they gaze out of the window, holding on to each other. 'Look at that, the city's all lit up,' she acknowledges as a smile returns mobility to her face.

Hotel Room, an intended series pilot which would air on HBO as a one-off special, was launched at the Monte Carlo TV market in January 1993.

Although Propaganda Films sold many of the overseas rights, both for broadcast and video, it ended up being shown or released to precious few territories. (In the UK, for example, video rights are retained but the distributors never saw fit to release the film.) Forgotten flagship of an unrealised TV series, *Hotel Room* is another isolated oddity in a wildly uneven career: neither representative of the movie painter's own haunting style, nor worthy of dismissal, it ultimately makes an unforeseen bridge between the absolute nadir of public indifference and critical disapproval and the obsessively personal project yet to come.

Meanwhile, the director's 24-year-old daughter – first introduced to the family business via the *Twin Peaks* novelisation tie-in – was going through strange days of her own.

Boxing Helena was a personal project for Jennifer Chambers Lynch, a screenplay she had worked on since before her father's *Peaks* glory days of the early '90s. Originally offered to her as a concept when she was still just 20 years old by independent producer Philippe Caland, she found herself disturbed by the idea but intrigued enough to try her own hand at a first draft screenplay.

Developing a concept close to the obsessive infatuation premise of *The Collector* (1965), Caland suggested they take everything further by having a socially-crippled surgeon, reduced to an emotional blank by his abusive childhood, keep the subject of his hopeless affections prisoner by amputating first her legs, then her arms – hoping, above all hope, that her total dependence on him will make her fall in love. As Jennifer's involvement grew, it fertilised an obsession with bringing the project to the screen – which, even with the backing of independent Mainline Productions and a respectable budget, would still take the best part of a draining half-decade.

Five weeks before the production was due to start shooting in July 1991, lead actress Kim Basinger called the first-time director to express last-minute reservations about her character – an unremittingly hard bitch, despite her traumatic ordeal, right up until her emotional submission towards the end.

On 10 June, Ms Basinger withdrew her services from the film, leading to the course of action which eclipsed any extra-legal debate of the film's relative merits. Mainline Productions drew up a lawsuit against Kim Basinger and her agents, seeking $5 million in damages for potential loss at the box office.

Undaunted by implicit recognition that the film's producers were suing for lack of a female star, Sherilyn Fenn gamely (and perversely) curtailed any appearance by the character Audrey Horne in David Lynch's *Twin Peaks – Fire Walk With Me* to sign up for notoriety in his daughter's debut feature.

By the time *Boxing Helena* received its much delayed premiere at the January 1993 Sundance Festival in Utah, Ms Lynch was still the youngest woman ever to direct a

Jennifer Chambers Lynch (top) tried taking on her father's mantle as director of 'Weird Americana' with **Boxing Helena** *(1993), the youngest woman ever to direct a Hollywood film. Sherilyn Fenn (bottom) precluded the possibility of her character, Audrey Horne, appearing in* **Twin Peaks – Fire Walk With Me**, *by taking the title role of a desirable amputee held prisoner by her obsessed admirer. Sadly, the film was far more anodyne than its outrageous premise, seemingly curtailing Ms Lynch's film career.*

Hollywood film. 'I'm not sure if people have opened many doors,' she empathised of her contemporaries. 'We sort of had to knock our own down.'

Certain agape observers were compelled to point out that Ms Lynch – oblivious to industry nepotism as she may have been – was still a newcomer with no cinematic experience, at the helm of a $5–6 million movie with a bizarre premise which would get any other film maker – apart from, perhaps, David Lynch, though his bankability was much in question – kicked out of the producer's office. Dad's credentials as the King of Weird Americana seemed to make her backers believe she could deliver in the same field.

Screen International saw no reason to pull punches in their Sundance review, setting the tone for the consensus which would bury the film: '. . . the best that can be said about Jennifer Lynch's *Boxing Helena* is that she had the audacity to make it at all . . . late-night cable television is more dangerous . . . Lynch shows that she knows what to do with the camera in this confident directorial debut. What's lacking, however, is some of her father's sinister edge and deadpan black humour.'

Indeed, much of the film's disappointment derived from how Ms Lynch stripped her bad-taste scenario of inherent grotesquerie. Without her father's aesthetic love of the grotesque, *Boxing Helena* is an anodyne, though beautifully photographed, extended pop video, awash in '80s-style synthesised strings on the soundtrack, too scared of disrespectability to take its premise to any wild imaginative conclusions.

On the few occasions the film comes alive visually, it almost seems as if Ms Lynch, aware of its failings, is desperately trying to emulate her father: a caged bird flutters in shuddering slow motion as the legless captive throws ornaments from her bed, semi-industrial percussion playing on the soundtrack; flashback dream images intercut with the same electrical flashes which signify chaos in *Eraserhead*, *Blue Velvet* and *Twin Peaks*.

Within two short months, the nature of the film itself became a strictly secondary matter, when Kim Basinger appeared in the Supreme Court to defend herself against Mainline Productions' charges of violating a 'verbal, informal or simplified' agreement. Bitterness was never far from the surface, the defence calling Jennifer Lynch a 'pornographer' and a 'liar', Mainline countering that Ms Basinger had never been slow to shed her clothes early on in her career, her route into acting made possible solely by a 1983 *Playboy* centrefold.

While the case itself was not entirely unprecedented, the jury took the historic step of imposing punitive penalties on a defendant for the first time: an award of $8.92 million made against Ms Basinger. (It was increased to $9.5 million by court costs, enough to make a former A-list Hollywood starlet like Ms Basinger file for bankruptcy.) The money, as some failed to appreciate at the time, went entirely to the producers rather than to Jennifer Lynch.

Ms Lynch retired from the project's five-year history a sadder, wiser woman. 'It has not been a happy experience,' she conceded, understatedly. 'Being on the witness stand in superior court is not where I expected to be at age 24.' As for future cinematic plans, she conceded, 'I don't know that I'll ever fall in love with anything as much again.' For the immediate future, she would, she said, be happy to 'write novels and have babies'.

When last heard of, Jennifer Chambers Lynch was devoting herself to the former activity, with no further precarious plans for aspiring to that cinematic art of everyday surrealism, American style, which bears the stylistic patent of the father who stayed diplomatically silent during the whole farrago.

At the same time, Lynch *père* was still locked in the same creative impasse he'd been in since pre-production failed to take place on *Ronnie Rocket*.

'I just couldn't fall in love with anything,' he'd later say of the cinematic lay-off following *Fire Walk With Me*. 'I wasn't disillusioned. I wasn't depressed. This same thing happened after *Blue Velvet*; it was four years before I did *Wild At Heart*. I don't know why it happens. I'm looking for stuff, thinking, sitting in my chair going as fast as I can. But until it hits you, and hits you hard, you really can't do anything.'

While this is just a little on the disingenuous side – skirting around the little matter of *Twin Peaks* filling the gap between *Blue Velvet* and *Wild At Heart*, and how the financial backers continually blew hot and cold on *Ronnie*, *One Saliva Bubble* and the planned Kafka project – it does at least explain how David Lynch came to lend his name to a film on which he did no work whatsoever.

Crumb (1994) is credited as 'A David Lynch presentation of a Superior Pictures production'. (In the autumn of 1990, opera director Peter Sellars' film *The Cabinet of Dr Ramirez* had started shooting with Lynch credited as executive producer. A badly-received attempt to update Robert Wiene's 1919 Expressionist classic, *The Cabinet of Dr Caligari*, semi-silent with a music-only soundtrack, it utilised dancer Mikhail Baryshnikov as a vagrant under the murderous control of a powerful hypnotist. Reckoned to be disastrously short of its own pretensions when it played the 1991 Cannes Festival, it's now all but impossible to see. By the time of its particularly short release to the festival circuit, Lynch's name was

Terry Zwigoff's **Crumb** *(1994) is a true-life piece of 'Weird Americana' to which Lynch lent his name and personal endorsement. Seen here is the film's eponymous, lecherous subject, legendary cartoonist Robert Crumb, with an admirer.*

removed from the production credits – testament either to his own over-commitment in the early '90s, or to possible disappointment with the project as it evolved.)

On *Crumb*, David Lynch neither raised finance nor worked in any kind of production capacity before the film was completed – instead, he agreed to lend his name to the documentary as a kind of brand-name endorsement of its very American strangeness.

First conceived by director Terry Zwigoff – a long-time friend of the film's subject – back in the mid-'80s, this intensely funny and disturbing piece of fly-on-the-wall documentary examines the life of the only 1960s underground comic book artist (creator of Fritz the Cat, Mr Natural and other even less wholesome counter-cultural icons) to be recognised by the mainstream.

For two years, Zwigoff and his French-born cinematographer, Maryse Alberti, put Crumb's off-kilter life into perspective by dogging most of his movements via the camera. As well as surprisingly animated montage shots of the still comics – backed with the early, piano-based jazz or acoustic blues recordings beloved of Crumb himself – they produced a squirmingly honest underview of middle-America's tragicomic side.

Like the older William S. Burroughs, Crumb comes on as so square he's hip – and maybe a little unnerving too, despite his innate nerdishness. (Lynch has some of this 'cool rube' appeal, too – though his buttoned collars and suit jackets have long erred on the side of designer chic, and, unlike either Crumb or Burroughs, he's far too clean a customer to have any serious history in the drug culture.)

Most alluring to Lynch was the presentation of Crumb's personal and familial history – the type of family which the young David Lynch, with his pathologically tidy and stable background, may once have lamented as being beyond his wildest dreams.

167

Crumb's brothers, Charles and Maxon, put their gloriously dysfunctional psyches on display in a manner befitting the most sympathetic Lynchian grotesque. Uncomfortably enough, however, it was all for real. Charles is revealed as a charming, housebound neurotic who has only had a job for one year in his life; now toothless and heavily medicated, living with his mother and confessing to a suppressed desire to kill his successful younger brother.

Seen through the camera's eye, his claustrophobic living space (with Beatrix, the Crumbs' mother, hollering in the background for Charles to come fix a jammed window) is as compellingly awful as the environment of *Eraserhead*. Almost poetically, the strange matriarchy that remains of the Crumb family are long-term residents of Philadelphia – the city of Lynch's bad dreams which formed the background to his startling debut.

Within a year of the interview, the socially and emotionally withdrawn Charles Crumb – having opened up his internal existence in a manner both harrowingly confessional and bravely humorous – finally managed to commit suicide. The film subsequently bore the dedication, 'For Charles'.

Maxon, the younger brother, lives as a street beggar in a San Francisco flophouse, where he assumes a yoga position atop a bed of nails for two hours a day. Max – also an artist, obsessively producing oil paintings of the female form – shows his brother the pencil drawing of a beautiful Chinese woman he once approached in a drugstore. As a sudden camera pan to his manic, shaking hand indicates, Max has certain difficulties with women – in fact, he has a long history of arrests for molestation.

In one surreal sequence, which would be attacked for its freakshow element if it appeared in a David Lynch script, Max sits in full-lotus position on his bed of nails slowly swallowing a 30-foot length of nylon cord to clean his intestines – a process he claims to undergo every six weeks, though, he says, it can take several days to pass completely through his system.

The film ends with Crumb moving out of his Californian home to escape the 'horror of modern America' which the artist and his wife, both uncomfortably adrift in the consumerist age, can no longer withstand – trading six of his sketchbooks for a chateau in the South of France.

Terry Zwigoff was ultimately perplexed when Crumb, the artist, told him that he'd added *Crumb*, the film, to his list of hated modern Americana. So ended the most critically successful, and by far the most uncomfortably real, piece of Weird Americana associated with David Lynch for several years – whose name, much to Robert Crumb's chagrin, had been instrumental in finding the film a theatrical distributor.

Lynch's involvement, though less than peripheral, roused some of the critics who joined in the panning of *Fire Walk With Me* to wonder aloud why there had been no firm news of any personal big screen project for a couple of years.

Credit for getting Lynch much more centrally involved in an extra-curricular production belongs to his third wife.

Mary Sweeney had acted as editor on the little-seen *Hotel Room*, and had worked on every Lynch project going back to *Blue Velvet*; since the turn-of-the-decade end of his 'bi-coastal' (i.e. conducted at a distance) relationship with Isabella Rossellini, both had also nurtured a close personal involvement, culminating in marriage in 1992.

Encouraging the cinema-shy director to take an interest in current film, Ms Sweeney showed him two independent features by a young American named Michael Almereyda – *Twister* (1989) and *Another Girl, Another Planet* (1992).

The latter, a nihilistic trawl through the love life of a lowlife in his crummy Manhattan apartment, was chiefly remarkable for juxtaposing black and white 16mm footage with scenes shot on a $45 plastic PXL 2000 toy video camera (launched by Fisher-Price in 1987, the item proved more popular with impoverished underground film-makers than with the intended juvenile market, its line now discontinued). Fragmenting images in a strangely symmetrical blur, 'Pixel Vision' reproduced the method of 'pixellation': rectangular face-masking, often to prevent legal identification. As well as the cheapness of the equipment, the young independents who used the Pixel bought into its accidental alienation technique – all the focus of the viewer's attention directed (so the theory goes) to the film's essence and mood, away from the primitive method of production.

More impressed by 'his writing and his potential' than Almereyda's worthy little films themselves, Lynch was immediately interested in raising funding for the underground director's proposed next feature – for which Ms Sweeney would produce. In fact, in the capacity of executive producer, Lynch wasted little time passing the begging bowl around potential investors by putting his own money in the project.

Produced in 1994 in a surprisingly effective mix of black and white 35mm and Pixel Vision, *Nadja* (1995 – 'David Lynch Presents a Kino Link production') is an off-kilter, fragmented but sincere subversion of the gothic vampire myth – recreated here as a series of distracted (though hypnotic) conversations and vignettes.

Nadja, the title character – seemingly named after the heroine created by Andre Breton, author of *The Surrealist Manifesto* – is a distinctly mid-European and strikingly handsome young woman, with heavy brow and aquiline profile, played with a romantically troubled air by Hal Hartley regular Elina Lowensohn. As we see early in the film, she's also a predatory creature of

the night, feasting on a young man she picks up in an East Village bar. Both this erotic vampirisation and the impalement by stake of her father are shown through the alienating piece-imagery of pixellation.

As the daughter of Transylvania's most illustrious ex-patriate, she also brings a novel agenda to the film: how to set the brood of Dracula among the ice-cool night life of modern Manhattan, without descending into parody or kitsch. With a languorous pace and an air of doomed romanticism, *Nadja* is an uncredited, de-melodramatised update of Garret Fort and Lambert Hillyer's rarely-screened 1936 classic, *Dracula's Daughter*.

Nadja herself is able to wander through late night Manhattan in vampiric cowl and cape without anyone sneering or double-taking at the pop-cultural cliché. (Lynch is unmistakable in a brief walk-on, as the

*Michael Almereyda's **Nadja** (1995) is a languid, dream-like subversion of the horror genre, for which Lynch acted as executive producer and took a walk-on part. Elina Lowensohn is seen here in the title role, as a sensual vampiress sleepwalking through her existence.*

tousle-haired attendant of the mortuary where the vampire's staked body is held – his daughter identifying the historical context of this mythic and ethnic archetype by airily announcing, 'We have come for the body of Count Voivode Armenios Ceaucescu Dracula.')

'The idea was to cross the Dracula legend with parallel plots involving a dysfunctional family and unstable marriage,' said Almereyda at the time of *Nadja*'s Sundance presentation. 'I wanted to locate horror movie anxiety, strangeness and fear within the heart of common experience.' The measure of its quiet success is how the film manages to be constantly referential while maintaining its passive, dream-like mood and never sinking into camp pastiche.

For the most part, *Nadja*'s theme of vampirism is assimilated into a dreamy world-weariness – the genuinely oneiric vision (the novel camera techniques, particularly the Pixel footage blown up to 35mm, suggest a recognisably vague dreamworld where certain things are half-glimpsed or intuitively felt, rather than vividly surreal) complements the story of a beautiful young woman floating through an urban(e) existential crisis, instead of going foaming mad with bloodlust. As the story diffuses through the sextet of main characters, reinforcing the sense that Nadja is always watching the people of her private world through the monochrome veil of her dreams (this, presumably, being Lynch's main attraction to the project), there's a complete and consistent absence of any conventional horror film tension.

The imagery reaches its apogee in the penultimate scene where the faces of the lesbian lovers, Nadja and Lucy, are suspended beneath water – not drowning, but floating somewhere beyond the realm of earthly emotions – and in the final scene where Nadja's still-living face is isolated in a wild natural setting after her death, intercut with the face of Lucy, the lover she now 'inhabits'. Far from the now-standard horror movie epilogue which shows the killer or ghoul triumphant, the closing image is that of lingering love and reconciled emotions. Both are pure pop surrealism, as if Man Ray was filtered via the ethereal gloss of Lynch's Obsession perfume ads.

After favourable responses at the 1994 Toronto and the 1995 Sundance Film Festivals, CiBy Sales – the distribution wing of CiBy 2000, Lynch's European backers – picked up worldwide rights. *Nadja* continues to play in international repertory; performing unexceptionally on a commercial level, it nonetheless has the gradual momentum of a minor cult, with an evocative soundtrack album to consolidate its elitist appeal.

Simultaneous to *Nadja*'s release to the festival circuit came Lynch's announcement that he had recently completed his first collaborative script with Barry Gifford, except it wasn't so much an announcement as a coy admission.

'I just don't feel like talking about it,' the movie painter told *Screen International*, despite admitting to being 'super-excited' about the project. 'Somehow the more you talk about something, the power of it drains out. It's a tricky thing because it's so long from the start of a film to the end.'

Confirmed to begin shooting in Los Angeles in late 1995, the film would be, staggeringly belatedly, the first under the three-picture CiBy 2000 deal struck back in the spring of 1991. Purportedly an obsessive love story, its co-creator's reluctance to talk about it may have stemmed in part from all the baggage that would ride with the project – several years of unrealised concepts and unfulfilled expectations.

CHAPTER TEN

Lost Highway:

The Highway Back

If anything were truly indicative of how David Lynch, absent from the media spotlight since the early 1990s, was likely to re-emerge into a world where his most esoteric visions seemed more timely than ever, it was the belated publication of his photographic collection, *Images*.

Consisting of shots of the weirdly mundane – electricity plants and garden snowmen – and the obsessively contrived – Lynch's original 'industrial symphony' paintings, Pollockian abstracts with mathematical formulae, plus much more interesting organic constructs – alongside a selective career scan of film stills, publication was first excitedly announced in a 1990 interview with *Time*.

'I've got a real lot of beautiful industrial landscapes,' enthused Lynch. 'And I'm real interested in dental hygiene, so I'm going to have a chapter on that. Maybe something on fictitious archaeology: I'd like to bury some things, then wait a little while and dig them up. I like to photograph plastic people in little scenes. Then I might have a chapter on spark plugs. Kind of amazing things, spark plugs; our lives revolve around them.'

Though Lynchiana was supposedly all the rage at the time, the book failed to meet its 1991 publication deadline (coincidentally enough – or perhaps not – this period coincided with the start of his fall from media grace); deadlines continued to be missed, until, after a change of publisher, Hyperion finally brought out an updated, glossy hardbound volume in winter 1994/95. The imagery of David Lynch – the publishers of *Images* were confident – was due back on the cultural agenda.

Containing evidence of Lynch's life-long fascination with the aesthetics of biology, the book offers a rare chance to glimpse the self-assembled 'animal kits' created during the early days of his career as a professional film-maker.

'One is a fish kit that I made in London right after *The Elephant Man*,' explains Lynch. 'I bought a mackerel. The kits are based on the model airplane kits where you get a box and you take out the parts and you have to read the instructions and assemble them. So these things end up being photographs of parts of things and some instructions about how to put it together. Then it says to put it in water when it's finished.

'And then I did a chicken kit in Mexico, but it didn't come with feathers, you had to purchase them extra. And so it's a naked chicken.' ('Do not set fire to your chicken or people will eat him,' warn the classically *faux-naif* Lynch instructions of the dismembered mass of raw poultry and innards.)

'And then I was all set to do a mouse kit in *Blue Velvet*. I had about 12 mice in my freezer, and I never did the kit. The house was a rental, so I'm sure the landlord found them.'

At his peak of media hipness – summer 1990, at the time of *Wild At Heart*'s release and between the two seasons of *Twin Peaks* – Lynch was asked by an interviewer for *Rolling Stone* whether it was true that his legendary collection of organic matter and fossilised animal parts included the uterus of a female film producer, which he'd reputedly asked her to save after a hysterectomy.

'It wasn't that way at all!' countered Lynch. 'This woman was having an operation and asked the doctor to save it for me, as something she felt that I would want to have.'

Like those infinitely less sociable mid-Western obsessives, Wisconsin boys Ed Gein and Jeffrey Dahmer, Lynch was fascinated enough by the visceral textures of the body to decorate his home with them. Appearing in the recently-published hardback edition of *Images*, alongside pristine, coldly fetishised shots of a female nude obscured by cigarette smoke, is a selection from the movie painter's domestic collection of biological *objet d'arts*: an excised pancreas, sclerosed kidneys, an amputated gangrenous foot. 'It's like, there's many things I have in my house, right? But some things have stuck with certain people as very interesting things. So I guess that could be one of them.' Sadly, the pickled womb makes no apperance in the book. As its creator attests, however, dentistry makes its debut as one of the lesser chronicled Lynch obsessions – particularly scenes of dental and orthodontic treatment which, even in their antiseptic form, still retain their ability to put the observer's own dentistry on edge.

The fascination even extended as far as the cover of the original draft screenplay co-written by Lynch and Barry Gifford, as the basis of the first project in the three-film CiBy 2000 deal.

Featuring a photo from a textbook on dental emergencies, their unwitting cover star was an unfortunate guy with one side of his face normal, the other grotesquely swollen by oral decay and disease which threatened to overwhelm his entire head. Refreshingly perverse, Asymmetrical, Lynch's production company, were initially interested to find out whether the orally-diseased patient might grant copyright clearance, regarding use of the startling image on the poster and published screenplay for the film: *Lost Highway*.

'A 21st Century *Noir* Horror Film,' reads the opening description of the *Lost Highway* screenplay. 'A graphic investigation into parallel indentity crises. A world where time is dangerously out of control. A terrifying ride down the lost highway.'

Forever ploughing his personal furrow of hardboiled Americana, Barry Gifford had recently seen the screenplay of his novel *Perdita Durango* (sequel, of a kind, to *Wild At Heart: the Story of Sailor and Lula*) cease filming early in 1995, when Spanish writer/director Bigas Luna left the independent European production. (Shooting resumed in 1996 with Alejandro de la Iglesia taking over directorial duties.)

Called to work again with Lynch (their slowly-evolving partnership producing a collaborative screenplay for the first time), Gifford brought the classic trappings of hardboiled fiction into play – the blood, booze, desperate men and double-dealing women, and the fatalistic relentlessness of the most pessmistic vintage *noir*.

'There's a human condition there,' recognises Lynch, 'people in trouble, people led into situations that become increasingly dangerous. And it's also about mood and those kind of things that can only happen at night.'

Like its more literal, monochrome ancestors, Lynch and Gifford's irrational narrative traps the main character in a scenario which not only denies self determination or escape, but undermines his whole sense of reality.

Lost Highway, an Asymmetrical Production for October Films, began its 54-day shoot in December 1995, finally wrapping in the last week of February 1996. Contrary to the small-town ethic that informed Lynch's visions of Weird Americana for a decade, the film was to make use of the metropolis that had been his home for over 20 years.

So many years on from the childhood memories which set the scene for *Blue Velvet* and *Twin Peaks*, or even the uneasy urban experience of *Eraserhead*, Lynch was finally ready to take Los Angeles – an automotive terrain of highways and freeways – on board as the city of his dreams. He concedes the film could well have taken place elsewhere – 'but you don't know how it would affect it. The place, the light and the feel – all these things come with the knowledge that you are looking for things to flesh out your ideas, make them more right. For me, LA was the right place.'

So localised a vision is *Lost Highway* that the house where its two main characters (played by Bill Pullman and Patricia Arquette) live is one of three owned in the same street by Lynch himself, including his own living residence.

The office of Asymmetrical Productions is also contained in this suburban street just outside Hollywood. Set on a hill with a steep gradient, the office building's entry and kitchen are on the top floor, placing the rest of the building below ground level. Lynch's office is only locatable via a descending spiral staircase leading down to a solid grey door – enclosed below the earth, it's the kind of claustrophobic sanctum of dreams one would expect to find inhabited by his more obsessive characters.

The neighbouring house which serves as Pullman and Arquette's home is strangely opaque from the outside – until the camera reaches close range, revealing many small windows which allow a more intimate peek. During filming, Lynch also adapted the interior design to conform to his overall vision, building a long hallway which ensured entry to the main house required walking into darkness.

'I always like to have the people stand out, so the furnishings have got to be as minimal as possible so you can see the people. There were many things that had to be built for the story to work,' confirms the director, having expanded his own manual activities to include furniture design for the film.

Back at the directorial helm for the first time in four years, Lynch, plus several dozen crew members, set up in location sites around the perimeters of LA, including desertland outside of city limits. Cast and crew seemed appreciative of playing a hand in something potentially unique – even if interpretations of the same project differ so much as to reflect happenings in a different space-time continuum. (Probably as apt a summation as Lynch or Gifford could possibly hope for.)

Put at ease by Lynch's eternally youthful enthusiasm and microscopic attention to detail, they responded well to his cryptic directions, to his almost pathological politeness and folksy mannerisms – even to boyish habits like running off to piss in a ditch whenever nature called on location, unwilling to disturb the film's momentum by meandering down to the Portakabin. (This incontinent quirk of Lynch's is well known and universally tolerated

– testament to the diuretic properties of caffeine and his own love of coffee. His collaborators on *Twin Peaks* affectionately parodied him in Episode 17, where Agent Cooper relieves his coffee-filled bladder while Major Briggs disappears in a flash of electricity.)

The idiosyncratically-picked cast (by Lynch veteran Johanna Ray, keeping the faith alongside fellow regulars Mary Sweeney, Angelo Badalamenti and production designer Patricia Norris) included:

Bill Pullman, reliable Hollywood factotum whose many credits include *Sommersby* with Jodie Foster (1993), *Sleepless in Seattle* (1993), *Wyatt Earp* (1994), John Dahl's brilliant modern noir, *The Last Seduction* (1994), *Independence Day* (1996 – in which he played the US president) and *The End of Violence* (1997);

Patricia Arquette, who previously made a striking impression in *True Romance* (1993), and *Ed Wood* (1994);

Balthazar Getty, young heir of that legendary dynasty who appeared in *Lord of the Flies* (1990), *White Squall* (1996), and in a support role for *Natural Born Killers* (1994);

Robert Loggia, formidable stage and screen presence who made his film debut in *Somebody Up There Likes Me* (1955) with Paul Newman, and appeared in a string of the 1980s best crime dramas: *Scarface* (1983), *Prizzi's Honor* (1985), *Jagged Edge* (1986);

Gary Busey, reliable character actor, Oscar-nominated for the title role in *The Buddy Holly Story* (1978), occasionally cropping up in underrated features like *Carny* (1980), and as Joe DiMaggio in Nicolas Roeg's *Insignificance* (1984);

Natasha Gregson Wagner, daughter/lookalike of Natalie Wood and relative newcomer to the screen.

As for supporting cast, the slew of semi-familiar faces is a movie cultist's/trainspotter's dream: Robert Blake, still vaguely recognisable as whiningly pathetic killer Perry Smith from *In Cold Blood* (1967), is cast as the Mystery Man – a widow's-peaked modern variant on the incubus legend, luring an urbane sophisticate to psychic destruction; longtime-unseen comedian Richard Pryor makes a comeback from ill health as an auto repair boss; brutalist post-punk rocker/raconteur and musclebound martial artist Henry Rollins – an increasingly frequent second-stringer in the movies – is a prison guard; John Waters veteran Mink Stole makes a brief aural appearance (her scene excised from the final print) as the forewoman of a jury; shock rock star Marilyn Manson is, fittingly perhaps, a transexual porn star, as well as a contributor to the soundtrack; and good ol' Jack Nance is there because he simply has to be – though, sadly, for the last time.

The oddly diffident character actor, whose career consisted mainly of noticeable bit parts, was most often employed in non-Lynch roles due to a director's personal regard for him, or for Henry Spencer. (In the film lover's mind, Nance will always *be* Henry.) Barbet Schroeder gave him a part in *Barfly*, on the back of author Charles Bukowski's rare love for a film: *Eraserhead*; Dennis Hopper recruited him to the cast of his street-gang thriller, *Colors*, and his neo-*noir The Hot Spot*, impressed by the little guy's downbeat charisma when playing one of Frank's gang in *Blue Velvet*. These roles – and Wenders' *Hammett* – aside, Nance was basically notable for being the most enduring member of the Lynch Mob.

'He's a strange guy and doesn't go out looking for work,' Lynch said at the time of shooting *Lost Highway*. 'If you wanted him for a film, you'd have to go get him and dust him off.'

Lynch had dusted his long-time friend off for the last time, however. Good ol' Henry is no longer with us, and will be much missed. On December 30, 1996, the Pasadena police entered Jack Nance's apartment to find him dead. With cause of death currently unconfirmed, it's only known he took a blow to the head on the day before in a fight at his local doughnut store.

'Jack had a quality . . . it's hard to put into words,' Lynch reflected in the immediate aftermath, 'but in my mind Jack was a real Kafka character, Gregor Samsa (hapless man-into-insect of *The Metamorphosis*), which means to me: he understands trouble. He's trying to do the right thing, but he's also sensing the darkness and confusion of the world. That was pretty much Jack. He really had a rough life, and it was rougher because he was a thinking person.'

Ultimately, it seems, though the late Jack Nance will forever personify the worry-wart 'wild pain' of *Eraserhead*, nothing was more Lynchian about his life than the bizarre circumstances of his leaving it.

Lynch and Gifford's script, while it yields up character motivation and cinematic clues, remains an open-ended mystery, tailed by a severe identity crisis or nervous breakdown. Though too psychologically subjective to endure much rational analysis, it makes pure expressionistic sense – not a concept widely appreciated in corporate Hollywood.

Despite the film's Californian setting, lack of Hollywood interference (Lynch's paymaster based in Paris) allowed for an uncompromised vision – with Gifford's input of refined, hardboiled style, Lynch finally produced the surrealist-*noir* hybrid that's been formulating ever since the first draft of the *Blue Velvet* screenplay, back in the '70s. Without the temperance of sentimentality, *Lost Highway* has become Lynch's darkest and most aesthetically exacting work since his Weird Americana *ouevre* first found a place at the edge of the mainstream.

Talking one-to-one with leading cast members between takes, the director gave no firm orders as to how individual lines should be read, nor what the meaning of a particular scene might be – just very basic verbal sketches of their characters' states of mind.

'Actors ask a lot of questions,' confirmed Lynch, skirting round the edges of truism. 'But they're strange, because they seem to understand things – abstract things – pretty easily. They can buy into an abstraction without too much trouble. In the beginning we rehearsed certain scenes because somehow those scenes – in our minds – defined the characters in some way. Once they got those scenes, the rest fell into place. But then there's always some scene that needs more explaining than others.'

'I wouldn't say that I understand the script completely,' admitted Natasha Gregson Wagner during shooting, 'but I like that. I know that when I see the movie I'm going to be surprised by how it all fits together. We all have our own fantasies about what the secret of *Lost Highway* is. At times, in David's direction, he'll give you an idea and you'll think you're on to something. Then the next day it will be completely the opposite.'

(Ms Wagner, in the breathless tradition of Laura Dern, effuses how her director is far from merely the sum of his more disturbing obsessions: 'He's such a dignified, handsome, nice man. Such a great contradiction.' As gushing as it may seem, it's a consensual viewpoint of the cast, who found the pleasantness and almost eerie calm of the man himself much at odds with his preternaturally unsettling vision.)

'This movie is just about an obsessive love affair,' opined Patricia Arquette, cast in the Hitchcockian role of an icy blonde who appears to be the reincarnation of a dead woman. 'It doesn't have to make sense to anybody else. It's like stepping into the mind of someone who's obsessed.

'Usually I'm cast as a character of hope, or love,' she reflects. 'But this is about the darkness of woman. The destructive element of woman. It's a man's concept, but I've never played that before. And I've never done a lot of nudity, so that was a whole other confusing problem. Not just in film, but in my whole life,' she adds candidly. 'So I thought that maybe I should go through the gates of hell and face up to all my fears.'

In her climactic love-making scene with co-star Getty, the allure of Ms Arquette is intensified by a beauty that, while far from Junoesque, is sufficiently 'of the flesh' to create a textural eroticism uncommon to modern cinema. Although no one has drawn him on the subject, the untoned flesh of a beautiful woman – even, perhaps, the slight lure of gravity upon her breasts – seems to hold an aesthetic fascination for Lynch's painterly eye, as did the bruised pulchritude of Dorothy in *Blue Velvet*.

'It's a dangerous thing to say what a picture is,' Lynch ultimately reflected, rejecting his and Gifford's own multi-genre synopsis of the screenplay. 'If things get too specific, the dream stops. There are things that happen sometimes that open a door that lets you soar out and feel a bigger thing. Like when the mind gets involved in a mystery. It's a thrilling feeling. When you talk about things, unless you're a poet, a big thing becomes smaller.

'To fall into a mystery and its danger . . . everything becomes so intense in those moments. When most mysteries are solved, I feel tremendously let down. So I want things to feel solved up to a point, but there's got to be a certain percentage left over to keep the thing going.

'You understand it, but you don't understand it, and it keeps that mystery alive. That's the most beautiful thing.'

LOST HIGHWAY (1997)

Opening credits play to the point-of-view shot of a night-time highway, its yellow lines merging into one as the driver's vision is blurred by his car's velocity – as per 'Frank's wild ride' in Blue Velvet.

In the first of many short fades in and out of black, structuring the first third of the film, we see Fred Madison (Bill Pullman), thirty-something, sitting alone in the early morning quiet of his Hollywood Hills home.

His buzzer rings, and he's disturbed by the (meaningless, to him) message: 'Dick Laurent is dead.' He goes to the window but finds no one there.

Believe it or not time: Lynch claims the progenitor for his and Gifford's tortuous, semi-circular chain of events was an anonymous intercom call which relayed exactly the same message as received by Fred: 'Dick Laurent is dead.' Needless to say, Lynch has no idea who Dick Laurent may have been, and his caller had vanished by the time he looked from the window.

Fred's alienated relationship with his wife, Renee (Patricia Arquette in brunette wig), and lack of trust, is apparent in their banal conversation. When he tries to reassure himself by saying, 'It's nice to know I can still make you laugh,' and she answers with, 'I like to laugh, Fred,' it's as blank as the dialogue of any cheap, old-school porn or gore movie. But the blankness is as pregnant with tension as anything by Pinter.

Fred is a free-form jazz saxophonist; he plays a gig at a local club, where his post-bebop honking drives them as wild as the most uninhibited rock 'n' roll. But Renee's not there. When Fred phones her after leaving the stage, he receives no answer. When he gets home, he finds her sound asleep in bed.

Renee plays Fred a videotape she's received in the mail. It's a brief camera sweep through their own home. She says it must have come from a real estate agent.

Fred wildly and frantically fucks Renee while she lays inert, physically and emotionally unmoved. As he comes down from his orgasm, he tells her of a dream he had last night: the scene is replayed in languid flashback, moving to the menacingly sedate pace of the film's opening scenes. Fred follows Renee's voice through the dense darkness as she calls to him. The camera cuts in to a sudden close-up of Renee in bed, her face in total terror.

Fred Madison (Bill Pullman), the jazz musician whose psychic fragmentation ('psychogenic fugue') provides the subjective reality of **Lost Highway (1997)***. Lynch's cast claimed their director made no attempt to impose any rationale on the script during shooting, and that its internal logic only became totally clear on viewing the finished film.*

Another videotape is received; this time it's disturbingly obtrusive, with images of both of them in bed, taken by an unidentified intruder.

As the disorientated couple sit watching this televisual invasion of privacy, the threateningly irrational mood is mirrored by three expressionistic paintings hanging above their couch; these are not original works by Lynch, but paintings by his first wife, Peggy, mother of Jennifer and 'star' of *The Alphabet*.

The cabinet that contains the looming VCR was built by Lynch himself, as part of his foray into furniture design.

The cops are called. Al and Ed, two traditionally bluff movie detectives examine the interior of the house as if expert in the art of handheld camerawork. Fred explains to them why he won't keep a camcorder in the house: 'I like to remember things my own way . . . Not necessarily the way they happened.'

Inexplicably, the next tape they receive freezes on a facial close-up of Fred with an expression of extreme terror, kneeling by Renee's side of their bed. Unnerved by the impossibly intrusive images, Renee calls the cops back. She's incensed to find Fred hasn't bothered to turn the burglar alarm system on while they've been asleep at nights.

Fred and Renee go to a Hollywood party attended by her friends, a set of sleazy third-raters he obviously feels uncomfortable with. As Renee socialises with them, Fred is approached by the 'Mystery Man' (Robert Blake) – a strange, pallid, almost pierrot-like figure who claims to have met Fred before back at his home – surrealistically, he claims he's back at the house right now. He urges Fred to phone his home number, to find him answering at the other end of the line. When Fred, disorientated and angry, asks him how he got into his house, the Mystery Man claims, just like the vampire or incubus of legend, that he never goes where he isn't invited.

Fred enquires of Renee's mustachioed, sleazebag friend Andy, with whom she's been spending most of her evening, who exactly the Mystery Man is. When told he's a friend of Dick Laurent, he impulsively replies that he's dead – to which Andy asks where he got his information from, and how he knows Dick.

On the drive home, Fred verbally attacks Andy and his 'fucked-up friends', but can't bring himself to mention the metaphysically impossible conversation with the Mystery Man. Renee is cagey about how she got to know Andy, telling him they met at a place called Moke's and he once offered her a job.

Fred stands in front of the mirror, staring hard at his own face as if he finds it hard to recognise. Renee finds herself alone in the darkened house, calling to Fred but unable to see or hear him – in direct reversal of Fred's dream.

Fred (Bill Pullman) and Renee (Patricia Arquette) at the Hollywood party where his sense of reality starts to become severely deranged. Future echoes of the personal tragedy - Renee's murder - which accompanies his identity crisis have already started to replay themselves, in a never-ending sequence of events.

The last of the spy videos shows Fred standing over Renee's mutilated body. Chillingly, we soon realise this is a reality. He has no memory of her murder, but, under arrest for the crime, he begs Al and Ed to tell him he didn't do it, as if unsure of his own actions. He's rapidly charged with murder, convicted and sentenced to death. Escorted to his cell by two sardonic guards, he's told to make himself at home and to 'just call the concierge' if he needs anything.

'I'm really glad that I'm not going to be executed this evening,' reflected Lynch, once he finished checking technical details over the phone with a prison official from his teenage home state of Virginia – where the electric chair is still retained.

Ultimately, however, the old-fashioned execution scene (of another Death Row prisoner) would be excised from the completed print, the prison scenes concentrating solely on the personal hell of Fred.

In the prison yard, during his limited exercise period, Fred suffers such severe head pain that he begs to be taken back inside. 'Shit, that wife killer's lookin' pretty fucked up,' concedes a slightly troubled Guard Henry, who can do little to assist him. 'Which one?' laughs his buddy.

In a vivid scene of biological surrealism, Fred's pain-wracked head turns into a bloody blur, transmogrifying into that of a younger man.

The younger man appears in a dream sequence of a cabin fire out in the desert, off of the lost highway. A girl (Natasha Gregson Wagner) is standing in front of the cabin trying to call to him. It becomes apparent that the fire is running in reverse motion. – the cabin is left completely reformed, just a single light above the door illuminating the desert night.

The man who awakes on Death Row is no longer Fred. The warden is panicked into running a fingerprint check on his identity, the prisoner temporarily unable to talk and identify himself.

He's identified as a 24-year-old garage mechanic from the San Fernando Valley named Pete Dayton (Balthazar Getty), with nothing more than a five-year-old stolen car rap to his name, his fresh face looking as if it recently received emergency surgery. He lives with his parents, middle-aged ex-bikers, who are called in to try to explain the situation but can proffer nothing more than that they haven't seen him for two days. Pete can neither explain nor grasp the reality of his own presence in the condemned cell; forced to concede defeat by the inexplicable circumstances, the authorities release him but put a police tail on his movements.

With Balthazar Getty wearing a prosthetic fleshwound on his forehead at this point, the director reminded the young actor that his character was 'still a bit in never-never land'. Moving from disorientation into psychosis and 'psychogenic fugue', it's fair to say Pete remains in this state of mind all throughout the action.

Adapting Kafka's theme of spontaneous metamorphosis into a *noir* idiom, Lynch extends the basis of one more unmade pet project into something altogether more unnervingly identifiable. As per the obsessive Dorothy and Frank in *Blue Velvet* – whose enjoyment of oral assault and manic profanity respectively seem to reflect the conditions algophilia and Tourette's syndrome – Lynch believes he may have identified a classic syndrome sufferer, despite his complete lack of psychoanalytical grounding. 'Psychogenic fugue,' he observes, is a syndrome that 'fits Fred Madison perfectly. When Barry and I were working we didn't know the term, but it's when a person suddenly takes on a completely different personality, different friends, everything.'

But of course, Fred's very literal metamorphosis takes *Lost Highway* out of the realm of the purely psychological, into the subjective reality of the fantastic and surreal. Lynch, however, insists that the Fred/Pete metamorphosis, and similar phenomena, 'are not inexplicable'.

'There are explanations for a billion things in life that aren't so understandable, and yet inside – somewhere – they are understandable. There are things that happen to people that can be understood in terms of jealousy, or fear, or love. Maybe not in a rational, intellectual way.

'It's like when you are sitting alone, you sometimes have the feeling that there are different parts of you. There are certain things that you can do and there are certain things that you would never do unless there was a part of you that took over. So, in a way, it's kind of logical.'

Out with his buddies for the evening, Pete is still disorientated and trying to figure out what happened to him. They pick up Sheila (Natasha Gregson Wagner), his girlfriend, and go to a bowling alley. She tells him how strange he was acting the other night, which he can't remember; he wants to know more, but the subject disturbs her so much she clams up on him.

Returned to his workplace, where he's been much missed, Pete finds that his employer, Arnie (Richard Pryor), has been told by Pete's mother that he's had a fever. He tells him that Mr Eddy, a faithful customer, has been asking after him.

Richard Pryor is virtually unrecognisable from his heyday as a brilliant stand-up comedian and notable character actor, very visibly suffering from muscular dystrophy. Apart from leaving him skeletally thin, with eyes popping from his head, the illness markedly affects his speech. Sadly, while the former stand-up genius may regard *Lost Highway* as an all-too-rare legitimate acting role, there's little doubt he's a piece of 'novelty casting', the culmination of Lynch's forte for presenting incidental characters as part of a general everyday weirdness.

He's still ill at ease when Mr Eddy (Robert Loggia), a local businessman-cum-hood and regular customer, turns up. Mr Eddy's tickled by the good repair job Pete's done on his 600 Pullman, taking him out for a leisurely cruise along Mulholland Drive. Singing the praises of his beloved car, Mr Eddy's quietly outraged when some clown in a silver Infiniti starts to tailgate him. As he pulls over to let the pushy overtaker pass, the Infiniti driver gives him the finger. Mr Eddy floors the gas and rear-ends the Infiniti till it runs off the road into some trees. Eddy pulls the terrified overtaker from his car, splitting his face with the butt of a .44 Ruger. The goons who have been riding with their boss train their .45s on the tailgater. 'Sorry about that, Pete, but tailgating is one thing I can't tolerate,' his host tells him.

Dropping Pete back at the garage, Mr Eddy offers to lend him a videotape: 'You like pornos? Give ya a boner?' Pete declines. Outside the garage, Hank and Lou, another standard pair of movie cops who are chasing Pete's tail, identify Mr Eddy as Dick Laurent.

Back at the garage next day, Pete's aching head is offended by the free-form sax blowing of Fred Madison on the radio, making Phil, the aging grease monkey he works with (Jack Nance, in his final blink-and-miss-it role), turn it off.

Mr Eddy returns. He has a blonde ladyfriend named Alice, a painted beauty with a 1940s Veronica Lake hairstyle – also played by Patricia Arquette, she's a ringer for Fred Madison's murdered wife with a change of hair colour. Pete can't make out why he seems to know her, or why his own life has started to seem so unfamiliar. Mr Eddy watches the magic moment, amused but wary of the effect his girl has had on Pete.

At this stage of the film, Renee could be assumed to lead a double life – changing her name, her hair colour and complicating her already duplicitous private life even further – like the dual Kim Novak character who drives tormented James Stewart to the edge of sanity in *Vertigo* (1958). 'The only problem,' reminds Lynch, 'is that Renee was already killed.'

'My first concept was that they were two different people,' says Patricia Arquette of the twin roles of Alice and Renee. 'But then David said, "No, no, no. They're the same person." So then you have to cross over a reality border, because they can't be the same person and one of them die. I was adrift there for awhile. So maybe one of them is an hallucination.

'I play two different interpretations of the same woman. I think it's about a man trying to recreate a relationship with the woman he loves so that it ends up better. Fred recreates himself as Pete, but the element of distrust in him is so strong that even his fantasy turns into a nightmare.'

Despite the disorientation of their two meshed male personalities, each one's existence clearly becomes a mirror image of the other's – experiencing the same trap through a social dimension warp.

'They're living the same relationship,' concedes a reticent Lynch of Fred and Pete, 'but they're living it in two different ways. They're victims in different ways, in both worlds.'

'Let's say you don't want to be yourself anymore,' explains Barry Gifford, providing the voice of rationality. 'Something happens to you and you just show up in Seattle, living under the name Joe Smith, with a whole different reality. It means that you're trying to escape something, and that's basically what Fred Madison does. He gets into a fugue state, which in this case means that he can't go anywhere – he's in a prison cell, so it's happening

Twin **femme fatales** Renee, left, and Alice, above, both portrayed by Patricia Arquette. Lynch insisted that Ms Arquette play both as if they were the same woman with different hair colours, irrespective of the fact that Renee has been murdered before Alice appears, and both of them appear in a photograph together. Renee/Alice carry echoes of Madelaine (Kim Novak) in **Vertigo** (1958), one of Lynch's abiding cinematic influences. Whereas the Novak character was a seemingly reincarnated beauty playing a duplicitous psychological game, Ms Arquette's twin role personifies the psycho-sexual trap which ensnares Fred (Bill Pullman). As he discovers after his personal metamorphosis, personalities are amorphous, reality has become fluid – but his predicament is inescapable.

Alice (Patricia Arquette) phones to make a date with a sleazy 'client'; Pete Dayton (Balthazar Getty), the confused young man Fred has metamorphosed into, will be recruited to rob her date but will stumble into murder instead.

internally, within his own mind. But things don't work out any better in the fugue state than they do in real life. He can't control the woman any more than he could in real life. You might say this is an explanation for what happens. However, this is not a complete explanation for the film. Things happen in this film that are not – and should not be – easily explained.'

Pete takes Sheila for a ride in his car; they pull up and make love passionately, watched by the two cops.

Next day, Alice, Mr Eddy's squeeze, shows up at the garage. Against Pete's better instincts, she talks him into taking her to dinner – then forgetting the dinner, just taking her home. 'Fucker gets more pussy than a toilet seat,' grouches one of the spying cops. They go to Harmon's Hideaway Hotel, where they fuck wildly, passionately, the antithesis of her doppelganger's bloodless coupling with Fred Madison. Pete is under her spell and agrees to see her again, despite the risk.

When Alice blows out a date because she has to see Mr Eddy, adrift Pete goes looking for Sheila. He finds her with his buddies out on Van Nuys Boulevard. He deals with a couple of drunken creeps putting the squeeze on her, to Sheila's surprise as she didn't see him when he was gazing straight over at her. He takes her back to Harmon's Hideaway, where he had his illicit scene with Alice, and fucks Sheila with a similar sense of wild desperation.

Neither Sheila nor his parents will tell what happened to him on the night he went missing. His dad, Bill (Gary Busey), admits that Sheila brought him back home with a man he'd never seen before, but when Pete asks him to elaborate, his old man's eyes fill with tears and he refuses to answer.

Mr Eddy calls in at the garage. He makes a casual point of telling Pete that if he knew anyone was going with his girl, he'd push his gun up their ass till it came out their mouth, then shoot 'em between the eyes. Alice calls Pete, telling him to meet her at another cheap, sleazy motel, the Starlight. She confides that she's almost sure Eddy knows about them; they have to get some money and get away together. She plans to rob a sleazebag pornographer Mr Eddy sometimes makes her fuck for money – when she confesses to Pete they met at a place called Moke's, where he offered her a job, it becomes clear that this is Andy, the moustached creep similarly acquainted with her alter-ago Renee.

In a flashback sequence, Alice remembers her first meeting with Andy and Mr Eddy – in a private office, watched by their cronies, she's forced to strip at gunpoint. Nervous at first, she gradually puts more erotic rhythm into her movement until Mr Eddy beckons her over. She sinks her head between his legs to fellate him, wearing a sensual smile on her face. On hearing her tell the story Pete accuses her of liking what she was forced to do, and it's hard for the viewer not to concur.

'I want to rehearse but first I want to see all the underwear,' said Lynch to cast and crew, prior to shooting scenes at the seedy sex rendezvous. 'Just remember, panties and death, same thing.' As the audience should by now realise, psychosis and sex are at least as closely entwined as lingerie and death.

Alice arranges to 'party' with Andy tomorrow night; distasteful as it is to Pete, he agrees to let her have two hours alone with Andy before he breaks into the house at 11.15 p.m. to crack him over the head while she mixes drinks.

Sheila waits outside Pete's house for him to return home. She doesn't see him until he stands directly in front of her, then seems to have a delayed vision of him in the car with another person. She accuses him of fucking another woman, punches him and gets hysterical in the street till Pete's dad comes out to calm things down. She accuses Pete of being a different person, insisting Bill Dayton tells him exactly what they saw the other night. Bill finds it too painful to talk. Sheila gives up, promising never to bother his family again, and walks away.

Inside the house, Pete receives a call from Mr Eddy, who sinisterly claims he just wants to check that Pete is 'doing okay'. He hands him over to a friend he has on the line – the sardonic, vampire-faced Mystery Man, who claims to have met him before at his house. The Mystery Man matter-of-factly claims they've just killed two people, then reflects aloud on the Far Eastern mode of execution wherein the prisoner never knows when a bullet will be aimed at the back of his head. Unsurprisingly, Pete's unease increases.

As Pete climbs into Andy's house, he can see the pair of them watching a porno film which features Alice at the centre of its group-sex scene. He tightens as she seems to enjoy anal sex on screen; as the sex becomes more brutal, Pete bites hard and brings a statuette down on Andy's head. Dazed Andy retaliates, wrestling with Pete till the younger man manages to send him flying. With a visceral crack, the sharp corner of the coffee table pierces deep into Andy's cranium. Impaled through the forehead, his corpse remains suspended in a kneeling position like a piece of surreal body furniture.

Pete is shocked but Alice is quietly impressed. After she strips the dead Andy of his jewellery and money, they make to clear out but Pete spots a photograph on the wall: it's a group shot featuring Andy, Mr Eddy, Alice and the dark-haired Renee. Pete asks her which one she really is, which she finds a nonsensical question; his head is starting to ache again and his nose is bleeding. As they prepare to leave the house, he's unsure whether the Alice he sees is real, or the porno actress being butt-fucked on the video screen.

They drive out to the desert, where Alice claims she knows a fence who can convert Andy's valuables into cash. Alice seduces the bewildered Pete in the desert night air; after they make love, he tells her how much he wants her. 'You'll never have me,' she contradicts. Walking naked toward the fence's cabin, the earlier image, witnessed by the transforming Fred, of the cabin fire playing backwards, repeats itself.

This recurring scene, the most hypnotic in the film, was shot in a converted furniture warehouse in downtown LA, with one five-foot section convincingly converted into a microscopic stretch of the Mojave desert. At one point Ms Arquette, her body clad in black velvet and held stiffly upright by various restraining contraptions, appears invisible apart from her head – which is suspended still in the desert night air. As an artificial breeze runs across her face, electricity suddenly flashes – that Lynchian industrial lightning that can only signal psychic chaos.

As the fragmented Pete raises his head from his hands, he's no longer Pete at all – he's Fred Madison. About to make off in the car, he hears a voice behind him: it's the quietly demonic Mystery Man. Free to move around space and time, the Mystery Man is suddenly standing on the porch of the re-integrated cabin. Fred follows him in, looking for Alice. 'Her name is Renee. If she told you her name is Alice, she's lying,' claims Fred's greasepainted pursuer. We see his point of view through the camcorder he's using to shoot Fred, of the same grainy black and white quality as the intrusive tapes seen earlier.

Fred pulls up at the Lost Highway Hotel. He finds a passageway identical to that in Andy's house, where he opens the door to find Alice having anal sex just like in the video film.

Back at Andy's house, all four police detectives regard the photo portrait which shows Fred Madison's wife with Dick Laurent (Mr Eddy). Pete Dayton's prints are all over the house. Ed opines there's no such thing as a bad coincidence, which may as well be the maxim the whole film is based around.

At the Lost Highway Hotel, Fred finds dark-haired Renee, seemingly resurrected, in bed with Mr Eddy/Dick Laurent. He waits quietly in the wings for her to leave, then abducts her boss/pimp at gunpoint, shutting him in the trunk of his own Mercedes Pullman. From the window of the hotel, the Mystery Man is shooting the whole thing on his camcorder.

Fred pulls over on a piece of shrubland; as he releases Eddy/Laurent from the trunk, they fight desperately, but Fred cuts his throat when passed a knife by someone standing behind him. A gun is trained on the wounded big guy by the Mystery Man. 'What do you guys want?' gurgles Eddy/Laurent through his own blood. The Mystery Man holds out a portable mini-TV, which shows the hardcore porno film featuring Alice being played out on a screen back at Andy's house; as the sex becomes more violently deviant, hinting that it may in fact be a 'snuff movie', the camera pans to show Renee, turned on by watching the movie with Eddy/Laurent and Andy. The picture suddenly changes to show Fred and the Mystery Man standing complicitly together. The Mystery Man instructs the dying Eddy/Laurent to hand the TV back; the big old guy laughs sardonically, knowing the game's up. The demonic intruder fires the gun point blank into him. He then whispers into his partner Fred's ear. As the camera moves back, Fred is holding the gun. He drives off alone. Was the Mystery Man ever really there at all?

As day breaks, Fred speaks into the intercom of his own house, to give himself the message: 'Dick Laurent is dead.' Reality has arrived back at the same point of madness, as if a twisted Moebius strip.

As the cops give chase, Fred heads back out onto the highway. His head starts to ache and throb, distorting its shape as he begins to lose his identity again.

The credits close on the same opening image of the yellow-lined lost highway.

Of all the component parts of the film to which Lynch plays obsessive attention, music is by now a long-established device for building the atmosphere of a Lynch project – both on soundtrack and on set.

With the main compositional duties taken by Badalamenti, *Lost Highway* marks the long-overdue use of a specially-commissioned secondary score by Barry Adamson, credited as 'additional music composer'. Gaining well-deserved critical acclaim (but little commercial success) by composing soundtracks to imaginary movies for the last decade, the British ex-Magazine/Bad Seeds bass guitarist has evolved a style and atmosphere of his own that can chill or warm the bone marrow.

The secondary soundtrack was painstakingly compiled by Lynch and his music editor,

Marc Vanocur. 'I listened to tons of music,' Lynch confirms, 'and some of it talks to me for this scene or that. I don't really know why, but each piece that ends up in the film supports the scene and makes the whole greater than the sum of the parts.'

(The hypnotic cabin fire scene, for example, makes eerie use of This Mortal Coil's icily romantic cover of Tim Buckley's 'Song to the Siren'. As the cabin reforms, the final notes of the song, just after the unheard closing words – 'Here I am. Waiting to hold you.' – play out just before the desert night re-appearance of the Mystery Man. 'Here I am,' are his first words to the Balthazar Getty character, implicitly echoing the song.)

With a soundtrack album released prior to the film by Interscope Records, the musical tie-in – veering from Badalamenti and Adamson's urgent melodies to updated cover versions and cacophonic noise rock – seems a conscious effort to herald the film as a mixed-media event, as per the best-selling soundtrack album to *Natural Born Killers* (1994), compiled and produced for Oliver Stone by Trent Reznor of Nine Inch Nails – who subsequently took on the same role for David Lynch.

David Bowie, long-time Lynch admirer and perpetrator of a dreadful cameo *in Fire Walk With Me*, also contributes the aptly-titled 'I'm Deranged'. Formerly a skilful recycler of the *zeitgeist*, Bowie recently returned a certain ferocity to his sound by tapping into the generation of noise-rockers, such as recent collaborator Trent Reznor, just as he once copped his attitude from rock 'n' roll mavericks like Lou Reed. 'I'm Deranged' is, appropriately, the film's theme tune, playing over the opening and closing credits, against footage of the highway itself.

In this incestuous generational cross-over, Lou Reed also appears on the soundtrack singing a cover of 'This Magic Moment', by his late friend Doc Pomus (composer of 'Suspicion' and 'Viva Las Vegas' for Elvis) – the intention to signify Pete Dayton's first glimpse of the predatory Alice with the song indicated in the original screenplay.

The aesthetic of the *Lost Highway* soundtrack is one in which thematic melody and background noise both conflict and combine; this, for non-musician Lynch, is the atmospheric concept of pure sound.

'Sound is almost like a drug,' testifies the artist who once described himself as more of a soundman than a director. 'It's so pure that when it goes in your ears, it instantly does something to you. The thing that I'm after is when the whole becomes greater than the sum of the parts. It's so beautifully abstract. The great thing is that it can't be picked to death, because it's so fantastically complicated. It's a beautiful realm to experiment in. There's a magical thing that happens that elevates it to another place. And it can't happen until everything is there. It can jump in those last moments, and it has to do with sound and picture working together in a certain way. It's such an abstract thing. It's just impossible to guarantee it happening.'

Though Lynch himself is credited for 'sound design' on the film, he's clearly indebted to the influence of his early collaborator Alan Splet, who died of cancer, age 58, in December 1994. As an acknowledged influence on the more creative European industrial musicians of the 1980s–'90s, Splet originated a balance of noise and sound effects as an extra-musical aesthetic, rather than simple cacophony. As further testament to his influence, additional sound effects for *Lost Highway* are provided, in Splet's imaginatively improvised style, by his widow Ann Kroeber-Splet.

'I'm not a musician,' Lynch once reminded the *Hollywood Reporter*. 'I've been brought into the world of music by Angelo and by sound effects. Actually, I think sound effects are music. You can suddenly have a feel for things, and you don't really know where it comes from. And I just have a love for sound effects as music.'

Though the stalled CiBy 2000 three-picture deal now has a schedule of seven years, supposedly leaving little time for extra-curricular artistic projects, Lynch, characteristically, has responded to overtures by British musician Robin Rimbaud, who – as if adopting the surname of the French Romantic poet wasn't enough – goes under the professional title of Scanner.

Acknowledged as a 'telephone terrorist' who marries intercepted and found conversations to electro-rhythms and keyboard music (kind of a musical/conceptual CIA operative), Rimbaud suggested a collaborative project which looks likely to take place in 1997 – an album treating the recorded sounds of the human body as music. Given Lynch's fascination with the human organism as a factory of strange by-products, it seems he may finally fulfil an ambition which survived the wasteful *Dune* era – to make a definitive album of sound-effects-as-music.

At the height of his early 1990s activity, Lynch found himself engrossed in a number of extra-curricular projects – musical, visual art, performance. In recent years, he has lent his name to other directors' films, as an endorsement of their own peculiar forms of Weird Americana. In part, a measure of the artistic success of his long-awaited new film may be how it sparks off other areas of enthusiasm and creativity; alternatively, a poor international reaction could mean such sideline projects become an increasing mainstay of his career.

With the soundtrack album making a prior release to the film, *Lost Highway*'s backers are clearly hoping for an under-35s phenomenon; something which appeals to the fickle, pop-culturally literate movie fan – an audience whose sensiblities have been formed as much by rock music and cult TV as by celluloid.

Lost Highway, with a far more linear structure and plot than was imaginable back in the art school/*Eraserhead* days, however irrational its narrative, makes the headlong dive into the subconscious which *Blue Velvet*, Lynch's second genuine masterpiece, was ultimately restrained from. (And which *Fire Walk With Me*, the movie painter's little valued *third* genuine masterpiece, ventured much further into, though few seemed to notice or care.)

The commercial response may largely depend on how many under-35 cinemagoers buy the distributor's line that Lynch is the godfather of today's purveyors of post-modern violence – but with an imaginative and emotional resonance that lingers in the mind.

Ultimately, *Lost Highway* may well determine how many of Lynch's remaining CiBy 2000 projects are realised with a full budget – certainly, how uncompromised the rest of his career will be, now that he's reached his early fifties. While unsympathetic commentators might be happy to see his obsessive vision fade from view, only the most churlish would refuse to admit the painstaking construction of *Lost Highway* fulfils its very dark promise.

'I'm trying to find my next film,' claims Lynch, regarding PR on *Lost Highway* as just one more unavoidable chore, 'and it's not here yet. I'm fishing and maybe tomorrow it will bob to the surface.'

While Lynch, the artist, doubtless spends much time digging in his subconscious, the word on his latest project suggests it may well be adapted from a novel by Joe R. Lansdale, the crime novelist who updates the conventions of the genre with a more eccentric American gothicism.

Moreover, the literary agents of boxing journalist Katherine Dunn have confirmed Lynch/Asymmetrical hold an option on the rights to her classic 1980s novel, *Geek Love*. This would truly be a marriage made in a distorted heaven. Telling the tragi-comic tale of a quartet of twisted, gifted children purposely conceived with deformities by their carny mother, Dunn's celebrated prose is equal parts showmanish, compassionate and fixated on the grotesque. If Lynch brought his vision to such a project, it might extend the prurient/profound freakshow ethic to its logical, aesthetic extreme – far beyond the pallid, cautious efforts of his daughter to place deformity centre-stage.

For now, all depends on how many can be enticed into sharing the sanity-threatening journey into identity crisis, down the lost highway. At this strange juncture, at the end of the American century – where much of the US population, as well as a large contingent of western society, seem to live in a nostalgic love affair with an idealised past they never really knew, while indulging a near-apocalyptic fear of the future – Lynch's vision may yet come into its own time.

More than half a decade on from the peak of his public profile – back when his name carried definite associations for every media-literate person, even those who knew him as nothing more than a guy who did 'weird stuff' – Lynch is still competing only on his own terms.

As the mass media continues to prove itself adept at assimilating violent imagery, sexual titillation and mild fetishism into its money-making machine, there's even a danger that a rarefied vision like Lynch's may appear overly polite to the more jaded consumer.

But that, perhaps, is as it should be; the grotesquerie of Lynch's vision was always a 'ticket to another world', a tool to help gain entrance to the richer, more vivid reality of a singularly all-American subconscious. At no point has he ever entered any kind of pop-cultural transgression contest. As he once said, making people recoil just for the sake of it is no fun at all.

The rapid-fire profanity of Frank Booth, *in Blue Velvet*, was a larger-than-life idiosyncrasy, rendering him a comical slave to his own impulses – rather than just a character who could out-cuss the post-Scorsese school of screen gangsters; similarly, the sexual perversion in that film was a twisted subversion of Frank and Dorothy's own, irreconcilable romantic longings.

The monochrome squalor and DIY gore of *Eraserhead* created, with benefit of hindsight, a private dreamworld which is surprisingly sentimental – as much concerned with the responsibilities of parenthood, and the small mercy of a 'dream lover', as with cold urban angst.

Even the bleak, severely underrated *Fire Walk With Me* lent meaning to the disappearing life of a young abuse and murder victim: dying from multiple stab wounds, Laura could remember a thrift-store painting on her bedroom wall and find herself in the protecting arms of a guardian angel.

Now, a much colder psycho-sexuality delineates Lynch's personal dream of LA – a product of its times, as well as its creator's obsessive vision. As visually rich as it is thematically dark, *Lost Highway* is the love story that our age of insecurity demands.

Lynch, in his least compromised moments, has nurtured a sincere personal vision he continues to paint for the screen. A vision born at a point where inner reality and waking dreams make their mark on the small wonders of everyday living.

In the late 1990s, such a peculiar earnestness may still prove to be his strength – or may yet be his commercial undoing. But still, David Lynch has the life-affirming sentimentality to make us remember those quirky little things that make life worth living – and then again, he has the unflinching, painterly eye of a Goya or Bacon, making the ugliness he describes too compellingly beautiful to turn away from.

Bibliography
Magazine/newspaper articles

Andrew, Geoff. 'Blue Murder: Sex Shocker or Cult Classic?' *Time Out* (4/3/87).

Bilbow, Marjorie. 'Herbert – full of praise for Lynch.' *Screen International* (5/1/85).

Billson, Anne. 'Blue Murder: Cult Classic or Sex Shocker?' *Time Out* (4/3/87).

Bloom, Philippa. 'Mark Frost: Director/Writer/Peakie.' *Empire* (July 1992).

Borden, Lizzie. 'The World According to Lynch.' *Village Voice* (23/9/86).

Bouzereau, Laurent. '*Blue Velvet* – An Interview with David Lynch.' *Cineaste* (volume XV number 3, 1987).

Briskin, David. 'Amazerhead.' *Rolling Stone* (September 1990).

Chambers, Veronica. 'Young At Art.' *Premiere* (May 1993).

Chute, David. 'Out to Lynch.' *Film Comment* (September/October 1986).

Ciment, Michel and Nioguret, Hubert. Interview with Lynch – part of 'David Lynch Dossier'. *Positif* (October 1990).

Collis, Clark. 'Terry Zwigoff.' *Empire* (June 1995).

Cook, Richard. 'Would You Buy a $45m Epic From This Man?' *New Musical Express* (15/12/84).

Corliss, Richard. 'Czar of Bizarre.' *Time* (1/10/90).

Dawson, Jeff. 'Laura Palmer Lives!' *Empire* (November 1992).

Ferry, Jeffrey. 'Blue Movie.' *The Face* (February 1987).

Film Review. 'It Took Courage To Film This True Story . . .' (writer uncredited – October 1980).

Foster Wallace, David. *Premiere* (October 1996).

Franklin, B. J. 'De Laurentiis' $40m *Dune* ends principal photography in Mexico.' *Screen International* (17/12/83).

Fuller, Graham. 'Call of the Wild.' *The Listener* (10/5/90).

Gentry, Ric. 'Alan Splet and Sound Effects for *Dune*.' *American Cinematographer* (December 1984).

Gilmore, Mikal. 'The Lost Boys.' *Rolling Stone* (6/3/97)

Godwin, K. George. '*Eraserhead*: The story behind the strangest movie ever made, and the cinematic genius who directed it.' *Cinefantastique* (September 1984).

Hinson, Hal. 'Dreamscapes.' *American Film* (December 1984).

Hoberman, J. 'Bloodsuckers Invade Sundance.' *Premiere* (June 1995).

Hollywood Reporter. Production reportage on *Twin Peaks*: from Season One to pre-production on *Fire Walk With Me*. (31/5/90, 23/7/90, 21/8/90, 2/10/90, 26/10/90, 1/11/90, 12/11/90, 14/11/90, 8/1/91, 25/2/91, 27/2/91, 5/3/91, 25/4/91, 29/4/91, 6/6/91, 12/6/91.)

Klein, Andy. 'Like a Drug . . .' *Hollywood Reporter TV & Music Special Issue* (24/8/90).

L'Ecuyer, Gerald. 'David Lynch: Out-of-Bounds.' *Interview* (March 1987).

Lindroth, James. 'Down the Yellow Brick Road: Two Dorothys and the Journey of Initiation in Dream and Nightmare.' *Literature/Film Quarterly* (volume 18, number 3, 1990).

Lipman, Amanda. 'Pleasure and Pain.' *City Limits* (9/4/87).

Lofficier, Randy and Jean-Marc. 'The Long, Long Road to *Dune*.' Rod Serling's *The Twilight Zone Magazine* (December 1984).

Magid, Ron. '*Blue Velvet* – Small Town Horror Tale.' *American Cinematographer* (November 1986).

Mandell, Paul. 'Photography and Visual Effects for *Dune*.' *American Cinematographer* (December 1984).

Marsh, David and Missler, Andreas. 'David Lynch.' *Cinema Papers* (March 1987).

Pizello, Chris. 'Peeking Through Crumb's Keyhole.' *American Cinematographer* (July 1995).

Riddle, Patricia. 'The Master Builders of *Dune*.' *Prevue* (July/August 1984).

'The Legend Maker of *Dune*.' *Prevue* (November/December 1984).

Rodley, Chris. 'David Lynch: Mr Contradiction.' *Sight and Sound* (July 1996).

Romney, Jonathan. 'Songs For Swinging Loggers.' *City Limits* (8/11/90).

'*Eraserhead*'s human heart.' *The Guardian* (14/1/97).

Rugoff, Ralph. 'David Lynch and Laura Dern Cut Loose.' (*Premiere*, September 1990.)

Salisbury, Mark. 'Jennifer Lynch: Director.' *Empire* (June 1993).

Sammon, Paul M. 'David Lynch's *Dune* Journal.' *Cinefantastique* (September 1984).

Sammon, Paul M., Jones, Stephen and Levy, Frederic Albert. 'Versions of Arrakis you'll never see.' *Cinefantastique* (September 1984).

Stein, Michael. 'Frank Herbert's Masterful Epic *Dune* Now Becomes A Mammoth Film.' *Fantastic Films* (March 1984).

Transcript. 'David Lynch's *Fire Walk With Me*: the press conference.' *Cinema Papers* (August 1992).

Vaines, Colin. 'Film-maker Bizarre.' *Screen International* (1/12/79).

Various writers. 'David Lynch Dossier.' *Starfix* (September 1990).

'Why Mel's repaying a debt . . .'. *Screen International* (20/10/79).

Yates, Robert. 'Crumbs!' *Premiere* (UK – July 1995)

Filmography

THE ALPHABET

An H. Barton Wasserman Production.
Sole cast member: Peggy Lynch. Written, Produced, Directed, Animated, Photographed, Recorded and Edited by David Lynch. 1968. 4 mins.

THE GRANDMOTHER

The American Film Institute presents A Film by David Lynch.
Cast: BOY(Richard White), GRANDMOTHER (Dorothy McGinnis), MOTHER (Virginia Maitland), FATHER (Robert Chadwick).
Crew: Sound Effects: David Lynch, Margaret Lynch, Robert Chadwick, Alan R. Splet. Sound Editing and Recording Alan R. Splet. Music and music effects Tractor. Assistant script consultants Margaret Lynch/C. K. Williams. Written, Produced, Directed, Animation, Make-up and Photography by David Lynch. 1970. 34 mins.

ERASERHEAD

The American Film Institute Center for Advanced Film Studies presents A Film by David Lynch.
Cast: HENRY SPENCER(John Nance), MARY X(Charlotte Stewart), BILL X(Allen Joseph), MRS X(Jeanne Bates), BEAUTIFUL GIRL ACROSS THE HALL(Judith Anna Roberts), LADY IN THE RADIATOR(Laurel Near), LANDLADY(V. Phipps-Wilson), MAN IN THE PLANET(Jack Fisk), GRANDMOTHER(Jean Lange), BOY(Thomas Coulson), BUM(John Monez), PAUL(Darwin Joston), ERASER FACTORY BOSS(Neil Moran), PENCIL MACHINE OPERATOR(Hal Landon, Jr.), LITTLE GIRL(Jennifer Lynch), LITTLE BOY(Brad Keller), PEOPLE DIGGING IN THE ALLEY(Peggy Lynch/Doddie Keller), MAN WITH CIGAR(Gill Dennis), FIGHTING MAN(Toby Keller), MR ROUNDHEELS(Raymond Walsh).
Crew: Sound Effects: Alan R. Splet/David Lynch. Sound Design Alan R. Splet. 'Lady in the Radiator Song' composed and performed by Peter Ivers; organ music by 'Fats' Waller. Photography Frederick Elmes/Herbert Cardwell. Special Photographic Effects Frederick Elmes. Production Assistant Catherine Coulson. Production Manager Doreen Small. Written, Produced, Directed; Special Effects, Make-up and Editing by David Lynch. 1976. 89 mins.

THE ELEPHANT MAN

A Brooksfilms Production.
Cast: FREDERICK TREVES(Anthony Hopkins), JOHN MERRICK(John Hurt), MRS MADGE KENDAL(Anne Bancroft), CARR GOMM(John Gielgud), MOTHERSHEAD(Wendy Hiller), BYTES(Freddie Jones), NIGHT PORTER(Michael Elphick), MRS TREVES(Hannah Gordon), PRINCESS ALEXANDRA(Helen Ryan), FOX(John Standing), BYTES' BOY(Dexter Fletcher), NURSE NORA(Lesley Dunlop), MERRICK'S MOTHER(Phoebe Nicholls), FAT LADY(Claire Davenport), SKELETON WOMAN(Orla Pederson), DISTRAUGHT WOMAN(Patsy Smart), ALDERMAN(Frederick Treves), FIRE EATER(The Great Stromboli), NURSE KATHLEEN(Nula Conwell), FIGHTING WOMEN(Bernadette Milnes/Brenda Kempner), TART(Carole Harrison), LADY WADDINGTON(Kathleen Byron), LORD WADDINGTON(Gerald Case), MAN WITH WHORES(David Ryall), WHORES(Deidre Costello/Pauline Quirke), PLUMED DWARF(Kenny Baker), GIANT(Chris Greener), MIDGETS(Marcus Powell/Gilda Cohen), SIAMESE TWINS(Lisa and Teri Scoble), JAPANESE BLEEDER(Eiji Kusuhara), LITTLE JIM(Robert Day), SCREAMING MUM(Patricia Hodge).
Crew: Special Sound Effects David Lynch. Sound Design Alan R. Splet. Make-up Application Wally Schneidermann. Elephant Man Make-Up Christopher Tucker. Costume Design Patricia Norris. Music Composed and Conducted by John Morris. Production Designer Stuart Craig. Editor Anne V. Coates. Director of Photography Freddie Francis. Assistant Directors Anthony Waye/Gerry Gavigan/Nick Daubeny. Executive Producer Stuart Cornfeld. Producer Jonathan Sanger. Written by Christopher De Vore, Eric Bergren and David Lynch. Based upon the books, *The Elephant Man and Other Reminiscences* by Sir Frederick Treves and *The Elephant Man – A Study in Human Dignity* by Ashley Montagu. Directed by David Lynch. 1980. 124 mins.

DUNE

Universal Pictures present a Dino De Laurentiis Production.
Cast: PAUL ATREIDES(Kyle MacLachlan), LADY JESSICA(Francesca Annis), BARON HARKONNEN(Kenneth McMillan), FEYD-RAUTHA(Sting), PADISHAH EMPEROR(Jose Ferrer), GURNEY HALLECK(Patrick Stewart), THUFIR HAWAT(Freddie Jones), REVEREND MOTHER MOHIAM(Sian Phillips), CHANI(Sean Young), BEAST RABBAN(Paul Smith), PRINCESS IRULAN(Virginia Madsen), DR KYNES(Max Von Sydow), PITER(Brad Dourif), DR YUEH(Dean Stockwell), DUKE LETO(Jurgen Prochnow), REVEREND MOTHER RAMALLO(Silvana Mangano), SHADOUT MAPES(Linda Hunt), NEFUD(Jack Nance), DUNCAN(Richard Jordan), STILGAR(Everett McGill), JAMIS(Judd Omen), ALIA(Alicia Roanne Witt).
Crew: Sound Design Alan R. Splet. Creative Make-Up Giannetto De Rossi. 'Stillsuit'

Construction/Development Don Post. Costume Design Bob Ringwood. 'Prophecy' Theme by Brian Eno/Daniel Lanois/Roger Eno. Music Composed and Performed by Toto. Optical Effects Van Der Veer Photo Company. Additional Special Visual Effects Albert J. Whitlock. Special Visual Effects Universal City Studios Matte Department. Special Photographic Effects Barry Nolan. Mechanical Creatures Carlo Rambaldi. Mechanical Special Effects Kit West. Production Designer Tony Masters. Editor Antony Gibbs. Second Unit Photography James Devis/Frederick Elmes. Director of Photography Freddie Francis. Assistant Director / Associate Producer Jose Lopez Rodero. Producer Rafaella De Laurentiis. Screenplay by David Lynch. Adapted from the novel by Frank Herbert. Directed by David Lynch. 1984. 137 mins.

BLUE VELVET

A De Laurentiis Entertainment Production.
Cast: JEFFREY BEAUMONT(Kyle MacLachlan), DOROTHY VALLENS(Isabella Rossellini), FRANK BOOTH(Dennis Hopper), SANDY WILLIAMS(Laura Dern), MRS WILLIAMS(Hope Lange), BEN(Dean Stockwell), DETECTIVE WILLIAMS(George Dickerson), MRS BEAUMONT(Priscilla Pointer), AUNT BARBARA(Frances Bay), TOM BEAUMONT(Jack Harvey), MIKE(Ken Stovitz), RAYMOND(Brad Dourif), PAUL(Jack Nance), HUNTER(J. Michael Hunter), DON VALLENS(Dick Green), YELLOW MAN(Fred Pickler), DR GYNDE(Philip Markert), DOUBLE ED(Leonard Watkins), DOUBLE ED(Moses Gibson).
Crew: Casting Johanna Ray. Sound Recording Ann Kroeber. Sound Design Alan R. Splet. Titles and Opticals Van Der Veer Photo Company. Special Make-Up Effects Dean Jones. Music Composed and Conducted by Angelo Badalamenti. Song 'The Mysteries of Love' (music: Badalamenti/lyrics: Lynch), performed by Julee Cruise. Additional Songs 'Blue Velvet' performed by Bobby Vinton; 'In Dreams', Roy Orbison. Special Effects Greg Hull/George Hill. Production Designer Patricia Norris. Editor Duwayne Dunham. Production Assistant Jennifer Lynch. Key Production Assistant John Wildermuth. Director of Photography Frederick Elmes. Assistant Directors Ellen Rauch/Ian Woolf. Executive Producer Richard Roth. Producer Fred Caruso. Written and Directed by David Lynch. 1986. 120 mins.

LE COWBOY ET LE FRENCHMAN

An Erato Films Production, in conjunction with *Figaro* Magazine.
Cast: SLIM(Harry Dean Stanton), FRENCHMAN(Frederic Golchan), COWBOYS & INDIANS(Tracey Walters/Jack Nance/Michael Horse).

Crew: Editor Scott Chesnut. Sound Engineer Jon Huck. Choreography Sarah Elgart. Production / Costume Design Patricia Norris/Nancy Martinelli. Director of Photography Frederick Elmes. Written and Directed by David Lynch. 1988. 20 mins.

TWIN PEAKS

A Lynch–Frost/Propaganda Films Production, in association with Worldvision Enterprises Inc.
For original cast and central characters early in the first season, see Chapter Six.
Later Cast Members: ALBERT ROSENFIELD(Miguel Ferrer), GORDON COLE(David Lynch), WINDOM EARLE(Kenneth Welsh), ANNIE BLACKBURN(Heather Graham), MAJOR BRIGGS (Don Davis), BETTY BRIGGS(Charlotte Stewart*), RONNETTE PULASKI(Phoebe Augustine), MAN FROM ANOTHER PLACE (DWARF)(Michael J. Anderson), GIANT (Carel L. Struycken), GERARD, THE ONE-ARMED MAN(Al Strobel), ROADHOUSE SINGER(Julee Cruise), BLACK LODGE SINGER(Jimmy Scott), JACQUES RENAULT(Walter Olkewicz), JEAN RENAULT(Michael Parks), BERNARD RENAULT(Clay Wilcox), DICK TREMAYNE(Ian Buchanan), BLACKIE(Victoria Catlin), ANDREW PACKARD(Dan O'Herlihy), HAROLD SMITH(Lenny Von Dohlen), 'COUSIN JONATHAN'(Mark Takano), MIKE NELSON(Gary Hershberger), DENISE/DENNIS BRYSON(David Duchovny), THE LATE CAROLINE EARLE(Brenda E. Mathers), THOMAS ECKAHART(David Warner).
Crew: Casting Johanna Ray. Sound Design Douglas Murray. Make-Up Lizbeth Williamson. Special Effects Greg McMickle. Production/Costume Design Patricia Norris. Editor Duwayne Dunham. Art Director Patricia Norris (pilot)/Richard Hooker (series). Music Angelo Badalamenti. Songs 'The Nightingale', 'Into the Night', 'Falling', 'Rockin' Back Inside My Heart', 'The World Spins': all sung by Julee Cruise; 'Sycamore Trees' sung by Jimmy Scott. All songs, music: Badalamenti/lyrics: Lynch. Director of Photography Ron Garcia (pilot)/Frank Byers (series). Producers (of individual episodes) David J. Latt/Harley Peyton/Robert Engels/Robert D. Simon/Monty Montgomery/Philip Neel. Supervising Producer Gregg Fienberg. Associate Producer Monty Montgomery. Executive Producers Mark Frost/David Lynch. Story by David Lynch and Mark Frost. Written by David Lynch and Mark Frost (pilot, episodes 1 and 2); see Chapters Six/Eight for other writers. Directed by David Lynch (pilot, episodes 2, 8, 9, 14 and 29); see Chapters Six/Eight for other directors. TV series. Two seasons. Produced 1989–91. Pilot: 110 mins. Episode 8: 95 mins. All other episodes 45 mins.

WILD AT HEART

A Propaganda Films Production, in association with Polygram Filmed Entertainment.
Cast: SAILOR RIPLEY (Nicolas Cage), LULA PACE FORTUNE(Laura Dern), BOBBY PERU (Willem Dafoe), MARIETTA FORTUNE (Diane Ladd), SANTOS(J. E. Freeman), JOHNNIE FARRAGUT(Harry Dean Stanton), REGGIE (Calvin Lockhart), PERDITA DURANGO(Isabella Rossellini), COUSIN DELL(Crispin Glover), JUANA(Grace Zabriskie), MR REINDEER(W. Morgan Sheppard), DROPSHADOW(David Patrick Kelly), BOBBY RAY LEMON(Gregg Dandridge), GIRL IN ACCIDENT (Sherilyn Fenn), UNCLE POOCH(Marvin Kaplan), GEORGE KOVICH (Freddie Jones), SPARKY(John Lurie), BUDDY(Pruitt Taylor Vince), O. O. SPOOL(Jack Nance), PACE (Glenn Walker Harris, Jr.), GOOD WITCH (Sheryl Lee).
Crew: Special Make-Up Effects David B. Miller/Louis Lazzara. Special Effects Don Power/David Domeyer. Casting Johanna Ray. Script Supervisor Mary Sweeney. Production Design Patricia Norris. Editor Duwayne Dunham. Sound Design Randy Thom. Original Music Angelo Badalamenti. Song 'Up in Flames' (music: Badalamenti/lyrics: Lynch), performed by Koko Taylor. Additional Music 'Bomada', performed by Les Baxter; 'Wrinkles', The Big Three Trio; 'Chrysanthemum', 'Avant de Mourir', Shony Alex Braun; '1st Movement', Duke Ellington; 'Streamline', John Ewing's Allstars; 'Smoke Rings', Glen Gray; 'In the Mood', Glenn Miller; 'Kosmogonia', Kryzstof Penderecki; 'Slaughter House', Powermad; 'Im Abendrot', Richard Strauss; 'Buried Alive', Billy Swan. Additional Songs 'Far Away Chant', performed by African Head Charge; 'Love Me', 'Love Me Tender', Nicolas Cage; 'Wicked Game', 'Blue Spanish Sky', 'In the Heat of the Jungle', Chris Isaak; 'Baby Please Don't Go', Them; 'Be-Bop-a-Lula', Gene Vincent. (Promotional video for Chris Isaak's 'Wicked Game' directed by David Lynch.) Director of Photography Frederick Elmes. Assistant Directors Margaux Mackay Myers/Steven Hirsch/Deepak Nayar/W.Thomas Snyder. Executive Producer Michael Kuhn. Producers Monty Montgomery/Steve Golin/Sigurjon Sighvatsson. Written by David Lynch. Based upon the novel, *Wild At Heart: the Story of Sailor and Lula* by Barry Gifford. Directed by David Lynch. 1990. 124 mins.

INDUSTRIAL SYMPHONY NO. 1

A Propaganda Films Production.
Cast: HEARTBROKEN WOMAN(Laura Dern), HEARTBREAKER(Nicolas Cage), DREAMSELF OF THE HEARTBROKEN WOMAN(Julee Cruise), FEMALE DANCER(Lisa Giobbi), MALE DANCER(Felix Blaska), WOODSMAN (TWIN A)(Michael J. Anderson), CLARINET SOLOIST (TWIN B) (Andre Badalamenti), TALL SKINNED DEER (John Bell).
Musical Director Angelo Badalamenti. Songs/Musical Dramas 'Up in Flames', 'I Float Alone', 'Into the Night', 'Pinky's Bubble Egg (The Twins Spoke)', 'Dream Conversation', 'Rockin' Back Inside My Heart', 'The World Spins': (all music: Badalamenti/lyrics: Lynch); 'The Black Sea (Badalamenti/Lynch). Producer John Wentworth. Conceived and Directed by David Lynch. Video Production Crew: Production Manager Bruce Roberts. Head of Production Tim Clawson. Editor Bob Jenkis. Executive Producers Monty Montgomery/Steve Golin/Sigurjon Sighvatsson. Producers David Lynch/Angelo Badalamenti/Rob Jason. Directed by David Lynch. Recorded live at the Brooklyn Academy of Music Opera House, 10/11/89. Video production 1990. 50 mins.

TWIN PEAKS — Fire Walk With Me

Francis Bouygues (in association with Lynch–Frost Productions and *Twin Peaks* Productions) presents a CiBy Picture.
Cast: SPECIAL AGENT DALE COOPER (Kyle MacLachlan), LAURA PALMER (Sheryl Lee), LELAND PALMER(Ray Wise), SPECIAL AGENT CHESTER DESMOND (Chris Isaak), DONNA HAYWARD (Moira Kelly), BOBBY BRIGGS(Dana Ashbrook), CARL RODD(Harry Dean Stanton), SARAH PALMER(Grace Zabriskie), JAMES HURLEY (James Marshall), PHILLIP JEFFRIES(David Bowie), AGENT SAM STANLEY(Kiefer Sutherland), NORMA JENNINGS(Peggy Lipton), TERESA BANKS(Pamela Gidley), GORDON COLE(David Lynch), SHELLY JOHNSON(Madchen Amick), ALBERT ROSENFIELD(Miguel Ferrer), RONNETTE PULASKI(Phoebe Augustine), LEO JOHNSON(Eric DuRe), HAROLD SMITH(Lenny Von Dohlen), MRS TREMOND (CHALFONT)(Frances Bay), MRS TREMOND'S GRANDSON (Jonathan F. Leppell), LOG LADY (Catherine E. Coulson), ANNIE BLACKBURN (Heather Graham), SHERIFF CABLE (Gary Bullock), BOB(Frank Silva), MAN FROM ANOTHER PLACE (DWARF)(Michael J. Anderson), JACQUES RENAULT (Walter Olkewicz), PHILLIP GERARD (ONE-ARMED MAN) (Al Strobel), IRENE (Sandra Kinder), WOODSMAN (Jurgen Prochnow), LIL THE DANCER (Kimberly Ann Cole), ROADHOUSE SINGER (Julee Cruise), ANGEL IN TRAIN CAR (Karin Robinson), ANGEL IN RED ROOM (Lorna McMillan).
Crew: Casting Johanna Ray. Editor Mary Sweeney. Special Effects L.A. Wizards, Inc. Sound Design David Lynch. Production/Costume Design Patricia Norris. Unit Production Manager Gregg Fienberg.

Music Angelo Badalamenti. Songs 'A Real Indication', 'The Black Dog Runs At Night', performed by Thought Gang (vocals: Badalamenti); 'Questions in a World of Blue', 'She Would Die For Love', Julee Cruise. All songs music: Badalamenti/lyrics: Lynch. Additional Music David Lynch and David Slusser. Director of Photography Ron Garcia. Assistant Directors Deepak Nayar/Richard Oswald/Bill Jennings. Executive Producers David Lynch/Mark Frost. Associate Producers Johanna Ray/Tim Harbert. Producers Gregg Fienberg/John Wentworth. Written by David Lynch and Robert Engels. Directed by David Lynch. 1992. 135 mins.

ON THE AIR

A Lynch–Frost Production for Worldvision Enterprises.
Regular Cast: LESTER GUY(Ian Buchanan), BETTY HUDSON(Nancye Ferguson), BUDDY BUDWALLER(Miguel Ferrer), with: Gary Grossman, Mel Johnson, Jr., Marvin Kaplan, David Lander, Kim McGuire, Marla Jeanette Rubinoff, Tracey Walter.
Crew: Editor Mary Sweeney. Music Angelo Badalamenti. Executive Producers Mark Frost/David Lynch. Producers Gregg Fienberg (pilot)/Deepak Nayar (series). Written by Mark Frost and David Lynch (pilot – see Chapter Nine for other writers). Directed by David Lynch (pilot – see Chapter Nine for other directors). 1992. 22 minutes per episode.

HOTEL ROOM

Asymmetrical Productions and Propaganda Films present an HBO Production.
Cast: Part 1: MOE(Harry Dean Stanton), LOU(Freddie Jones). Part 3: DANNY(Crispin Glover).
Crew: Casting Johanna Ray. Sound Design David Lynch. Production Design/Costume Design (Part 1) Patricia Norris. Editor (Part 1) Mary Sweeney. Editor (Part 3) David Siegel. Music Angelo Badalamenti. Director of Photography Peter Deming. Production Manager Deepak Nayar. Executive Producers Monty Montgomery/David Lynch. Associate Producer John Wentworth. Producer Deepak Nayar. Concept by Monty Montgomery/David Lynch. Written (Parts 1 and 3) by Barry Gifford. Directed (Parts 1 and 3) by David Lynch. 1993. 30 mins. per segment.

CRUMB

A David Lynch presentation of a Superior Pictures production.
Crew: Photography Maryse Alberti. Producers Lynn O'Donnell/Terry Zwigoff. Directed by Terry Zwigoff. 1995. 119 mins.

NADJA

David Lynch Presents a Kino Link production.

Cast: CASSANDRA(Suzy Amis), LUCY(Galaxy Craze), JIM(Martin Donovan), COUNT DRACULA/DR VAN HELSING(Peter Fonda), RENFIELD(Karl Geary), EDGAR(Jared Harris), NADJA(Elina Lowensohn), MORGUE RECEPTIONIST(David Lynch).
Crew: Editor David Leonard. Production Design Kurt Ossenfort. Music Simon Fisher Turner. Photography Jim Denault. Executive Producer David Lynch. Producers Mary Sweeney/Amy Hobby. Written and Directed by Michael Almereyda. 1995. 100 mins.

LOST HIGHWAY

Asymmetrical Productions present a CiBy Picture.
Cast: FRED MADISON(Bill Pullman), RENEE MADISON/ALICE WAKEFIELD(Patricia Arquette), PETE DAYTON(Balthazar Getty), MR EDDY/DICK LAURENT(Robert Loggia), BILL DAYTON(Gary Busey), SHEILA(Natasha Gregson Warner), ARNIE(Richard Pryor), MYSTERY MAN(Robert Blake), CANDACE DAYTON(Lucy Butler), AL (John Roselius), ED(Lou Eppolito), PARTY GIRL(Jenna Maetlind), ANDY(Michael Massee), GUARD HENRY(Henry Rollins), GUARD MIKE(Michael Shamus Wiles), GUARD IVORY(Ivory Ocean), GUARD JOHNNY MACK(Jack Kehler), JUDGE(Leonard Termo), DR SMORDIN (David Byrd), WARDEN CLEMENTS(Gene Ross), CAPTAIN LUNEAU(F. William Parker), PRISON OFFICIALS(Guy Siner/Alexander Folk), HANK (Carl Sundstrom), LOU(John Solari), CARL(Al Garrett), LANIE(Heather Stephens), STEVE V(Giovanni Ribisi), TEDDY(Scott Coffey), GIRL #1(Amanda Anka), JUNKIE GIRL(Jennifer Syme), MR EDDY'S ASSISTANTS(Matt Sigloch/Gil Combs), TAILGATE DRIVER (Greg Travis), PHIL(Jack Nance), MARIAN(Lisa Boyle), RAQUEL(Leslie Bega), PORNO STARS(Marilyn Manson/Twiggy Ramirez), FOREWOMAN (Mink Stole).
Crew: Casting Johanna Ray/Elaine J. Huzzar. Editor Mary Sweeney. Production Design Patricia Norris. Additional Sound Effects Ann Kroeber-Splet. Sound Design David Lynch. Music Editor Marc Vanocur. Original Music Angelo Badalamenti. Additional Music Barry Adamson/Angelo Badalamenti and David Lynch. Songs: 'I'm Deranged', David Bowie; 'Videodrones', 'Driving Down', 'The Perfect Drug', Nine Inch Nails; 'Eye', Smashing Pumpkins; 'This Magic Moment', Lou Reed; 'Apple of Sodom', 'I Put a Spell on You', Marilyn Manson; 'Insensatez', Antonio Carlos Jobim; 'Rammstein', 'Heirate Mich', Rammstein. Unit Production Manager Deepak Nayar. Assistant Directors Scott Cameron/Simone Farber. Director of Photography Peter Deming. Producers Deepak Nayar/Mary Sweeney/Tom Sternberg. Written by David Lynch and Barry Gifford. Directed by David Lynch. 1997. 135 mins.